Student Politics in AMERICA

Foundations of Higher Education

Student Politics in America

A HISTORICAL ANALYSIS

Philip G. Altbach

WITH A NEW PREFACE AND INTRODUCTION BY THE AUTHOR

TRANSACTION PUBLISHERS

New Brunswick (U.S.A.) and London (U.K.)

New material this edition copyright © 1997 by Transaction Publishers, New Brunswick, New Jersey 08903. Originally published in 1974 by McGraw-Hill, Inc.

This book is printed on acid-free paper that meets the American National Standard for Permanence of Paper for Printed Library Materials.

Library of Congress Catalog Number: 97-597
ISBN: 1-56000-944-6
Printed in the United States of America

Library of Congress Cataloging-in-Publication Data

Altbach, Philip G.
    Student politics in America : a historical analysis / Philip G. Altbach, with a new preface and introduction by the author.
        p.   cm. — (Foundations of higher education)
    Originally published: New York : McGraw-Hill, 1973.
    Includes bibliographical references and index.
    ISBN 1-56000-944-6 (pbk. : alk. paper)
    1. Student movements—United States. 2. Students—United States—Political activity—History—20th century. I. Title. II. Series.
LA229.A69   1997
378.1'98'10973—dc21   97-597
                                                            CIP

CONTENTS

Preface to the Transaction Edition   vii

Introduction to the Transaction Edition   xiii

Preface   xli

Chapter 1   Introduction   1

Chapter 2   The Stirrings of Student Activism:
1900-1930   17

Chapter 3   The Thirties: A Movement Comes of Age   57

Chapter 4   The Postwar Years: Liberal Currents
Amidst Apathy   109

Chapter 5   Radicals and Others in the Fifties:
In and Out of the Wilderness   141

Chapter 6   The Revival of Student Activism:
The Late Fifties   177

Chapter 7   Continuity and Change: The New Left
in the Context of American Student
Activism   209

Appendix   235

Index   239

PREFACE TO THE TRANSACTION EDITION

This book has a particular history and was written out of particular interests and concerns. Published in 1974, it was an effort to provide a broad historical perspective to the turbulent decade of the sixties. The book does not discuss the sixties in significant detail, but rather deals with the history of student politics prior to that decade. My conviction was that American students were unaware of the history of campus politics, and indeed of the history of higher education, and that an understanding of the organizational and political realities of student politics was necessary for both an understanding of the activism of the period and for effective political involvement. Indeed, the failure to understand the lessons of earlier periods significantly diminished the success of the student movements of the sixties.

My interest in student politics goes back to my involvement in the early stages of the campus movements of the sixties, just prior to the emergence of the New Left. The Student Peace Union (SPU), for which I served as national chairman between 1959 and 1961, was at the time the largest left-of-center student organization in the United States, with chapters on more than fifty campuses.[1] Concerned primarily with the arms race and with nuclear testing, the SPU was one of the first activist organizations to be concerned with the beginnings of American military involvement in Vietnam. It protested this involvement at a time when few had ever heard of the country and when the focus of the peace movement and the liberal community was on the arms race and the dangers of nuclear confrontation between the United States and the Soviet Union. This was the height of the Cold War, when issues of disarmament were immediately enmeshed in the ideological struggles of the period. It was also at the end of the period of McCarthy repression, when emerging political movements relating to civil liberties, civil rights, and issues of war and peace were testing the limits of the right to protest and engage in direct action politics, and participants felt that there were potential personal risks. It was a period of emerging activism rather than massive demonstrations. Those involved in the social movements of the period did not have the feeling, so common—and so wrong—in the later sixties, that political protest held unlimited possibilities and that, with sufficient pressure, the capitalist system might be destroyed.[2] In 1963, for example, I wrote an article in the *New Leader* that argued that the campus was quiet and lamented that conditions in society and in the universities were not favorable for activist movements.[3] Just a few years later, the largest and most significant activist movement in American history emerged.

Student Politics in America was influenced by the saga of the American student movement of the 1960s, which played itself out between the mid-sixties and the time that the book was published in 1974. I felt that one of the reasons that the movement of the 1960s did not reach its potential for influencing American society was that the activist movement failed to grasp either the broader issues of student activism or the specific history of American student politics. Similarly, I felt that the authorities responding to activist politics and protest in the universities and in government misjudged the nature and character of the student movement. This misunderstanding led to poor decisions on the part of academic administrators, which exacerbated an already difficult campus situation.

Many of the analysts of campus activism had themselves been involved in student politics. Seymour Martin Lipset[4] and Nathan Glazer[5] are among a large number of 1930s activists, many from that hotbed of radical politics at City College of New York, who became social scientists and turned their attention to the analysis of student politics in the 1960s. It is interesting to note that some of that generation of the 1930s felt betrayed by a later generation of activists, whose tactics—especially whose attacks on the university as an institution—were seen as highly negative. Lewis S. Feuer developed a full-scale theory of generational conflict.[6] Hal Draper, who wrote one of the influential propaganda pamphlets of the Berkeley student revolt, was involved in the student movement of the 1930s and wrote of its history.[7] Several of the activists of the sixties became social scientists and wrote about student politics—including Richard Flacks,[8] Todd Gitlin,[9] Cyril Levitt,[10] and several others. Although student activism, and the research and writing on student politics, declined in the aftermath of the sixties, the tradition of activists writing about activism has by no means disappeared. Robert Cohen, author in 1993 of the definitive history of the student movements of the 1930s, was himself in the student movement.[11] It is not surprising that movement veterans were attracted to careers in academe, with its intellectual as well as service elements, and to the study of student politics.

I became interested in student politics as a phenomenon even while a student. In the early 1960s, I had the opportunity to meet several of the leaders of the Japanese radical movement Zengakuren while they were on an American tour, and wrote one of the earliest articles published in English on Japanese student politics.[12] Around the same time, I had an opportunity to observe at close hand several Cold War–related international student organizations, the International Union of Students—headquartered in Prague and financed by the Soviet Union—and the International Student Conference, with offices in Holland and financed, as we learned only later, largely by the U.S. Central Intelligence Agency.[13] Somewhat later, I wrote a doctoral dissertation dealing with student politics in India,[14] and the broader theoretical implications of student politics.[15] My work on student political activism was significantly deepened by a year spent in 1966–67 as a postdoctoral fellow, working with Seymour Martin Lipset at Harvard University on his major international inquiry into student political activism.[16]

While a faculty member at the University of Wisconsin-Madison, and later at the State University of New York at Buffalo, I maintained an interest in student politics. *Student Politics in America,* originally published in 1974, was the product of research funded by the National Endowment for the Humanities at the University of Wisconsin. At Madison, I witnessed the most radical phase of the Vietnam protest movement, including the bombing of the Army Mathematics Research Center. I coedited a book dealing in part with the University of Wisconsin's reaction to the protests and the implications of the rapid expansion of American higher education.[17]

Although American student politics subsided after the mid-1970s, this was not the case worldwide. I focused my attention on the international status of student activism in my 1989 international survey.[18] Although I do not believe that a truly international student movement has ever existed, patterns of activism in one country have from time to time influenced or provided examples to groups in other nations. This was certainly the case during the sixties, when the international mass media focused on student politics worldwide. As Todd Gitlin discussed, the "whole world was watching"—at least in the sense that student activism received considerable attention from the media.[19]

There was, in the late 1980s, a modest temporary revival in student activism, focused on racial issues and to a lesser extent on apartheid in South Africa. This resurgence stimulated Robert Cohen and me to consider the saga of student politics in the post-sixties era. That article, originally published in 1990 in the *Journal of Higher Education,* forms the basis of the introductory chapter of this book.[20]

This volume is thus part of my longstanding interest in student politics in the context of higher education, both in the United States and abroad. The motivation for this interest comes in part from my concern with the workings of universities and the relationship of academic institutions to the broader society, and in part from my own involvement in campus activism in the era just prior to the emergence of the major movements of the sixties. I am indebted to David Webster, editor of this series, and to Irving Louis Horowitz, the editorial chairman at Transaction Publishers, for their interest in *Student Politics in America.*

PHILIP G. ALTBACH
Chestnut Hill, Massachusetts
January 1997

NOTES

1. The Student Peace Union is discussed to a limited extent in this book, but it has never received a full-scale analysis. See Howard Metzenberg, "Student Peace Union: Five Years Before the New Left" (bachelor's thesis, Oberlin College, n.d.).
2. For a generally positive discussion of the sixties, see Todd Gitlin, *The Sixties: Years of Hope, Days of Rage* (New York: Bantam Books, 1987).
3. Philip G. Altbach, "The Quiet Campus," *The New Leader* 46 (August 5, 1963), 12–14.

4. See Seymour Martin Lipset and Sheldon S. Wolin, eds., *The Berkeley Student Revolt: Facts and Interpretations* (Garden City, N.Y.: Doubleday Anchor Books, 1965) and other books.

5. Nathan Glazer, *Remembering the Answers: Essays on the American Student Revolt* (New York: Basic Books, 1970).

6. Lewis S. Feuer, *The Conflict of Generations: The Character and Significance of Student Movements* (New York: Basic Books, 1969).

7. Hal Draper, "The Student Movement of the Thirties: A Political History," in *As We Saw the Thirties: Essays on Social and Political Movements of a Decade,* ed. Rita James Simon (Urbana: University of Illinois Press, 1967), 151–89.

8. Richard Flacks, *Youth and Social Change* (Chicago: Markham, 1971). See also Jack Whalen and Richard Flacks, *Beyond the Barricades: The Sixties Generation Grows Up,* (Philadelphia: Temple University Press, 1989).

9. Gitlin, *The Sixties.*

10. Cyril Levitt, *Children of Privilege: Student Revolt in the Sixties* (Toronto: University of Toronto Press, 1984).

11. Robert Cohen, *When the Old Left Was Young: Student Radicals and America's First Mass Student Movement, 1929–1941* (New York: Oxford University Press, 1993).

12. Philip G. Altbach, "Japanese Students and Japanese Politics," *Comparative Education Review* 7 (October 1963), 181–89.

13. Philip G. Altbach, "The International Student Movement," *Comparative Education Review* 8 (October 1964), 31–38. See also Philip G. Altbach, "Spies for C.I.A. or Deserving Students?" *Christian Century* 83 (March 15, 1967): 352–54, and Philip G. Altbach and Norman T. Uphoff, eds. *The Student Internationals* (Metuchen, N.J.: Scarecrow Press, 1973).

14. Philip G. Altbach, *Student Politics in Bombay* (Bombay: Asia Publishing House, 1968), and Philip G. Altbach, ed., *Turmoil and Transition: Higher Education and Student Politics in India* (New York: Basic Books, 1968).

15. Philip G. Altbach, "Students and Politics," *Comparative Education Review* 10 (June 1966), 175–87.

16. See Philip G. Altbach and Seymour Martin Lipset, *Students in Revolt* (Boston: Houghton Mifflin, 1969), and Philip G. Altbach, *A Select Bibliography on Students, Politics, and Higher Education,* rev. ed. (Cambridge: Center for International Affairs, Harvard University, 1970).

17. Philip G. Altbach, Robert S. Laufer, and Sheila McVey, eds., *Academic Supermarkets* (San Francisco: Jossey-Bass, 1971).

18. Philip G. Altbach, ed., *Student Political Activism: An International Reference Handbook* (New York: Greenwood Press, 1989). This volume brought together 33 essays from as many countries.

19. Todd Gitlin, *The Whole World Is Watching: The Mass Media and the Unmaking of the New Left* (Berkeley: University of California Press, 1980).

20. Philip G. Altbach and Robert Cohen, "American Student Activism: The Post-Sixties Transformation," *Journal of Higher Education* 61 (January/February, 1990), 33–49.

INTRODUCTION TO THE TRANSACTION EDITION

American Student Politics:
Activism in the Midst of Apathy

The 1960s, of course, saw the flowering of American student political activism.[1] The American university was in turmoil, and students, for the first time since the 1930s, were playing on a national political stage. A sitting president, Lyndon Johnson, decided not to run for re-election in part because of student demonstrations against his Vietnam policies. Students were also at the forefront of a major change in American values and attitudes—particularly in areas such as relations between the sexes, reproductive rights, music, and social norms. For a short period in the late 1960s, public opinion polls indicated that the most important concern of the American population was campus unrest. It is certainly true that the two decades following the sixties have, in contrast to the decade of turbulence, been characterized by quiet. In reality, the situation is much more complex. There has been some activism, and the revolution in attitudes and values started in the sixties has not completely disappeared.[2] The one major upsurge of student activism, the anti-apartheid "divestment" movement of 1984–86, involved thousands of students nationwide and indicated a new trend in student activism. The quarter century since the sixties has seen a few blips of activism, but seems apathetic only in contrast to the benchmark decade. It may, in fact, be just about at the norm for activism on campus.

Several things are clear about the past quarter century. The first is that activism is not entirely dead. There have been modest upsurges from time to time. There was a flurry of concern about such issues as Nicaragua and campus racism, and there was significantly more involvement with the anti-apartheid movement. It is significant that these are precisely the sorts of issues that have energized American students in the past—issues that have a clear moral content and that may relate to foreign policy. It is also clear that although American student attitudes have become somewhat more conservative politically, the campus remains fairly liberal in orientation on issues of political ideology and particularly on "life-style" questions.

Some have detected the embers of activism on campuses, and that the right combination of circumstances might reignite a major student movement.[3] These analysts point to a range of localized student political efforts, and the existence of several national liberal and left-oriented groups. Others look at student volunteerism and the willingness of significant numbers of students to spend time on social service activities as an important force on campus and perhaps a harbinger of political activism.[4] However, the circumstances of both American politics and American higher education in the 1990s are so different that such a resurgence seems very unlikely.

At the same time, American students have certainly turned "inward" in many respects. They have become more concerned with careers in a difficult economy, and the increase in interest in religions—first "alternative" faiths such as Hinduism and Zen Buddhism and, more recently, fundamentalist Christianity and conservative Judaism—shows a concern for spiritual issues.

In sum, the period since 1970 exhibits a variety of somewhat contradictory trends among American students. There is neither sustained activism nor total apathy; neither complete "careerism" nor widespread altruism. The fact is that the past two decades have been characterized by brief sparks of activism in a general context of quiet and even political apathy. There are undercurrents of concern for social issues, with a significant minority of students participating in social service volunteerism. But there are no national or regional activist organizations with significant campus support or the ability to project a political voice for students nationally.

THE LEGACY OF THE SIXTIES: CAUSES OF DECLINE

The contemporary campus scene is frequently seen in the mirror of the sixties—despite the fact that this era was quite atypical. The legacy of that decade may have some lessons for the recent period. The student movement of the sixties declined for a number of complex reasons. It is not possible to provide a quantifiable explanation for the decline or even to assess accurately the relative weights of the causes. Nonetheless, it is important to catalog some of the key factors.

1. The key motivating force for student activism, the war in Vietnam, gradually wound down during the early 1970s. The war was the factor that mobilized the largest number of students and generated the most dissent. The Vietnam War was a unique phenomenon in American history—it was, at least by the late sixties, widely unpopular not only on campus but among the American middle classes.[5] Students were being drafted into the army, and there was an undercurrent of guilt and resentment among large numbers of students. The end of the war brought an immediate end to mass student activism.

2. The economic situation dramatically changed. The prosperity of the sixties helped to generate a feeling among students and the middle classes generally that individual economic success was assured in the context of a steadily expanding economy. In this respect, among others, the sixties were a rather unique decade. The economic "costs" of activism were seen to be minor in terms of risks to careers—through temporarily suspending studies, and the like. Economic realities changed dramatically in the following decades. The 1970s were characterized by rapid inflation, several "oil shocks" with resulting economic dislocation, fairly high levels of unemployment, and a generally gloomy feeling about the economy. Basic structural changes in the American economy also became evident. American world economic hegemony ended with the rise of Japan and other Pacific Rim nations as major industrial and technological forces. Productivity declined as global competition increased and trade deficits grew. Students began to worry about the job market and how to fit into an increasingly uncertain economy.

Not only were traditional middle-class jobs declining, but the employment market was in the process of significant change. Students increasingly chose "safe" fields for majors, such as business administration, computer science, pre-law, and pre-medicine—fields in which job prospects were perceived to be favorable. Enrollment patterns on campus shifted dramatically, with majors in the traditional liberal arts declining.

3. The fields that became increasingly popular—in the sciences and professions—were not fields that tend to contribute to activism. Many activists traditionally came from the social sciences, and these fields rapidly lost popularity during the 1970s.

4. The tactics and to some extent the ideology of the student movement of the sixties, particularly in its later, more militant, and sometimes violent phases, did not lead to success. On the contrary, the majority of American students were alienated by both violent tactics and the hyper-revolutionary rhetoric of the Weathermen and other factions.[6] It must be remembered that the activist leaders of the sixties felt that they were unsuccessful in their major goals—ending the Vietnam War and stimulating revolutionary social change in America. Many were bitter, and some turned to ever more radical approaches, including bombing buildings, violent bank robberies, and super-militancy on campus. The movement itself sowed some of the seeds of its own destruction. In some ways, the ideological and tactical self-destruction at the end of the sixties made it more difficult for activist movements in the following decades.

5. Media attention was an important part of the student movement of the sixties, and when the mass media turned to other topics, the activist movement lost an important focus.[7]

6. The changing American political climate had a key influence on the decline of the student movement. American politics moved sharply to the right and has remained there throughout the past two decades. The election of Richard Nixon as president in 1968 was the beginning of this trend, and the "Reagan Revolution" of the 1980s solidified it. There is no question that the political center in America has moved significantly to the right. Traditionally, student activist movements have benefited from a relatively liberal social milieu.

7. The student population itself significantly changed. Expansion slowed, and the proportion of students from working-class and minority backgrounds increased. Many more students studied part-time, and the percentage of students working while studying ballooned. These

demographic facts tend to diminish the potential for activism, since activists have traditionally been middle-class in social class origins and full-time students with the time to devote to extracurricular activities.

The decline and, by 1972, virtual collapse of perhaps the largest student activist movement in American history left a tremendous vacuum on the campus. Ever since then, the trend has been to compare activist campaigns to the sixties, a comparison that is unfair, because the more recent period has not been characterized by the social unrest and crisis of the sixties. Recent activist movements have had to grow in the shadow of both the accomplishments and the failures of the sixties.

A COMPLEX CONFIGURATION OF ATTITUDES

There is no question that student attitudes have become more conservative on many issues since the sixties. In 1987, only 2.3 percent of American freshmen identified themselves as being on the far left with another 22.2 percent liberal. On the other hand, only 1.3 percent claimed a far right affiliation, and 18.3 percent were conservative.[8] In 1995, these proportions remained fairly stable—with 2.7 percent claiming far left views, 21.1 percent liberal, 20.3 percent conservative, and 1.6 percent far-right. This is down, particularly in the far left category, from the 1960s. The large majority are "middle of the road." A configuration of attitudes concerning political and life-style issues indicates that students express a variety of liberal to middle-of-the-road attitudes. General trends in political and life-style attitudes remained fairly steady from the mid-1980s to the mid-1990s. For example, 23.8 percent favored the abolition of the death penalty in 1988. In 1995, 20.9 percent agreed. In 1988, there was majority support for nuclear disarmament, consumer protection, busing to achieve racial balance in the schools, and other items on the liberal agenda. A majority of students believed that couples should live together before marriage (52.1 percent), and 58.7 percent believe that abortion should be legal. Yet, only 19.3 percent support the legalization of marijuana and 23.8 back the abolition of the death penalty.[9] By 1995, 33.8 percent supported the legalization of marijuana, while support for the abolition of the death penalty dropped to 20.9 percent. Ninety percent of American students claim religious affiliation, and 80.6 percent in 1995 reported that they attended a religious service at least once in the previous year.

Religion is an interesting indication of change in student interest and perspectives. During the sixties, campus religious organizations continued to exist and some were involved in the activist movement. In the past two decades, there has been a resurgence of interest in religion, reflecting, it seems, a concern for personal values and orientations as opposed to societal issues.

Except during the 1960s, American student attitudes have not been notably different from those of the mainstream of the American population—particularly the middle class from which a large proportion of the students come. Student attitudes tend to be modestly more liberal on ideological issues and significantly more liberal on "life-style" questions. In 1984, for example, Ronald Reagan had 7 percent less support among students than he had among adults. All in all, however, there is general consistency.

Students in the 1980s and 1990s indicated that they did not participate to any great extent in political activities. Only 14.8 percent in 1995 indicated that they discussed politics frequently, and 7.6 percent worked in an off-campus political campaign. On the other hand, 70.3 percent performed volunteer work during the previous year.[10]

Arthur Levine and Keith R. Wilson have written persuasively about the "me-generation" that they felt dominated campus culture during the 1970s and, for the most part, up to the present time.[11] The "me-generation" is characterized by student attitudes that place much greater stress on individual values and needs than did the socially conscious students of the 1960s. "Me-generation" students have chosen academic fields that promise the best and most lucrative opportunities for jobs and careers, and when asked, they have named the achievement of wealth as an important goal. They have been interested in a variety of self-fulfillment movements, from EST to Hare Krishna, and there has been a modest return to traditional religious faiths. During this period, Americans, in general, expressed a lack of confidence in social institutions of all kinds: for example, confidence in the U.S. Supreme Court dropped from 50 percent in 1966 to 31 percent in 1977. Confidence in institutions of higher education dropped from 73 percent to 55 percent in the same period; people tended to rely more on individual orientations and concerns.

"Me-ism" has had a significant impact on campus life. Self-help groups have, for example, expanded significantly. Students have been more willing to bring lawsuits against academic institutions and have been much more concerned with the quality of campus life. There has been more competition—for admission to the best colleges, for entry into the major fields that will yield high-paying careers, and for grades in courses and the like. Social and sexual mores also seem to be affected, although here causes—and effects—are less clear, in part due to the concern about AIDS.

"ME-ISM" AND ACTIVISM

The configuration of attitudes that emerged in the 1970s is reflected in a new style of campus activism. Without question, there is less activism and political concern in general. Further, the nature of the organizations changed during the 1970s, as did the tactics of student political groups. The rebirth of the student government organizations, which were a mainstay of campus life and one of the foci of political concerns during the 1950s, is an indication of the change.[12] Student governments have been concerned not only with the quality of campus life and with student service enterprises, but also with the representation of students in a wider forum within the university—and in some cases in a broader one.[13] These groups seem to remain a minority phenomenon, however, since only 22.7 percent of students in 1995 indicated that they voted in student government elections.

Directly related to student governments were student lobbies, which emerged in many states and at the national level in the 1970s and 1980s, but seem to have waned by the 1990s. The National Student Lobby has been sporadically active in Washington, trying to press for their interests in Congress and elsewhere. It was estimated that such lobbies were established on 22 percent of the nation's campuses in thirty-nine states by the early 1970s. The lobbies were mainly concerned with ensuring that student interests are respected; they have tried to maintain guaranteed student loan programs, opposed tuition increases at state universities, argued against restrictions on student rights, and so on. One of the most successful student lobbies was the Student Association of the State University (SASU) at the State University of New York (SUNY), but even this active group had run its course by the end of the 1980s, and has been less active, even in a period when SUNY experienced serious cuts. SASU represented most of SUNY's thirty-four campuses at the state capitol in Albany and employed a full-time staff to work with SUNY

officials and the state government. On many occasions SASU has cooperated with SUNY on legislative initiatives, but occasionally it opposed
SUNY officials on tuition increases. It occasionally sponsored large-
scale demonstrations in Albany to press for student issues. The organization also provided reduced rate travel, block concert tickets, and student
shopping discounts.

Another notable trend among student organizations during the 1970s,
which has seen a decline in the 1980s, was the re-establishment of the
Public Interest Research Groups (PIRG). The idea for the PIRG was proposed by Ralph Nader in 1970, and by 1978 PIRGs had been formed at 11
percent of American colleges and universities in twenty-eight states.[14]
The PIRGs, which do research on environmental and other social issues,
and also engage in lobbying for legislation and in public education, proved
to be popular. They were able to combine student concerns for social
issues that affected their own lives, such as the environment, with a tradition of social activism. The PIRGs were not generally involved in activist
demonstrations but rather worked with government officials, provided
educational materials, and tried to raise public consciousness about their
concerns. By the mid-1980s, however, the PIRGs experienced a dramatic
decline and were much less evident on most campuses. Although students continue to be committed to environmental concerns, they are not
active in this or in the other areas stressed by the PIRGs.

Although the "me-generation" was primarily focused on activism
and the level of campus political concern was at a low ebb during the
1970s, "me-ism" did have some political and social ramifications.[15] The
kinds of student organizations that seemed to be most effective during
the 1970s reflected student interest in issues that directly affected their
lives and futures. The ideologically based social action groups that were
much in evidence during the 1960s virtually disappeared from the campuses. It is significant that the areas of activism that have been most
successful in the 1970s and early 1980s were those that combined individual interests and social concerns.

THE EIGHTIES AND THE NINETIES—MODEST
CONCERN IN THE MIDST OF APATHY

The 1980s and to some extent the early 1990s show something of a
paradox in student political activism in the United States. On the one

hand, the configuration of attitudes evident in the post-sixties period
has continued without significant change, with the marked decline in
radical attitudes but with the continuing social concerns noted earlier.
There continues to be a strong focus on careers and worry about ensuring a safe position in the middle class. Yet, in the nineties, there has also
been a modest resurgence of interest in the social sciences, education,
and other fields that had lost favor in the previous two decades. There
has also been a sporadic resurgence of student activism.[16] It has been
activism more reminiscent of the nonviolent period of the early 1960s
than the hyper-militant late sixties student movement. Students have
also reacted with some activism to campus racial tensions that were
marked at the end of the 1980s.[17] As in earlier periods, most activism
and social concern has emanated from the liberal left, although there
has also been some conservative political involvement as well.[18]

A detailed analysis of the broader political and economic context of
the past two decades is beyond the scope of this discussion. However, it
is important to mention several key elements. The fairly severe economic problems of the 1970s abated considerably, although the middle
class did not fully regain its sense of prosperity. The impact of the several "oil shocks" wore off, and rampant inflation ended. Unemployment, while quite high early in the 1980s, also declined, although the
pattern of employment changed, with many jobs clustered in low wage
fields. Students remained concerned about finding good jobs, and choices
of majors reflected an uncertain job market.

The "Reagan Revolution" downplayed the welfare state. Wall Street
boomed and declined, a record number of large corporations merged,
the savings and loan industry collapsed, and the scramble for wealth
dominated the national scene more completely than it had at any time
since the 1920s. By the end of Reagan's first term, the campuses seemed
to be little more than yuppie breeding grounds, politically quiescent
places where by far the leading undergraduate major was business administration. A *Newsweek on Campus* cover story summarized this mood
in a cartoon showing collegians dropping the rebellious 1960s' slogan
"Don't trust anyone over 30," and replacing it with a more yuppie/80s'
sentiment, "Never trust anyone under $30,000."[19]

The rejuvenation of conservatism wrought by the Reagan revolution
from 1980 to 1988 inhibited progressive activism on the two key issues
that traditionally had mobilized the student left: peace and civil rights.

President Reagan effectively promoted a new Cold War nationalism against the Soviet's "Evil Empire," obtaining congressional funding for a significant military buildup. His invasion of Grenada in 1983 and the U.S. military victory there yielded much flag waving, which even affected the campuses, where rallies in support of the invasion outnumbered protests. Though there was some student involvement in the nuclear freeze movement and in demonstrations against the Contra war in Nicaragua, the conservative national mood prevented these causes from generating mass student support during Reagan's first term. Moreover, the Reagan administration's assault on affirmative action left civil rights groups reeling and promoted a campus backlash against minorities, which helped to stifle student activism on civil rights issues and stimulated a rash of campus-based racial incidents by decade's end.

The Reagan landslide in 1984 seemed initially to seal the fate of the student left as an impotent minority in a conservative era. Ironically, however, the landslide had the opposite effect, stimulating rather than suffocating campus protest. Because the election had made it clear that neither Reagan nor the nation's rightward drift could be halted at the polls, student activists now concluded that protest was the only way to challenge Reaganism. And this challenge would occur on the one issue upon which the Reagan administration (and American university administrators) seemed most vulnerable: South Africa.

ANTI-APARTHEID AND DIVESTMENT: AN EIGHTIES' ACTIVIST MOVEMENT

During the 1984–85 academic year, the apartheid regime in South Africa faced the greatest black insurgency in a quarter century. Black protest against white minority rule and the new "reform" constitution was met with repression that was brutal even by South African standards, culminating in March 1985 with a police massacre of unarmed demonstrators near Sharpeville. In response to these events and stimulated by extensive television and press coverage of them, a solidarity movement took root in the United States, centered in black churches and civil rights organizations. This movement demanded that the Reagan administration enact sanctions against South Africa. But the administration, clinging to its "constructive engagement" policy, vigorously opposed sanctions. The solidarity movement escalated its protests through a dramatic civil disobedience campaign, orchestrating sit-ins at which demonstrators, including prominent political leaders, were arrested at the South African embassy. The anti-apartheid protests in both the United States and South Africa captured the imagination of American undergraduates in spring 1985, sparking the largest student protests since the 1960s.[20]

Both on campus and off, the anti-apartheid movement grew substantially in the wake of a national day of protest held on April 4, 1985, commemorating the seventeenth anniversary of Martin Luther King, Jr.'s assassination. Some 4,000 demonstrators marched outside the South African embassy in Washington, D.C., and 58 were arrested. On this same day several hundred Columbia University students brought the anti-apartheid movement to their campus. Chanting and sitting outside the main entrance to Hamilton Hall, they vowed to stay until Columbia divested all of its holdings in companies doing business with South Africa.[21]

The Columbia protest lasted three weeks, and it inspired similar divestment protests on some sixty campuses. Several of these protests were far larger than the Columbia sit-in. At the University of California at Berkeley well over 10,000 students joined a one-day strike in protest against the arrest of 158 divestment protesters. More than 1,000 Cornell University students were arrested in a series of divestment sit-ins.

Though engaging in protests that evoked memories of the 1960s, the divestment movement sought to avoid the polarization of that earlier decade. The spring 1985 protests were nonviolent and directed more toward raising the divestment issue than disrupting or attacking the university. This tone was set from the beginning at Columbia, where the protesters sat outside rather than inside Hamilton Hall and posted notices that though they were blocking the main entrance, the basement entrances would remain open. "We don't hate President Sovern," explained one Columbia protest leader. "We think we have a better argument than he does." *Newsweek* noted that "compared to the purple-hazed 60s" the divestment protesters "are exceedingly polite." Students at the University of Colorado at Boulder, for example, carefully negotiated with school officials before staging a demonstration that one administrator called "the most civilized on the face of the earth."[22]

The divestment protesters also seemed more studious and "high tech" than their predecessors. Students at Columbia and other campus sit-ins rotated on the front lines of the protest so that they could attend their

classes. The activists also made good use of the personal computer revolution, quickly setting up a computer network linking over one hundred
campuses to share the latest news about their protests.

The unambiguous moral issue of apartheid was at the heart of student
protests. The activists focused most of their attention on pressuring the
university and the nation to use their economic leverage against Pretoria's
racist regime. But beyond South Africa itself, the divestment protesters
were seeking to send America the message that the political conscience
of the campus had not disappeared and that their generation was ready
and willing to raise its voice against the administration's right-wing policies. Soon after the divestment protests began, the *New York Times* reported that across the United States student activists were unanimous in
agreeing that among their strongest recruiting points were the Reagan
administration policies and even the personality of the president himself.
"A lot of what's going on is in reaction to Reagan," explained a Berkeley
divestment activist. "People are frustrated and aggravated with what's
going on in El Salvador and Nicaragua. People with a lot of pent-up energy finally see a chance to do things constructively."[23]

This was a revolt against not only the president's foreign policy, but
against the self-centered materialism of the Reagan era. The student
protesters were saying that morality must take precedence over profit-
ability, that regardless of the financial costs the university had a civic
obligation to sever its economic ties to South Africa. Moreover, student
activists were trying to make a similar point about themselves, seeking
to show that contrary to media stereotypes, many collegians were not
avaricious yuppies. Berkeley divestment leader Ross Hammond explained that at his university the movement was "in part a reaction against
the media for portraying Berkeley as a dead campus. That idea annoys
people no end, people who really care. This is still a progressive campus." Similar sentiments were expressed by student protesters across
the nation, including Yale divestment organizer Tom Keenan who
proudly credited the demonstrations with "disproving the idea that we're
one homogeneous student body heading for business suits."[24]

Though the surge of activism in spring semester 1985 was confined
primarily to divestment, there were also protests on behalf of peace and
affirmative action. At the University of Colorado, over 450 protesters
were arrested during a demonstration against CIA recruiters. Anti-CIA
protests also occurred at Yale, Wesleyan and the University of Wiscon-

sin at Madison—where students sought to make a citizen's arrest against a CIA recruitment officer. Minority students incorporated into their divestment protests a call for greater minority representation on campus. And at Brown University affirmative action took center stage, as minority students led a brief strike and building occupation in April, demanding increased minority admission, financial aid, and a more Third World-oriented curriculum.[25]

Underestimating the political strength and appeal of the divestment movement, most campus administrators initially turned down its demand for total severance of all university investments in companies doing business in South Africa.[26] The Columbia administration led the way in setting this hard line. Soon after the sit-in began, Columbia spokesman Fred Knubel announced, "Columbia has no plan to meet the students' demands." In justifying this refusal to negotiate, Columbia president Michael Sovern insisted, "no university can allow some of its members to force a position on it." Campus officials at many institutions stressed that total divestment would violate their fiduciary responsibilities, and some claimed that divesting would lessen America's economic leverage and its ability to press for reform in South Africa. The depth of this administration opposition meant that the movement would not win divestment overnight: a lesson driven home by the Columbia sit-in, which ended with no promises by the administration that it would move toward total divestment.[27]

Campus administrators also reinforced their anti-divestment position by clamping down on the demonstrators. They initiated disciplinary proceedings against leaders of sit-ins and in several cases denied diplomas to students who had broken campus regulations. College officials began holding national meetings to discuss ways to control protesters. This led to the enactment of tighter campus disciplinary procedures at Cornell and other activist-oriented universities and colleges. At Berkeley and Columbia, campus police were authorized to videotape demonstrations to facilitate the prosecution of students involved in unlawful protests. Divestment protesters denounced these policies, claiming that they could have a chilling effect upon free speech.[28]

What these administrators had not counted on in taking this hard line was the groundswell of public support that would quickly strengthen the divestment movement. Divestment leaders such as Jon Klavens of Columbia understood, as college officials had not, that America's revulsion against apartheid—exacerbated daily by the televised atrocities from South Africa—gave their movement an edge over campus administrators, who appeared Scrooge-like in refusing to part with their South African investments. "We have as much of a moral high ground as the abolitionists, maybe more," Klavens said. Despite early setbacks in the face of administration intransigence, divestment protesters remained confident that ultimately, in the words of Stanford organizer Steven Phillips, "we will be effective because apartheid offends everyone's sense of justice."[29] Such confidence was well placed.

The campus divestment movement had never stood alone in demanding a change in university investment policies. During the first week of the Columbia sit-in Rev. Jesse Jackson came up to Morningside Heights and warmed the rain-drenched divestment protesters with a speech praising them for "setting a moral example for America."[30] Similar praise came from Bishop Desmond Tutu. Joining these civil rights leaders were labor leaders, faculty, and hundreds of public officials across the nation who advocated divestment of state and municipal funds from banks with South African connections. The call for federal sanctions against South Africa was also beginning to gather support in Congress. This increasingly favorable public mood gave the divestment movement powerful allies in the community. When, for instance, UCLA and Berkeley students sat-in, demanding divestment, several California state legislators, including House Speaker Willie Brown, endorsed the protest and warned the university that its budget would get bottled up in Sacramento unless it divested. The combination of campus and community pressure led more than twenty-five campuses nationwide to partially or totally divest between April and October 1985.

The pressure for divestment increased dramatically during the 1985–86 academic year. Building on the organizational base constructed the previous spring, a national divestment mobilization in October 1985 orchestrated demonstrations on over one hundred campuses—nearly doubling the size and geographical scope of the movement.[31] If the 1983–84 academic year had been the year of the yuppie on campus, 1985–86 was the year of the shanty, as divestment protesters across the nation constructed shabby huts, and placed them on their campuses to symbolize the poverty and oppression of South African blacks.[32]

With the movement gaining momentum, university administrators, regents, and trustees began to back down from their original refusal to divest. The first big symbolic victory of the academic year came in October 1985 when the Columbia administration committed itself to total divestment. Columbia also provided other administrators with a face-saving argument for reversing their earlier anti-divestment position. The Columbia administration claimed that it had opted to divest not because of student protest, but because the recent state of emergency imposed in South Africa had created a new political environment and rendered unrealistic the hope that U.S. companies could, through their presence and egalitarian employment policies, reform that social system and end apartheid. But Columbia was only the beginning; by the end of the 1985–86 academic year 120 colleges and universities had divested their South African holdings either partially or completely.[33]

The biggest divestment occurred in July 1986, when the University of California opted to pull its $3.1 billion investment out of companies doing business in South Africa. This victory was perhaps the most striking demonstration of the degree to which the divestment movement had influenced public opinion and thereby caused a shift in the position of politicians. Where the previous spring California's governor, George Deukmejian, had vigorously opposed divestment, this conservative Republican now—up for reelection and recognizing the widespread and rising public support of the student movement's goal—endorsed divestment and used his considerable political influence with the Board of Regents to bring about a surprising reversal of its earlier vote against divestment.

THE END OF THE DIVESTMENT MOVEMENT

Unlike the student movement of the 1960s, which self-destructed because of its sense of failure (its leaders wrongly thought the movement was failing to stop the Vietnam War), the divestment movement's demise was a product of its own success. The movement not only won divestment on campuses across the nation, it helped transform public opinion sufficiently so that even President Reagan had been forced to modify his position by supporting very limited sanctions against South Africa. Having won so many major divestment battles, the movement now had to face the problem of determining a new goal and a more extended political agenda. But having, in effect, lost its raison d'être, the movement was unable to solve this problem or shift its focus; instead it faded in the 1986–87 academic year almost as quickly as it had emerged.

The movement's collapse was linked to the fading of another important motivation for the student activism—the need to halt Reagan and the nation's rightward drift. The Reagan revolution no longer aroused fear among students because it had dissipated in the wake of both the 1986 elections, which restored Democratic dominance in Congress, and the Iran-Contra scandal, which paralyzed the Reagan White House. With its two major opponents—university investments in South Africa and President Reagan—now weakened, the student movement of the 1980s came to an end.

The demise of the divestment movement left some activists wondering whether their much-lauded pragmatism and moderation had turned out to be a weakness rather than a strength. By focusing so intently on the limited demand of divestiture, the movement had inadvertently given the universities a way of opting out of the controversy: allowing administrators to render apartheid a nonissue on campus simply by purging their investment portfolios of South Africa-linked stocks. Thus, after winning many divestment battles in 1985–86, campus protests ended, though the apartheid regime continued its repression. The divestment movement's collapse, moreover, coincided with the press blackout instituted by the Botha regime, which kept news of South Africa's anti-apartheid struggle out of the reach of the American media. Movement activists watched helplessly as public interest in South Africa, which they had labored so hard to build, declined both on campus and off. The movement had mobilized campus opinion against apartheid, Reaganism, and yuppie-ism, but it could find no way of sustaining mass anti-apartheid protest in the United States once the issue of university complicity with South African racism had been resolved.

Unlike the divestment effort, which tried to build a national movement through coordinated demonstrations and meetings, the anti-racism movement remained local and there was no national coordination. By the end of the 1987–88 academic year, there was little evidence of a significant campus protest movement. In addition to these two major activist thrusts in the mid-1980s, there has been concern about American policy in Central America, and significant campus opposition to supporting the Contras in Nicaragua. As in the past, civil rights issues and foreign policy were key elements of a modest rebirth of campus political concern. At the end of the 1987–88 academic year, there were no major national activist organizations seeking to coordinate political developments on campus.

CONSERVATIVE TRENDS: THE MEDIA EXAGGERATES

Not all students, however, welcomed these divestment victories and the appearance of shanties and mass protest on campus. Since the early Reagan years, small but well-organized and well-funded groups of right-wing student activists had appeared on campus. The most vocal and well-known of these groups was at Dartmouth. It published an ultraconservative magazine, the *Dartmouth Review,* which received financial support from conservative alumni. The *Review* was well connected to the right-wing Republican establishment; it drew attention and praise from William F. Buckley's *National Review,* and it served as an Ivy League recruiting ground for the Reagan White House–several editors went on to become administration officials. Dinesh D'Souza, who was one of the main organizers of the Dartmouth activities and was an editor of the *Dartmouth Review,* went on to write an influential book attacking affirmative action, multiculturalism, and other liberal initiatives on campus.[34] The *Dartmouth Review* was known not only for its conservative ideology, but also for its sarcastic and nasty editorials, which included gay bashing and minority baiting. A 1982 article opposing affirmative action charged that Dartmouth had lowered its academic standards in order to recruit blacks; it was headlined "DIS SHO AIN'T NO JIVE."[35]

With the emergence of an active divestment movement on the Dartmouth campus, the *Dartmouth Review* crowd had an opportunity to move beyond rhetorical attacks on the left. Enraged by the appearance of shanties on campus, a dozen right-wing students (ten of whom were *Review* staffers) went out late at night armed with sledge hammers and destroyed shanties in January 1986. The *Review*'s next issue praised the assault and crowed that it would have been even better had the shanties been destroyed much earlier.

This incident provoked a wave of indignation at Dartmouth, particularly since the destruction of the shanties had been timed to coincide with the Martin Luther King, Jr., holiday. In protest against the destruction of the shanties, students occupied the administration building for thirty hours, until the administration agreed to hold a day-long teach-in on racism. At the teach-in nearly two-thirds of the student body turned out and heard black students complain of the discriminatory environment they confronted at Dartmouth.[36]

The controversy at Dartmouth attracted national attention to the issue of collegiate fascism. "The shanty project," observed one reporter, "designed to focus attention on racism far away, forced many to face allegations of bigotry in their own backyard."[37] Similar attacks on shanties occurred at the University of Utah, Johns Hopkins University, California State College at Long Beach and at UC Berkeley. But such attacks were rare and aroused far more opposition than support among a national student body sympathetic to the anti-apartheid movement.

It is fair to say that there is little campus support for the right-wing politics expressed by the *Dartmouth Review* and similar newspapers and journals on other campuses. Conservative initiatives have been supported by right-wing foundations, which have provided funds to "conservative alternative" campus newspapers nationwide. These funds have permitted newspapers to continue to publish. By the 1990s, little remained of the modest conservative upswing—mainly the externally-funded newspapers. Conservative campus activism received considerable attention in the media, especially in conservative newspapers and magazines, in part because there has been very little other activism to report.

RACISM AND ANTI-RACISM

Many campuses experienced racial incidents aimed against African Americans and, to a lesser extent, other minority groups, in the mid-1980s and early 1990s. The causes for this surprising wave of campus racism are not entirely clear. The attitudes expressed by President Ronald Reagan and members of his administration opposing affirmative action and other programs to assist minorities, and the general lack of sensitivity to minority issues during this period, played a role. So, too, did growing resentment by many whites against affirmative action, set-asides, and other programs aimed at helping minorities, which were perceived by some as causing problems for whites. A racial climate punctuated by the Clarence Thomas court hearings, the beating of Rodney King and ensuing riots, and other incidents contributed to tensions on campus.[38]

While it would be an exaggeration to say that campus race relations dramatically deteriorated by the mid-1980s, there were a variety of racial problems at American colleges and universities, some of which remain unsolved. The most dramatic—and disturbing—issue was the emergence of acts of racism against minority students. It is difficult to estimate the number of incidents nationwide. The National Institute Against Prejudice and Violence cited 174 incidents of ethno-violence on college campuses in the 1986–88 academic years.[39] The same organization noted that one in five students of color indicated that they had been victims of some sort of harassment on the campus of the college they attended.[40] These incidents generally consisted of anonymous racist graffiti or slogans, defacing of posters or other petty incidents.[41] Such acts were deeply offensive to African-American students, and generally resulted in soul searching and sometimes in anti-racist activism on campus. Many colleges and universities adopted anti-hate speech codes intended to eliminate racist expression. Some faculty and students opposed these codes as violations of free speech and academic freedom, and in a few cases the matter was taken to the courts, where judicial rulings in some cases overruled the codes while in others supported them.

Campus racial and ethnic tensions proved to be a highly complex and contentious set of issues and concerns. The entire academic community agreed that expressions of racial and ethnic prejudice were reprehensible. There was less agreement about the trend toward dormitories and other facilities which were based on race or ethnicity, and many were dismayed by the noticeable self-segregation of groups on campus. Racial preferences in admissions and in the award of scholarships became controversial issues on campus in this period as well, and this further enhanced campus racial tensions.

The activist organizations that emerged to oppose campus racism were, in all cases, limited to single colleges and universities. No national movement emerged, and in general activism diminished once the specific racist incident was dealt with. Ad hoc student groups were organized to deal with the crisis, generally under the leadership of minority students, but these organizations did not last. In some universities—Stanford, Columbia, Cornell, and Arizona State University among them—the incidents were not handled sensitively by administrators, and protest escalated, resulting, in a few cases, in arrests.[42] In most cases, crises were soon defused, and the situation returned to normal. Anti-

racist groups succeeded in raising campus consciousness about prejudice and bigotry on campus, and focused discussion on racial issues.
They may have had a positive impact on campus relations. But they did
not engender a continuing student movement.

Campus race relations were, however, affected by these incidents.
National media attention exacerbated the situation by focusing attention on campus racial problems. Many African-American students felt
unwelcome on some predominantly white campuses. This feeling, combined with an already existing trend toward racial separation on campus, pulled African Americans out of the campus mainstream into
separate social groups, and sometimes into separate dormitories. By the
1990s, campus subcultures became based to some extent on race and
ethnicity, and in some cases, political activism devolved on these groups
to a considerable degree.

THE CURRICULUM AND "INTEREST POLITICS"

The undergraduate curriculum has undergone a number of significant changes during the past two decades. Students influenced these
changes to some degree. Perhaps the most significant change was the
re-establishment of the general education "core" curriculum on many
campuses. This restoration was mainly an initiative of the faculty, and
there was little student involvement, pro or con. Indeed, the general
education movement was in considerable part a reaction to the student-
induced abolition of specific curricular requirements in the sixties. As
students chose to major in pre-professional fields, engineering, and other
vocationally oriented subjects, and the humanities and social sciences
experienced low enrollments. The recent curricular "restoration" of the
general education movement was stimulated in part by faculty wishing
to restore the traditional base of the university, and in part as an effort to
increase enrollment in some fields.[43]

The new model general education curriculum that was put into place
differed, on most campuses, from the model that dominated American
higher education in the 1950s. It included, in addition to the traditional arts and sciences, a multicultural component, and often options
for such new fields as women's studies or minority studies. The inclu-
sion of these new fields in the curriculum, as well as the establishment
and nurturing of minority studies programs on many campuses, was

stimulated in considerable part by students and supported by influential student groups. In many cases, student activism to establish or institutionalize minority studies or women's studies programs and departments was of central importance. Traditional faculty members often opposed these new initiatives, with students providing the balance of influence.[44]

Without student support, women's studies and minority studies programs, would not have achieved their current level of success. In some cases, students were the initiating force for these programs, while in many others they provided central support for their establishment or maintenance. Women's and minority studies courses and programs are now entrenched in most universities, and are established as important fields of scholarship.[45] Feminist student groups are also widespread and have been active in both campus affairs and self-help for women students. Black student organizations are also widespread, and have had an impact on black studies academic programs. Newer phenomena are gay and Asian-American student groups. These have also been active in supporting academic programs to reflect their concerns, and by the 1990s academic programs in these areas were being established on some campuses.

None of these efforts have led to the creation of significant national organizations or regional or national student activist movement. The struggles have been focused on specific campuses. Many of the campus-based movements have attracted faculty support, and have been successful in establishing academic programs. Local organizations have, however, maintained their existence and have provided a focus for social and intellectual activity.

The establishment and maintenance of these new fields has been one of the most significant influences of students on American higher education, perhaps in the past century. It is, in this respect, worth noting that the various demands for university reform and the participation by students in academic governance made during the 1960s had little lasting impact. A small number of colleges and universities gave students significant voice in governance, but virtually all of these withdrew the reforms once student interest and faculty support waned in the 1980s. Students did gain participation in token numbers on academic committees in many institutions, but this did not significantly alter established patterns of governance.[46] While the history of the establishment and institutionalization of women's and minority studies program is a complex one, students played a central role.

OTHER CAMPUS POLITICAL DEVELOPMENTS

Students did not organize protest movements concerning the several American foreign policy involvements of the past decade. The case of the Persian Gulf War is especially interesting. The crisis built up over a number of months in 1990 and 1991. There was only minor campus concern, and few protests, although there was time for campus organizing and the crisis received considerable attention from the mass media. The large majority of students supported American policy in the Gulf.[47] There were more campus manifestations of support for the Gulf War (such as putting up American flags) than against it. No national protest movement emerged, and there seems to have been little coordination of campus activism. The Gulf crisis was relatively short-lived, involved few American causalities, and took place when students were not being compelled to enter military service. Yet, public opinion in the early period of the U.S. build-up in the Gulf was somewhat divided, and there was vocal congressional opposition to the use of military force. The lack of a strong student response is perhaps indicative of the significant changes in the American student population since the 1960s, as well as the general campus quiet during the past decade.

The collapse of the Soviet Union and the end of the Cold War had a modest impact on campus. One of the pillars of American foreign policy, opposition to the Soviet Union, was removed, as were many of the bipolar assumptions about America's role in the world. The collapse of communism was a blow to radical ideology, and the traditional stances of the left came into question. The small radical organizations on campus were affected. Other foreign policy initiatives during this period that might have aroused significant opposition were met with general campus apathy. The U.S. invasion of the Caribbean island of Grenada during the Reagan administration to topple a "pro-Castro" regime was widely opposed on campus, but attracted little activism. The ongoing crisis in the former Yugoslavia produced no student response or initiatives, nor was there any reaction when the United States decided to commit troops to the NATO peacekeeping mission in 1996. In short, foreign policy, traditionally the mother lode of student activism in the

United States, has not stimulated significant interest since the anti-Apartheid protests of the mid-1980s.

Students have, in small numbers and without a major national movement, been exercised about several issues. Environmental issues have always had considerable resonance on campus. When asked in surveys, students have supported environmental issues—in 1995, 83.5 percent of freshmen said that the federal government was not doing enough to control environmental pollution.[48] At the end of the 1980s, Earth Day had widespread campus support and was marked by meetings and demonstrations in many colleges and universities.[49] Greenpeace and other pro-environmental groups claim many campus chapters, and a dozen other organizations focus at least to some extent on campus environmental concerns.[50] Students support recycling efforts on campus. The environmental movement has not stimulated a national student movement, although several national organizations that work on campuses exist. The focus of most of the activism has been at the local campus level.

As noted earlier, participation in volunteerism has increased among students. While numbers are not available, it is likely that more students are involved in social service volunteer activity than in any other kind of activism, and perhaps more than all other kinds combined. Campus volunteerism is especially impressive because social service activity must compete with increasingly common part-time employment. Deborah J. Hirsch calls this volunteerism the activism of the 1990s and argues that it may pave the way for more militant activism.[51] So far this has not occurred, and if past trends are any indication, social service work focused on local organizations and relating to quite specific issues will not turn into campus-based national activist student movement.

CONCLUSION

The past quarter century has seen several campus trends, but overall it has been a period of general quiet. The one significant national political movement that emerged, the anti-apartheid struggle, was of short duration and little lasting significance. A deteriorating racial situation on campus in the 1980s was accompanied by some anti-racist involvement. There are few activist national student political organizations, and none that can claim significant campus support. Activism has been overwhelmingly focused on specific campuses and has not coalesced into a regional or national movement. The significant changes in the American economy and in the world situation have not favored campus activism. The composition of the student population has itself changed, and again these shifts do not favor political involvement. Fewer students are full-time, there is more diversity in terms of social class and ethnic background, and larger proportions of the student population are studying part-time and/or working to earn money to pay for their education.

The configuration of attitudes remains basically unaltered, although with a modest shift toward the center and away from leftist positions. On life-style questions as well as some social issues, students remain liberal in their views. There have been some interesting changes in curricular choices; the dramatic shift toward vocationalism in the late 1970s and early 1980s has been at least in part countered by a partial return to the liberal arts fields. There is some increase in interest in careers in teaching. Focus on the social science, traditional breeding ground of activists, is modestly up.

Compared to the volatile sixties, the past two and one half decades have, of course, been notably apathetic with regard to student political involvement. But in the broader historical context of American student activism, the recent period is by no means unusual. The decade of the 1970s might well have been below the norm for American activism, but that of the 1980s is probably somewhat above average. The basic patterns seem to hold. The issues that appear to motivate students are those with a high moral content—issues such as repression in South Africa, racism on American campuses, or U.S. intervention in Central America. The campuses that have exhibited most activism in the recent past are the same universities that were prominent in earlier periods—the more cosmopolitan and prestigious universities on both coasts, a sprinkling of major public universities in between, and some traditionally progressive liberal arts colleges. Students from the social sciences seem to be more interested in political participation than those in professional programs or the sciences. Thus, the basic configuration of American student political involvement seems to have been maintained over time.

Given the imposing historical reputation of the student movement of the 1960s, it is understandable that most commentators on student politics of the past two decades have used the heyday of the New Left as a benchmark for comparative analysis. But this is the faulty comparison. American society was in the process of change. American student activists during most of the 1970s and 1980s attended college when the nation as a whole was shifting rightward as it had in the 1950s.

The lobbying, electoral work, and nonviolent demonstrations that collegians organized on behalf of federal student aid, peace, affirmative action, women's, gay, and disabled rights over the past two decades transcends anything students were able to organize in previous conservative eras. Indeed, student divestment protesters in the mid-1980s achieved what no previous generation of campus activists had ever managed to do: they created a mass student movement during the term of a conservative president (in contrast to both previous mass student movements, in the 1930s and 1960s, which had been born during reformist eras when liberals occupied the White House). There has been a persistence of liberal values and modest activism despite the resurgent conservatism in the nation.

The early 1990s saw a downward trend in activism. No doubt influenced by the dramatic political changes on the world scene and the decline of the left in general, student activism has been at a very low ebb in terms of national organizations and movements. There has nonetheless been an increase in voluntary social service activity, indicating that students retain a sense of moral concern and involvement. And there have been some local student activist initiatives around environmental issues and incidents of racism on campus.

While it is impossible to predict the future of student activism, the immediate future does not look to be one of significant campus political involvement. Demographic, economic, and societal factors affecting the student population do not favor activism. Current foreign policy issues are not the sort that lend themselves to campus activism. It is hard to see a campus-based national movement flourishing under current circumstances. But circumstances change, and no one predicted the emergence of the student movement of the 1960s.

PHILIP G. ALTBACH
January 1997

NOTES

1. This introduction first appeared as an article in the *Journal of Higher Education* 61 (January-February 1990), 32–49. In that version, it was co-authored with Robert Cohen. It has been extensively revised and updated for this volume.

2. For a discussion of the sixties, see Todd Gitlin, *The Sixties: Years of Hope, Days of Rage* (New York: Bantam, 1987). See also Paul Berman, *A Tale of Two Utopias: The Political Journey of the Generation of 1968* (New York: Norton, 1996).

3. For two analyses which argue that activism is not dead, see Paul Rogat Loeb, *Generation at the Crossroads: Apathy and Action on the American Campus* (New Brunswick, N.J.: Rutgers University Press, 1994), and Tony Vellela, *New Voices: Student Activism in the '80s and '90s* (Boston: South End Press, 1988).

4. Arthur Levine and Deborah J. Hirsch, "Undergraduates in Transition: A New Wave of Activism on American College Campuses," *Higher Education* 22 (September 1991), 119–28.

5. See Tom Wells, *The War Within: America's Battle Over Vietnam* (New York: Henry Holt, 1994).

6. H. Jacobs, *Weatherman* (San Francisco: Ramparts Press, 1970). See also Cyril Levitt, *Children of Privilege: Student Revolt in the Sixties* (Toronto: University of Toronto Press, 1984).

7. Todd Gitlin, *The Whole World Is Watching: The Mass Media in the Making and Unmaking of the New Left* (Berkeley: University of California Press, 1980).

8. "Fact File: Attitudes and Characteristics of This Year's Freshmen," *Chronicle of Higher Education,* January 20, 1988, A36, and *Chronicle of Higher Education,* September 2, 1996, 19.

9. *Ibid.*

10. All of the data cited here is from the UCLA-American Council on Education annual survey of college freshmen as reported in the *Chronicle of Higher Education* and in Linda J. Sax et al., *The American Freshman: National Norms for Fall 1995* (Los Angeles: Higher Education Research Institute, University of California at Los Angeles, 1995). Attitudes for other categories of students may vary, although other research indicates general consistency.

11. Arthur Levine and Keith Wilson, "Student Politics in America: Transformation Not Decline," *Higher Education* 8 (November 1979), 636–38.

12. Philip G. Altbach, "The National Student Association in the Fifties: Flawed Conscience of the Silent Generation," *Youth and Society* 5 (December 1973), 184–211.

13. Helen Lefkowitz Horowitz, *Campus Life: Undergraduate Cultures from the End of the Eighteenth Century to the Present* (Chicago: University of Chicago Press, 1988).

14. Levine and Wilson, "Student Politics in America."

15. Arthur Levine, *When Dreams and Heroes Died: A Portrait of Today's College Student* (San Francisco: Jossey Bass, 1980).

16. For more positive analyses, see Loeb, *Generation at the Crossroads* and Vellela, *New Voices.*

17. For a general discussion of the campus racial climate, see Philip G. Altbach and Kofi Lomotey, eds., *The Racial Crisis in American Higher Education* (Albany: SUNY Press, 1991).

18. One of the most visible examples of conservative activism was at Dartmouth College, where a right-wing student newspaper was quite active in the 1980s.

See Dinesh D'Souza, *Illiberal Education: The Politics of Race and Sex on Campus* (New York: Free Press, 1991).

19. "The Conservative Student," *Newsweek on Campus,* March 1985.
20. J. Nesses, "Student Struggle: Agenda for Change," *Guardian Supplement* (Spring 1986), 3.
21. Eric L. Hirsch, "Sacrifice for the Cause: Group Processes, Recruitment, and Commitment in a Student Social Movement," *American Sociological Review* 55 (April 1990), 243–54.
22. "A New Wave of Campus Protest on Apartheid," *Newsweek,* April 22, 1985, 71.
23. *New York Times,* April 25, 1985.
24. "The Times They Are a Changin'," *Time,* April 29, 1985, 44.
25. *Chronicle of Higher Education,* April 24, 1984, 17.
26. *Ibid.*
27. "The Divestment Controversy," *Daily Californian Special* (Berkeley, Calif.) (1985), 1–4.
28. *Chronicle of Higher Education,* September 18, 1985, 25.
29. "A New Breed of Activism," *Newsweek,* May 13, 1985, 62.
30. "The Times They Are a Changin'."
31. *Chronicle of Higher Education,* October 6, 1985, 32.
32. J. Weiner, "Divestment Report Card: Students, Stocks and Shanties," *Nation,* October 11, 1986, 337.
33. *Ibid.*
34. D'Souza, *Illiberal Education.*
35. "Shanties on the Green," *Newsweek,* February 3, 1986, 63–64.
36. *Ibid.*
37. *Ibid.*
38. Philip G. Altbach, "The Racial Dilemma in American Higher Education," in Altbach and Lomotey, eds., *The Racial Crisis in American Higher Education,* 3-18.
39. Mfanya D. Tryman, "Racism and Violence on College Campuses," *The Western Journal of Black Studies* 16, No. 4 (1992), 222.
40. *Ibid.*
41. Denise K. Magner, "Racial Tensions Continue to Erupt on Campuses Despite Efforts to Promote Cultural Diversity," *Chronicle of Higher Education,* June 6, 1990, 1, 29-30. See also Jon C. Dalton, ed., *Racism on Campus: Confronting Racial Bias Through Peer Interventions* (San Francisco: Jossey-Bass, 1991).
42. Altbach and Lomotey, eds., *The Racial Crisis in American Higher Education,* 199-248.
43. See Allan Bloom, *The Closing of the American Mind* (New York: Simon and Schuster, 1987). This was one of several influential books arguing that American higher education had lost its direction, and advocating the restoration of a traditional core curriculum. See also Nicholas H. Farnham and Adam Yarmolinski, eds., *Rethinking Liberal Education* (New York: Oxford University Press, 1996).
44. For different perspectives, see Patricia Aufderheide, ed., *Beyond PC: Towards a Politics of Understanding* (St. Paul, Minn.: Graywolf Press, 1992) and Will-

iam Casement, *The Great Canon Controversy: The Battle of the Books in Higher Education* (New Brunswick, N.J.: Transaction Publishers, 1996).

45. Jayne E. Stake et al., "The Women's Studies Experience: Impetus for Feminist Activism," *Psychology of Women Quarterly* 18 (1994), 17–24. See also Frances A. Maher and Mary K. T. Tetreault, *The Feminist Classroom* (New York: Basic Books, 1994) and G. R. Bowles and R. Duelli Klein, *Theories of Women's Studies* (London: Routledge and Kegan Paul, 1983).

46. Alexander Astin et al., *The Power of Protest: A National Study of Students and Faculty Disruptions with Implications for the Future* (San Francisco: Jossey Bass, 1975).

47. Elizabeth A. Williams and Gary D. Malaney, "Assessing the Political Ideology and Activism of College Students: Reactions to the Persian Gulf War," *NASPA Journal* 33 (Winter 1996): 145–60.

48. "Attitudes and Characteristics of Freshmen," *Chronicle of Higher Education,* September 2, 1996, 19. See also Darren E. Sherkat and T. Jean Blockerm, "Environmental Activism in the Protest Generation: Differentiating 1960s Activists," *Youth and Society* 25 (September 1993), 140–61.

49. Julian Keniry, "Environmental Movement Booming on Campuses," *Change,* September-October 1993, 42-49.

50. *Ibid.,* 48.

51. Deborah J. Hirsch, "Politics Through Action: Student Service and Activism in the '90s," *Change,* September-October, 1993, 32–36.

PREFACE

This volume is intended to provide a basic historical overview to American student activism from 1900 to 1960. Short sections on the period prior to 1900 and on the post-1960 New Left are included, but my basic concern is the 1900-1960 period. The focus of this volume is on political activism among American college and university students, and I have chosen to analyze student organizations and movements devoted to politics and social concern as the means of this analysis. The volume makes a claim to discuss all aspects of American student life, and it gives more emphasis to liberal and radical activism than to conservative political efforts. This is true for two reasons. First, activism of the left has clearly been the most important trend on the American campus, at least during the period under analysis. Second, liberal and radical groups have left much more adequate records and documents, and have been much more adequately discussed in periodicals and other sources. This volume is largely focused on national and to some extent regional movements and organizations. Again, convenience and available data have dictated this choice. Much valuable information concerning specific campuses exists and case studies of activism are important. A discussion of the national scene, however, provides adequate information concerning trends and currents, and places student activism in its educational and political contexts. Thus, this volume has limited goals and is seen as a beginning for much needed future research which can provide detailed analysis of specific organizations as well as local situations. Research dealing with religious and conservative student groups is particularly needed.

The research for this volume was made possible by a grant from the National Endowment for the Humanities and the author wishes to thank the Endowment, and particularly Mr. Armen Tashdinian, for support. Two research assistants, Ms. Patti Peterson and Ms. Gail Kelly were invaluable to the project. The comments of Professors Seymour Martin Lipset and Arthur Liebman as well as those of James O'Brien are appreciated, although the responsibility for the volume lies with the author.

PHILIP G. ALTBACH

**STUDENT POLITICS
IN AMERICA:
A Historical Analysis**

CHAPTER ONE

Introduction

This volume considers student political and social activism in the United States from 1900 to 1960. It focuses on those periods during which students were most heavily committed to politics, notably the thirties, the late fifties, and the early sixties. The study is largely historical in nature and traces the development of student organizations and assesses their impact on universities and on society. For the most part, matters such as social class origins, psychological factors, and cultural currents are treated only when they directly influence student activism. Thus, the scope of this volume is modest—to provide the reader with a picture of organized student activism in the United States during the period of its development as a social force.

Within the framework of this study of student organizations and movements, this study concentrates on the actions, values, and ideologies of the organized student movements.[1] Too many analyses of student activism have dwelt on psychological and sociological variables, and have not seriously considered what those in the movement actually did. Focusing on this type of history, however, is problematic because of the lack of continuity. While some student groups, especially those linked to and financed by adult organizations, have been long-lived, most have been unstable. As a result, it is important to focus both on specific student groups and also continuing themes evident in American student activism. For example, the criticisms of society and the university raised by both religious and political student organizations in the late 1920s are important in understanding the more programmatic and active decade of the thirties. The concerns of the Student Peace Union in the late 1950s are reflected, to some extent, in the resurgence of the antiwar movement and the Students for a Democratic Society (SDS) in the sixties.

The organized student movement represented only a small fraction of the student population. For the most part, American students have not been notably radical or opposed to the status quo. In the midst of the turmoil of the past decade, it has often been forgotten that most students have few quarrels with the Establishment and that a powerful student movement has rarely existed on the campuses. Despite the fact that student activism has never represented the opinions of a majority of the student population, nor has even a significant minority of the students participated in activist campaigns, student activism does represent something of the "tip of the iceberg" of American student discontent. The level of discontent can be broadly measured by the success of activist organizations in mobilizing support on the campus.[2] It is important to keep in mind that student activist organizations and movements represent a constituency substantially larger than its own numbers would indicate. Throughout the period under discussion here, student groups with only a small membership were able to mobilize widespread support for particular causes.

This volume focuses on *organizations*—those manifestations of student activism or social concern which have taken on readily definable formal characteristics and which have some continuity over time. Although in many cases campus-based groups had strong nonstudent adult support and were frequently dominated by nonstudent elements, I am concerned in this study with organizations or movements composed largely of students on a college or university campus or with national organizations with local or regional campus-based affiliates, regardless of the outside affiliations of these groups. To some extent, spontaneous demonstrations, usually local in nature and based on a single issue, are considered because they are important elements in student activism.

Among student organizations, those which engage in political activism and social concern are the main focus of this volume. Political activism is defined rather broadly and extends from militant protest demonstrations to petitioning legislators, from paramilitary political ac-

tion to educational efforts. Student publications focusing on politics
are considered part of activism, as are ad hoc protests centered on local
campus questions. The issues which may motivate activism range from
food in the college dormitory to the war in Vietnam, from censorship
of a campus speaker or publication to support for a Socialist politician.
Those involved in activism range from the most sophisticated ideologue
to the student concerned only with a particular issue or demonstration.
Regional and national groups received the bulk of analysis, but more
limited groups have also been important and are considered, as are
ostensibly nonpolitical groups such as the campus YM-YWCA and the
Methodist Student Movement, which have taken an interest in social
issues and politics over the years. In short, while we have defined activism broadly and will consider many manifestations of student social
and political concern, the focus of this volume is on the organization of
student activism in America.

This study is limited, for the most part, to American student activism between 1900 and 1960. This period was chosen because it covers
the development of student activism in its familiar modern forms. While
students participated in movements of one sort or another prior to
1900, after 1900 ideologically oriented student political groups
emerged, and students began to be consistently concerned with issues
such as the depersonalization of the university, ROTC, peace, and social
change. Discussion of the post-1960 New Left has, for the most part,
been omitted from this text for several reasons: First, it has already
received a good deal of attention from a number of analysts. Second,
because it was perhaps the most influential force in its era of American
student activism and because many of its organizational and ideological
forms were different from those which preceded them, the New Left
should be treated more thoroughly than is possible within the scope of
this study, and a definitive study is now in progress.[3]

The post-1900 student movement marks a distinct period in the
history of American social protest, and there is a good deal of ideological and some organizational continuity within that movement. While it
has been argued by many that the New Left marks a sharp break with
the past, the roots of the New Left lie in earlier student organizations
and movements of the 1930s or even the 1920s. The dramatic impact
of the recent student movement does not obscure its earlier origins.
Certainly changing social conditions, most dramatically the Vietnam

war, and the increasing importance of the university in the society have contributed to the impact of the current student movement. Nonetheless, the history of the student left reveals much about the orientation and problems that confronted the New Left.

The American student movement contrasts rather dramatically with student movements in many other countries, especially with student movements in developing countries.[4] American student activism has never constituted an active threat to the stability of the political system—not even during the dramatic protests at the 1968 Democratic Convention or immediately after the events of the Cambodian invasion and the shootings at Kent State in 1970. This contrasts sharply with student movements in other countries, where students have toppled governments or created serious political disorder. In many industrialized countries, student activism has been annoying to the government and has even influenced the direction of politics in the society, but in very few have students, by themselves, constituted much of a real threat to political stability. France, in 1968, was one of the few cases in which students, with some initial support from workers, threatened the government's power.

American student activism has gone through a number of phases. In the 1930s, students focused attention on foreign policy issues at a time when public opinion was most concerned with domestic issues and kept the antiwar and anti-intervention sentiment strongly in the public eye during the pre-World War II period. Students were the key elements in the antiwar movements of the 1960s and focused national attention on Vietnam through the teach-ins and massive demonstrations. Later, students were instrumental in Eugene McCarthy's presidential bid, and had an impact in forcing Lyndon Johnson not to seek a second term in office. The student movement in all likelihood has at least entered into the equation of those in power concerning further intervention in Southeast Asia. But despite these successful political involvements, by and large American students have not been the political force that students have been in many other countries.

Student activism has also been generally ineffectual in the academic and political life of universities. Very rarely have student organizations taken an interest in university reform, curriculum, or governance. In some periods, notably the 1920s and 1960s, students strongly criticized the direction of higher education and the quality of instruction. Even in these instances, few students were actively involved in proposing and implementing specific reforms. Generally, while the student movement has been based on the campuses and directly influenced by conditions there, it has not shaped the direction of higher education. Ideologically oriented political groups have either felt that academic issues were irrelevant to revolutionary organizations or were simply involved in other struggles. There is a strong current in radical student thought against concern with academic issues on the grounds that these are inherently "reformist."

When student movements became involved in campus issues, they were more successful. The kinds of issues around which students have organized have been those campus questions which intersect with broader social concerns, such as ROTC or university involvement with military research. During the 1920s, student efforts to limit compulsory ROTC were related to antiwar issues. Similarly, in the 1960s student agitation against both ROTC and military-related research was widespread and directly linked to student concern over the Vietnam war. Yet, student agitation aimed at university issues, so evident in the 1960s, was something of an aberration, since the general focus of American student activism has not been the campus.

Some of the reasons why American students have been relatively unsuccessful in effecting social and political change are key to understanding the inner dynamic of the student movement as well as its relation to the broader society.

1. The American higher educational system, even in the early years of the present century, has been, in international terms, large and socially diverse. There has been no single geographical center for student activism; indeed, many of the most active campuses—Berkeley, Chicago, Madison, Ann Arbor—are located far from the center of political power in Washington, D. C. In addition, the levers of power are so geographically diffuse that "seizing" the government is virtually impossible. The universities are also administratively diffuse and there is no central authority which could, if inclined, introduce academic reform. Given this situation, American student organizations have found it very difficult to organize effective national movements or focus attention on a single source of political leverage when dealing with political or academic questions.

2. There has been little sense of community among American students. The student population has been large throughout the twentieth century, and while a majority of American students have been from the middle classes, there are major religious and regional differences among them. The higher education "system" is quite complex, and students at Harvard, for example, have little in common with their compeers at a community college in Oklahoma. In recent times, however, a temporary sense of community has developed during periods of intense activism, such as after the Kent State tragedy, and some regional identities often exist, such as among students in the Ivy League schools. But these examples are exceptions to the general rule.

3. American students have not had a strong tradition of political activism. While student political activism did not originate with the New Left or even the 1930s, student political involvement has not been considered a legitimate form of politics by either the general public or the government. Nor have students ever been effective in producing major political change in the United States. This lack of an accepted tradition of activism has made it difficult for activists to effectively organize on campus.

4. The American political infrastructure is highly complex and quite well developed. Thus, with many competing interest groups, an active mass media, and a large corps of educated individuals, the student movement has been only one element among many in pressing for political action. This contrasts sharply with many developing countries, where students have been one of the very few politically articulate elements in the population and have often expressed the desires of other less vocal groups.

5. The American student community has never been an "incipient elite" whose views and personalities might be valuable to society in the future. This situation is different from the situation in developing countries, where student leaders become members of the political elite. This lack of elite status (and consciousness) in the United States has limited the effectiveness of student political activism.

These factors only partially explain why the American student activists have been unsuccessful in creating an effective national movement and why students have not had a larger impact on society.[5]

CURRENTS IN AMERICAN STUDENT ACTIVISM

American student activism is marked by both continuity and change. On the one hand, there are political, cultural, and ideological currents which can be seen throughout the history of student activism; on the other hand, specific organizations have often been short-lived and activist movements have often disappeared when the particular issue which concerned them was resolved (or more likely, defeated). While this volume is organized basically along chronological lines, it is possible to discern a number of lines of political and organizational continuity. Figure 1 indicates some of these currents. It is not at all surprising that basic political currents should remain relatively stable over time, since the bases of ideological politics do not change dramatically. In addition, the participation in various adult organizations, political and religious, has added to this element of stability.

The three major streams in American student activism are the liberal-radical, the religious, and the conservative. The stress of this volume, as noted previously, is on the liberal-radical stream since it has provided the major leadership to the student activist movement in the United States. The liberal-radical stream is perhaps the most difficult one to trace over time, since it includes many different organizations and ideological tendencies. Nevertheless, within this stream, one can see a number of currents which have persisted. For example student organizations with a basically liberal ideology uphold similar analyses of American society and many common political programs. The radical groups exhibit more differences but, again, it is possible to see clear organizational and ideological currents over the sixty-year period. Student organizations tied ideologically and organizationally to the Communist party have changed names from time to time, but they exhibit more similarities than differences.

Student movements have often been oriented around a single issue and have maintained little continuity over time. Even in such cases, however, it is often possible to isolate a particular ideologically oriented group in a leadership position. While the issue of civil rights was a particularly important focal point of student activism in the late 1950s, key campus civil rights militants were members of ideologically oriented student groups (at least among the Northern white leadership). Similarly, the American Student Union, which was the key student organization of the mid-1930s, was oriented substantially to foreign

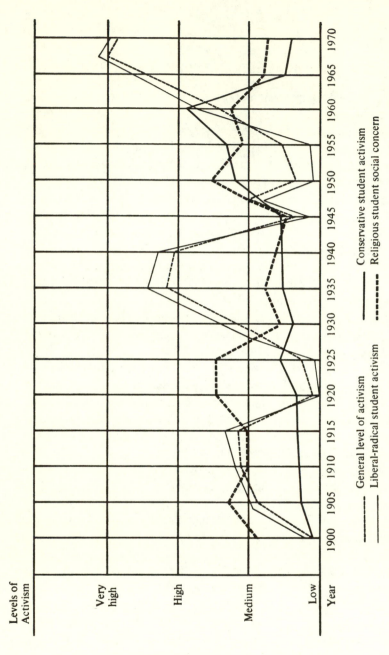

FIGURE 1 Levels of student activism in America, 1900-1970, measured by organizational strength, student participation in demonstrations, viability of student publications, and other general indicators.

policy issues and was under the strong leadership and at times domination by various radical student groups, particularly the Communists.

There are a number of issues of recurring importance in the development of student activism. Students have consistently focused on foreign affairs and questions of war and peace. The first large liberally oriented national student organization, the National Student Federation of America, was formed out of a concern for the League of Nations, the World Court, and other questions related to foreign policy in 1925. Similarly, the American Student Union, which had both Socialist and Communist leadership in the 1930s, was most successful when it organized around foreign policy questions. The brief upsurge of interest in student activism following World War II was in part stimulated by the United Nations, and the early strength of the revived post-McCarthy student movement of the late 1950s took its strength from the nuclear testing question, although civil rights later became the critical issue. This emphasis on foreign policy may well reflect the largely middle-class base of the student movement, which has made the more abstract issues of foreign affairs more meaningful than immediate questions of domestic import.

Civil liberties have also been a major concern of students. Student groups have been among the most active defenders of civil liberties, both on and off campus, during times when these rights were threatened, and particularly during the twenties and fifties. Students have often cooperated with faculty liberals and radicals in protecting academic freedom on campus and have engaged in many demonstrations to prevent outspoken professors from losing their jobs. While these battles have been lost more than won, students have been valuable to the faculty in maintaining freedom of expression in the universities in times when such freedom was under attack in the society at large.

Race relations has been a concern of large numbers of students but its significance has increased markedly since 1958 when the civil rights movements became militant. Since the beginning of the twentieth century, politically conscious students have been liberal on questions of race relations. The Cosmopolitan Club movement around 1910 had improved racial and international relations among students as its major aim, and the various political groups during the 1930s stressed the importance of including blacks in the student movement and in taking a strong stand on racial questions. Religious student groups also were concerned with race relations. Students were key elements in the founding of the Congress of Racial Equality (CORE) in 1943 in Chicago, and in stimulating the rebirth of the mass civil rights movement of the sixties through their participation in the Freedom Rides, sit-ins, and other militant activities. Despite this, however, the involvement of students in civil rights activities is of fairly recent origin.

It is logical to expect that student activists would have traditionally been concerned with conditions on their own campuses and also with the directions and programs of American higher education. While American students have traditionally had complaints about their universities, these complaints have not always been expressed in particularly militant ways. The two periods of greatest open dissatisfaction with the universities have been the 1920s and 1960s. Much of the most vocal criticism was aimed at the increasing impersonality and mass nature of the university. Throughout the period under consideration in this volume, sporadic concern and dissatisfaction with such matters as dormitory food, campus living conditions, and specific administrators or professors, were expressed by student newspapers and at times by student organizations.[6]

While much of the locally based dissatisfaction with the nature of higher education and with academic issues had little national importance, did not mean broader activism, and had few connections to ideological groups, at times educational reform questions were given serious attention by student activists. During the 1920s national student organizations and particularly the journal *New Student* focused attention on problems of higher education. For a period in the 1960s, the Students for a Democratic Society and the New University Conference stressed university issues, and related the university to broader social and political issues. Nationally coordinated campus demonstrations against the Dow Chemical Company's recruiting efforts at the universities because of the company's links with the Vietnam war were an effective means of pressing the antiwar movement. Similarly, the "student power" issue had a short period of prominence in the 1960s. Since before World War II, students have tried, with growing success, to eliminate vestiges of in loco parentis from the campus as well. But despite activism concerning academic issues and dissatisfaction with the nature of some aspects of higher education, student groups have seldom outlined comprehensive plans for the reform of higher education. Thus, while dissatisfaction was expressed, student activist groups did not spend much time or effort in formulating and pressing for comprehensive reform plans.

The United States is somewhat unique in its lack of a large and established radical movement or even a legitimate radical tradition. No Socialist, Communist, or even radical reformist political party has gained power and the various leftist (and for that matter rightist) political parties have remained small and generally isolated groups. Partly because of this lack of any possibility of attaining power, American radical movements have been noted for their factionalism and splintering.[7] Student activism has been affected by this and has been substantially weakened by the absence of a viable adult movement. Indeed, on a number of occasions, activist students have sought to build an adult movement on the basis of the student movement. The adult League for Industrial Democracy emerged from the campus-based Intercollegiate Socialist Society in the 1920s, and alumni of the Students for a Democratic Society in the late 1960s attempted to create an adult New Left—the Movement for a Democratic Society—in their image and published journals such as the *Radicals in the Professions Newsletter*. These efforts were not notably successful. Despite the absence of a viable leftist movement in America, adult radical groups have tried and, to some extent, have succeeded in controlling student groups.

What was the impact of student activism, on and off campus, during the first half of the twentieth century? This question is taken up in detail in the concluding section of this volume. The student movement has had some impact on the society, although it has been quite limited. Certainly students were among the most active proponents of neutrality prior to World War II and were instrumental in the peace movement of that period. More recently, student activists were in the vanguard of both the civil rights movement of the early 1960s and in the revival of radical politics known broadly as the New Left. But, as noted earlier, they did not come close to effecting major change in the social system. In addition, while student activism has impelled faculty members and university administrators to think seriously about the defects of American higher education, students have not had much control over the kinds of changes that have occurred.

The burden of this volume is not that "there is nothing new under the sun" and that student activism simply goes in predictable cycles. It is, rather, that in order to understand American student activism—and indeed modern American higher education and society, which are closely related to student activism—one must examine the historical development of organizations and movements on campus. While much attention has been devoted to analyzing the New Left of the 1960s, the most recent wave of campus activism is by no means the first manifestation of student concern with politics and society. Nor are the overtly political organizations, such as SDS, the only groups which have had an impact in terms of social and political action on campus. Indeed, one can argue that the New Left's importance increased because, among other things, it was, almost alone among the various elements of American society, pressing for political change in the sixties while the potent student movement of the thirties was just one among many social forces seeking to change society. The rest of this volume is aimed at placing the New Left in historical perspective and analyzing the various forces which interacted with the campus to create, and destroy, student organizations and movements during the first part of the twentieth century in the United States.

THE "PREHISTORY" OF AMERICAN STUDENT ACTIVISM:
A NOTE

This volume deals exclusively with the twentieth century. This is done for a simple reason—the emergence of student activism in coherently organized forms took place in this period, and relatively little activism of an organized nature occurred prior to 1900. It is, nevertheless, important to point to some of the important currents in American higher education and among students in the pre-1900 period in order to provide some relevant historical background.[8] Student activism cannot be divorced from its campus milieu, and it is no coincidence that at the same time that political involvement was taking place among students in the early 1900s, the American university was undergoing major change. The emergence of graduate schools and the expansion of higher education generally changed both the scope and many aspects of the curriculum of the American university in the early years of the twentieth century.[9] The student population grew from 52,000 in 1869 to 237,000 in 1900 and then climbed to 1,100,000 in 1929. New universities such as Stanford, Chicago, and Johns Hopkins were founded at the end of the nineteenth century, and became important elements of the university system by 1910. The great state universities—California, Michigan, Wisconsin, Illinois, and others—underwent massive growth at this time as well. Thus, American higher education was in the process of change, and by most yardsticks, substantial improvement and expansion, during the early years of the present century.

One of the elements of American higher education which has affected students up to the present time is the doctrine of in loco parentis. This concept goes back to the early years of American colleges, and has been the cause of much student unrest and many demonstrations through the years. In loco parentis, briefly stated, means that the university takes on the responsibilities of the parent regarding its students. Traditionally, this often meant that quite severe regulations concerning life styles, living arrangements, religious services, and other matters were enforced by the academic authorities, and that students had to obey these regulations. Many "revolts" against such regulations took place over the years, with compulsory chapel attendance one of the most heated issues. The doctrine of in loco parentis has been under attack, therefore, for a century or more and only in the last fifteen years has it been discarded to a substantial degree by many universities, particularly the more prestigious institutions and those in metropolitan areas. In loco parentis will emerge repeatedly in this volume as one of the causes for student unrest, particularly at the local campus level.

No major national student organizations devoted to politics emerged prior to 1900, but several currents in student activism can be detected. Student involvement in national affairs took place to some extent during the Revolutionary War and its immediate aftermath, although normal academic life was not seriously disrupted for the most part during this period. Students were also active during the Civil War period, when the antislavery issue aroused student activism in many Northern schools. Students were involved both in antidraft activities in New York and elsewhere during this period, and they volunteered in substantial numbers for service in the war.

Much local campus activism also occurred on an entirely spontaneous basis. Protests against dormitory food, specific professors, or other local issues occasionally aroused student discontent. Disciplinary procedures were stringent, and the usual result of a demonstration was the expulsion of substantial numbers of students from the affected college.

Religious activism was also part of nineteenth century campus life. At some schools, perhaps notably Harvard, Unitarianism and "freethinking" generally was the order of the day, while at many other colleges, led by Yale but including many newer church-related schools, the evangelistic fervor of the Great Awakening of the 1830s was a key element in campus life. While this religious activism produced few demonstrations and did not disrupt campus life (although at some colleges, freethinking professors were harassed by orthodox students), it was one of the important currents of the period.

Social concern during the late nineteenth century was expressed through several avenues. The settlement house movement involved thousands of students in urban social work. By 1911, 2,500 residents and as many as 15,000 volunteers, mostly college students, were involved in 413 settlement houses. As Jane Addams said, "Our so-called educated young people, who bear the brunt of being cultivated into unnourished, oversensitive lives," were the ones who perceived most sharply the contradiction between the existence of the middle and upper classes and the working classes.[10] While the numbers of students involved in settlement house work declined by the turn of the century, this kind of student participation continued and provided valuable and formative experience for prominent radicals like Norman Thomas and A. J. Muste. The YMCA movement was another outlet for both social and religious concern, and this organization continued to be important during the twentieth century as well. A specifically student wing of the YM-YWCA was formed in 1877 and the first full-time campus religious worker was appointed in that year. By 1885, Student Ys involved 10,000 students and this number grew impressively. In 1900, there were 611 student associations, not all of which were in colleges.[11] Students were also involved in missionary work, and by 1913, 2,500 students were involved in one or another kind of missionary activity. Overseas missionary work among college students was conducted by the Student Volunteer Movement, which was closely allied with the YMCAs. While it is clear that the main thrust of the campus Christian movement at this period was not social or political, it was one of the few agencies functioning in large numbers of American colleges which fostered some kind of social concern.

Thus, while no national or even regional political movements emerged prior to 1900, some of the currents which existed were important and must be kept in mind in the following discussion. Broader currents in American higher education influenced the students and student activism, and one of the most important transformations was taking place around the turn of the century. Historical trends such as in loco parentis also had a major impact on students and was a continuing cause of campus discontent. And the religious student movement which emerged in the late nineteenth century had a continuing impact on campus, perhaps especially in the 1920s.

NOTES

1. The problem of obtaining adequate data for this study has been a serious one. Student organizations have left fewer records than, for example, labor unions or political parties. Many groups are very short-lived, and much campus protest has been of a local nature. Further, there has in general been more adequate coverage of liberal and radical groups in the literature, in part because such groups had a greater historical sense.
2. Robert S. Laufer, "Sources of Generational Consciousness and Conflict," in P. G. Altbach and R. S. Laufer, eds., *The New Pilgrims: Youth Protest in Transition*, (New York: David McKay, 1972), pp. 218-237.
3. The analysis of the New Left is too lengthy to mention in detail here. For a variety of viewpoints, see the following works; Michael Miles, *Radical Probe: The Logic of Student Rebellion*, (New York: Atheneum, 1971), "The New Left and the Old," *Journal of Social Issues*, 27 (1), 1-200, 1971, Irving Howe, ed., *Beyond the New Left*, (New York: McCall, 1970), and Nathan Glazer, *Remembering the Answers: Essays on the American Student Revolt*, (New York: Basic Books, 1970). See also James P. O'Brien, "The Development of the New Left," in P. G. Altbach and R. Laufer, eds., *The New Pilgrims: Youth Protest in Transition*, (New York: David McKay, 1972), pp. 32-45. Dr. O'Brien is currently writing a definitive history of the New Left.
4. For some general discussion of the role of student movements in developing countries, see Philip G. Altbach, "Student Movements in Historical Perspective: The Asian Case," *Youth and Society*, Vol. 1, April, 1970, pp. 333-357 and S. M. Lipset, "University Students and Politics in Developing Countries," in S. M. Lipset, ed., *Student Politics*, (New York: Basic Books, 1968), pp. 3-53. The essays in Donald Emmerson, ed., *Students and Politics in Developing Countries*, (New York: Praeger, 1968), also provide valuable perspectives on this topic.
5. Many commentators have tried to put the student movement into perspective in America. For more thoughtful efforts, see Michael Miles, op. cit., E. Wright Bakke, *Campus Challenge*, (New Haven, Conn.: Archon Books, 1971), and S. M. Lipset, *Rebellion in the University*, (Boston: Little Brown, 1972).
6. A study of the levels of activism at two universities and a discussion of what segments of the campus community raised dissenting issues is by Shlomo

Swirski, "Changes in the Structure of Relations Between Groups and the Emergence of Political Movements: The Student Movement at Harvard and Wisconsin, 1930-1969" (Unpublished Ph.D. Dissertation, Department of Political Science, Michigan State University, 1971).

7. For analyses of the American radical movement, see S. M. Lipset and Earl Rabb, *The Politics of Unreason: Right-wing Extremism in America*, (New York: Doubleday, 1971), James Weinstein, *The Decline of Socialism in America, 1912-1925*, (New York: Monthly Review Press, 1970), and Irving Howe and Lewis Coser, *The American Communist Party*, (New York: Praeger, 1957), among other studies.

8. There is no full discussion of student activism prior to 1900. Several analysts deal more adequately than others with this period. For historical discussions, see particularly S. M. Lipset, *Rebellion in the University*, (Boston: Little Brown, 1972), Lewis Feuer, *The Conflict of Generations: The Character and Significance of Student Movements*, (New York: Basic Books, 1969), and Henry D. Sheldon, *The History and Pedagogy of American Student Societies*, (New York: D. Appleton, 1901).

9. For an excellent discussion of the dramatic changes which took place in American higher education in the late nineteenth century, see Laurence R. Veysey, *The Emergence of the American University*, (Chicago: University of Chicago Press, 1965).

10. Quoted in Lewis Feuer from Jane Addams. "The Subjective Necessity for Social Settlements," in Jane Addams, et al., *Philanthropy and Social Progress*, (New York, 1893), p. 6.

11. Commission on Student Work, YMCA, *What of the Future of the Student YMCAs?* (New York: National Student Council of the YMCAs, 1941), p. 5. For a more general discussion of the student Christian movement, see Clarence P. Shedd, *Two Centuries of Student Christian Movements: Their Origin and Intercollegiate Life*, (New York: Association Press, 1934) and Clarence P. Shedd, *The Church Follows Its Students*, (New Haven, Conn.: Yale University Press, 1934).

CHAPTER TWO

The Stirrings of Student Activism: 1900–1930

The period between 1900 and 1930 is a watershed in American history. The First World War, America's emergence as a major world power, and the economic and cultural movements of the twenties are the main landmarks of the period. Except for the war years, American higher education underwent sustained growth. Enrollments increased from 237,592 in 1900 to 1,100,737 in 1930, and from 4 percent to 12.5 percent of the age cohort. While the universities were not as prominent in the economy and culture as they were after 1945, their importance to the society was increasing. In the same period, for the first time national student organizations devoted to social action and politics developed and became an established part of academia. Ideological politics appeared on campus as socialism and communism became student concerns. Politically oriented activism on both regional and national levels grew as well. The 1900-1930 period did set the stage, both organizationally and ideologically, for the ascendancy of the massive student groups of the thirties. In short, this period marked the emergence of student activism in the organizational forms in which it has existed ever since.

The major currents of the period, which were particularly influential on campus, occurred after World War I. They were: (1) the disillusionment which many Americans, particularly the middle classes, felt following the war; (2) the rather peculiar prosperity of the period (the twenties were certainly economically "roaring" but the decade was also marked by large pockets of unemployment and by major economic shifts which left many insecure); (3) the Russian Revolution and its impact on the American left and to a lesser extent on the society generally; and (4) the cultural ferment of the period. The student activism and student organizations which are considered in this chapter are analyzed against the background of these (and other) factors.[1]

While it is often misleading to compare periods of American history, the 1920s becomes more comprehensible if compared to the 1960s.[2] Both periods were marked by massive cultural ferment and conflicts between segments of the older and younger generations. Many popular intellectuals on campus were openly antigovernment during part of both periods. In the 1920s prohibition was flaunted on campus and led to some disillusionment with established authority, just as student discontent with drug laws in the sixties contributed to antiestablishment sentiments. Traditional concepts of in loco parentis in the universities came under attack and, although they survived in somewhat weakened form in the twenties, paternalism was damaged. The much heralded "sexual revolution" of the twenties was documented by Alfred Kinsey, who noted a big jump in the proportion of females with premarital sexual experience. Seemingly, the proportion did not increase again, at least among college students, until the 1960s.[3] A final similarity between the two periods is the general lack of coordination between campus political and cultural movements and adult organizations, parties, and movements. This contrasts markedly with the activist thirties, when student groups were strongly linked to adult political parties.

The 1920s and the 1960s both saw substantial commentary on and criticism of higher education. Many blamed protest on the universities. The student organizations also focused on problems of the universities by calling for major academic reform without providing any detailed guidelines for it. Indeed, the criticisms of the universities of both periods are quite similar, for protests centered on the impersonal nature of instruction, over-expansion, and the emphasis on research to the detriment of teaching.

The 1900-1930 period can be divided into two distinct parts. The first is the pre-World War I period, between 1900 and 1917. It was a time of modest growth in campus political activism that showed some organizational development and very little generational conflict. The campus was not all that different from society as a whole in either attitudes or politics since political radicalism was on the upswing both on campus and off. The first politically oriented national student organization, the Intercollegiate Socialist Society, was formed during this period.

The second part of this era, 1918-1929, is more complex, for its encompasses the postwar red scare and the roaring twenties. This was a time of stress. It was an era of cultural ferment and the campus community was important in the counterculture of the decade. Students were avid followers of cultural movements from Dadaism to Couéism to various shades of Marxism. The twenties were also marked by cynicism on the campus; the outcome of the First World War and the failure of Wilson's Fourteen Points had been a profoundly disillusioning experience for many Americans, particularly the middle classes; the overwhelmingly materialistic orientation of most Americans during the twenties was resented by campus activists; the legal and moral restrictions of an "old" culture were being attacked even in adult society, and students, more than most segments of society, rebelled against such legalities as prohibition. The universities were also substantially changing as enrollments expanded and universities placed increasing emphasis on research. Combined with a growing articulateness among some segments of the student population and the development of national student journals, these changes meant that criticisms of higher education came regularly from activist students.

The twenties saw the growth of a number of politically oriented student organizations, some of which survived into the thirties. Political organizations of a liberal and radical orientation developed and, by the end of the decade, at least four national student organizations were functioning: the National Student Federation of America, the Young Communist League, the Young Peoples' Socialist League, and the League for Industrial Democracy—in addition to the various student-oriented religious groups, such as the YM-YWCAs. In addition, political parties took an interest in students. Christian student groups emerged that involved unprecedented numbers of students in their programs, many of which were related to social action. Few conservative organizations grew at this time despite the fact that many students expressed conservative sentiments.

The campus political culture was dominated by liberal and radical groups and by the aura of cultural radicalism. At the same time that these political groups were developing, particularly in the early twenties, some repression of student activists occurred. Academic discipline was much more severe than during later periods—administrators could still expel students at will and censor campus newspapers and journals with little compunction. Press reports from the period indicate that such repression was not uncommon, although it happened more often at the less prestigious institutions.

While radical student groups appeared, the campus was not marked by intense political awareness or cultural dissent. Indeed, the overall apathy and lack of political involvement on campus prevailed since only a minority of students and their organizations were activist. Political polls taken at the time indicate that the majority of students consistently favored the Republican presidential candidates and that support for progressive and radical candidates trailed behind that given off campus. According to *New York Times* reports, even the more "radical" schools such as Harvard, Columbia, Chicago, and Berkeley reported Republican majorities.[4] In one of the few editorials devoted to student affairs in the twenties, *The New York Times* noted that the American student was substantially more conservative and apathetic than his European counterpart. The *Times* explained this apathy by noting that students were satisfied with their country and that the campuses were, in any case, isolated from the mainstream of society.[5]

Student activism during the entire 1900-1930 period had little impact on the society at large. There were few, if any, major student demonstrations or campaigns directed at national issues and locally oriented protests were not usually effective. Students supported American membership in the World Court and lobbied for the League of Nations, but the government scarcely noticed them. Campus political life was generally focused on journalistic ventures, educational campaigns, and various kinds of meetings and conferences rather than on direct action. Thus, outside the universities, the existence of a political movement on campus had little impact and, while occasionally the subject of publicity in the mass media, student activism was not a major public concern. It is significant that the bulk of public debate about students in this period was over student morality and culture rather than the political dissent on campus.

Student activism in the 1920s, as at other periods, was limited to particular groups in the student body and to specific campuses. The politically oriented student organizations were not spread throughout the country but were, with few exceptions, limited to the campuses which in the sixties and seventies are known as the most radical schools. These were the larger Midwestern state universities and the prestigious private colleges and universities. Berkeley, Wisconsin, Harvard, Michigan, Swarthmore, Oberlin, and similar schools repeatedly were mentioned in the reports of the various political groups and in journals such as the *New Student.* Also, City College and Columbia University in New York were prominent as "radical" schools, perhaps reflecting the center of radicalism in the New York area. This was perhaps more accentuated in the twenties than it is at present. Students at smaller schools and at Southern and denominational colleges were almost completely inactive politically during this period. If one can surmise from the nature of the universities which were most politically concerned, it is likely that the activists of the twenties were similar to those of later periods in that they were bright, from cosmopolitan families, and from fairly affluent backgrounds.[6] In this respect, there seems to be a good deal of continuity over time.

THE EMERGENCE OF ORGANIZED STUDENT ACTIVISM

There were three major developments in terms of campus political activism between 1900 and 1917. The first, and in the long run most important, was the founding of the Intercollegiate Socialist Society (ISS) in 1905. The ISS, which later changed its name to the League for Industrial Democracy (LID), then to the Student League for Industrial Democracy, and finally the Students for a Democratic Society in 1962, was the first ideologically oriented national student organization in the United States. The second major development was the involvement of students in the settlement house movement. Thousands of middle-class students worked for varying periods of time in urban slums in settlement houses and other social service agencies. Many saw firsthand some of the problems of developing urbanization and not a few went into political or social service careers. The third critical development on campus was the continuing growth and influence of various Christian organizations. While only a small proportion of student Christian activity was directed at social action work, groups like the YMCA and the denominational student affiliates did expose many students to social service projects and to a degree of political education. This was particularly true in colleges where more general kinds of political action and discussion were not very prevalent.

The period prior to World War I was one of growth for radical and social reform movements. The problems of industrialism, which stimulated the muckrakers during this period and brought Upton Sinclair fame for his book, *The Jungle* (published in 1906), describing conditions in the Chicago stockyards, pricked the conscience of the middle classes and were influential among many campus intellectuals.[7] In 1912, the Progressive Party won 27 percent of the vote with Theodore Roosevelt as its presidential candidate and the Socialists' under Debs obtained 6 percent. The spirit of reform was in the air, and to a great extent the campus reflected this atmosphere of change. This period was one of expansion and differentiation for the universities. The founding of the great graduate-oriented universities such as Chicago, Stanford, and Johns Hopkins just prior to the turn of the century had a profound impact on American higher education, and the emphasis on research and graduate education, which has come to characterize higher education in the current period, developed at this time. Many complained that the undergraduate student was being left behind in the rush for research and publication, but there is little evidence that deteriorating conditions, if in fact they existed at the time, were evident to many students. There were very few overt complaints against the academic system and few active protests at the time. Campus issues were not the focus of student activism until after World War I.

The Intercollegiate Socialist Society (ISS) was the most important student organization of the period. The ISS succeeded in coordinating the various socialist and liberal clubs which existed in many universities and was the only nationally organized political group. It provided an ethos for campus radicalism. The ISS was never a doctrinaire organization and welcomed anyone with vaguely left-of-center views into its ranks. Indeed, it estimated that at least one-third of its members were nonsocialists in 1913.[8] The ISS was not an activist group. Its main activities were educational programs aimed at converting students to socialism and social reform or at providing socialist education for its own members. Prominent socialist speakers toured the campuses for the ISS and field workers provided regional and national coordination. Few campaigns were launched on either local or national levels. The ISS saw itself devoted to rational dialogue and education and not to activism.

This approach was quite successful in that ISS attracted many highly intellectual students, many of whom later became involved in national politics, both left and liberal.[9] In a sense the ISS was an "elitist" organization: it aimed at educating upper-middle-class college students about socialism, hoping that their commitment would extend beyond the college years. Here the ISS had more in common with the British Fabians than with Marxism.

While never a "movement" in the traditional sense, the ISS was influential on the campuses on which it was active and was an important part of the student "political culture." This was particularly true in the absence of other politically active groups. Indeed, the ISS was so successful only a few years after its founding that it attracted a good deal of negative commentary and opposition from adult conservative groups. ISS affiliated groups were often key elements on their campuses and campus intellectual centers.

The Intercollegiate Socialist Society was founded on the initiative of Upton Sinclair, then a young radical writer and author of the best-selling *The Jungle*, who felt that "since the professors would not educate the students, it was up to the students to educate the professors." [10] Sinclair brought together a small group of fifty-five people in New York in September 1905 to initiate an educational organization which would bring socialist ideas to the campuses. Among the people at this meeting were Clarence Darrow, Charlotte Perkins Gilman, J. G. Phelps Stokes, and Jack London—a good cross section of socialist intellectuals at the time. Only two students were present and only one, Harry Laidler of Wesleyan, was appointed to the first executive committee. Jack London was appointed president, although Upton Sinclair kept the organization going for its first years, with the financial assistance of a wealthy socialist jewelry manufacturer and a vice president of New York Life Insurance Company.

Although the idea that college students should be interested in socialism was new to the United States, the ISS found some support and quickly organized three chapters with a dozen members in each.[11] By 1906, ISS chapters were organized at Chicago, Wisconsin, Columbia, Wesleyan, Yale, and other schools, with a majority of members on the East coast. The major national activity of the ISS during its early years was national tours to campuses by ISS leaders who addressed large public meetings on topics related to socialism. A lecture tour by Jack

London in 1905, for example, was highly successful. Both Sinclair and Laidler also made numerous speaking tours for the ISS. In addition, the ISS was instrumental in getting courses on topics related to socialism started in many colleges. According to ISS Secretary Laidler, more than eighty such courses were initiated.[12] Other key activites of the ISS were the annual convention, usually held in New York, and summer institutes devoted to education on topics related to socialism. The conventions attracted around fifty delegates from campus ISS chapters, as well as many individual members from the New York area. (As many as 500 attended the convention dinners.) The summer institutes were held at a camp and were generally small.

While the ISS never became a mass movement on the campuses, its growth is fairly impressive in the years prior to World War I. When compared to the total student population of 400,000 in 1912-1913, ISS membership is not very impressive, although as S. M. Lipset points out, the ISS in its day had proportionally more members than did the Students for a Democratic Society in the 1960s, when SDS claimed 6,000 paid members out of a student population of almost 7,000,000.[13] Perhaps like the SDS, the importance of the ISS was in the kinds of students it attracted and the campuses on which it was active. Quite a number of individuals who were later well known in academic and intellectual circles were members of the ISS while at college in the prewar period. The ISS members included Paul Douglas,

TABLE 1 Growth of the Intercollegiate Socialist Society*

	1911	1913	1915	1917
Undergraduate members	750	1,000	1,332	900
Undergraduate chapters	38	64	70	39
Percentage of Socialists in ISS	59	–	50	36
Delegates to convention	50	33	42	50

*From Ann Topham, "Light More Light: The Intercollegiate Socialist Society, 1905-1918," (Unpublished paper, University of Wisconsin, 1971), p. 22. Data taken from *Intercollegiate Socialist.*

John Dewey, Walter Lippmann, Edna St. Vincent Millay, and A. J. Muste. In addition, ISS chapters, by 1913, were active at many of the country's more important campuses.[14] The ISS also had eleven alumni chapters in large cities in various parts of the country. These chapters provided funds for student activity and were an intellectual link among adult socialist intellectuals.

Something of a high-water mark in ISS activities was reached around 1913. In that year the first issue of the ISS journal, the *Intercollegiate Socialist*, appeared. The magazine was published on a bimonthly or quarterly basis until May 1919, when the name was changed to the *Socialist Review*. Edited by Harry Laidler and published from the ISS's New York offices, the magazine featured news of ISS activities on campus and articles related to theoretical aspects of socialism. While there is some attention given to student movements in other countries and to education, these were clearly subsidiary to the ISS's concern with spreading socialist ideas on the campus. While it is impossible to evaluate the impact of the *Intercollegiate Socialist*, the journal was the only student-oriented magazine devoted to political issues at the time and was probably influential where the ISS was active. In the Fabian tradition the ISS also published a series of pamphlets on socialism. None were devoted to education or university problems. The pamphlet series was augmented by a research program in which students participated. This research bureau was under the direction of Ordway Tead and looked into such questions as cooperatives and municipal socialism.

There was much variation among individual ISS chapters. Most limited themselves to educational activities and public meetings. Some, however, were more activist. At the University of Michigan, for example, the ISS chapter decided to broaden out from traditional activities of socialist study groups and lecture courses. Since many of the members (largely of working class origin) worked in the university's kitchens and dining rooms, they organized a union of working students and struck for reasonable working hours and clean food.[15] Local ISS chapters were also involved in antimilitary programs and were particularly active in trying to keep military training off campus.[16]

The Intercollegiate Socialist Society was able to maintain an active and fairly stable student organization for fifteen years. This is a particularly impressive feat since student organizations tend to be short-lived and political groups particularly, more often than not, succumb to factional quarrels. Part of the reason for this stability was the leadership of Harry Laidler, who worked for the ISS for this entire period. While students took an active role in running the organization, adults played a key role in funding it. In terms of membership, 1915 was the high-water mark for the ISS, with 1,332 members in seventy student and fifteen alumni chapters. Most of the chapters were fairly small, with fifty members a large group.

The ISS encountered problems after 1918, as did the American left generally. The First World War, particularly America's entry into the hostilities, and the Soviet revolution, were the turning points for the left. World War I presented radicals with two problems: the question of whether to support or oppose the war and how to deal with the repression of radical activities which accompanied and followed the war. The Socialist Party strongly opposed the war, and its presidential candidate, Eugene V. Debs, ran for office from prison and secured over one million votes. The ISS never took a firm position on the war although a number of ISS local groups opposed it. Radical activity in general suffered substantially during the war, due to the national stress on military defense. Many students volunteered or were drafted into the armed forces. Substantial pressures were placed on individuals and groups who opposed the war and, in some instances, students were expelled or professors fired from academic institutions for their opposition. Some radicals were prosecuted for antiwar activities during this period.

The antiwar movement predated World War I. Students had been active in protesting militarism and United States involvement in wars as early as 1904. In 1904, University of California students rioted against military programs on campus.[17] A poll taken in 1915 indicated that there were substantial opposition to both ROTC and militarism on campus; 63,000 out of 80,000 students polled opposed the introduction of military programs into the universities.[18] The ISS officially opposed ROTC as well, although it did not play an active role in anti-ROTC activities. Despite this tradition of opposing militarism on and off campus, much of the campus antimilitary activity quickly disappeared when the United States entered the war.

The Russian Revolution and the left's response to it marked the beginnings of major ideological differences among radicals. The ISS reflects this. In 1918 the *Intercollegiate Socialist* changed its name to the *Socialist Review*, in an effort to go beyond the campus. The journal also increased its coverage of international events and began to speak in terms of the strength of socialism in Europe. At the 1919 ISS convention there was a growing concern with the Soviet Union and an effort to deal with the effects of the Russian Revolution on American radicalism. While there is no evidence that the ISS was seriously split by factional problems created by this question, there are indications in the *Socialist Review* that there was a good deal of confusion about it. At least one observer claimed that the Russian Revolution caused a schism in the ISS and caused it to change both its name and its focus in 1921, when the ISS became the League for Industrial Democracy.[19]

The ISS never recovered either its numerical strength or its energy after World War I. It suffered greatly from the postwar repression of radicalism and loss of interest in socialism among most Americans. It was also subjected to the factional disagreements which wracked the entire radical movement. Indeed, Upton Sinclair went so far as to state that "The name of socialism became so unpopular . . . that the organization now calls itself the League for Industrial Democracy."[20] After World War I, campus radical movements in general suffered a setback and when a new set of organizations emerged, they were of a different nature.

While the ISS never became a mass student movement and did not have much of a direct impact on American politics or higher education, it did play an important educational role for its members and for many politically articulate students. It should be said also that the ISS never wished to be an activist movement. Its motto, "Light not Heat," is indicative of the educational orientation of the group. As noted previously, many of the critical intellectuals and some radical leaders of the twenties were alumni of the prewar ISS. The *Intercollegiate Socialist* was widely read among politically articulate students, and the ISS helped stimulate strong local political discussion groups. At Harvard, the ISS affiliated Socialist Club was among the most active organizations on campus. With fifty members in 1912, it served as a focus for some two hundred progressives concerned with women's suffrage, free speech, and other radical issues of the day.[21] The ISS also established for the first time a continuing radical political presence on the campuses, and this was no mean achievement. Upton Sinclair's original goal of making socialism an issue to be contended with on campus was achieved by the ISS, at least at the more prestigious colleges.

The Intercollegiate Socialist Society was by no means the only so-cially concerned organization on campus at this time. Although the focus of this section is on the ISS, it is important to mention some of the other groups as well. Two organizations with a more moderate political viewpoint than the ISS, although with similar types of pro-grams, were the Intercollegiate Civic League (ICL), founded in 1905, and the Cosmopolitan Club movement, founded in 1907. The Intercol-legiate Civic League aimed at bringing knowledge of practical politics to college students and encouraging their participating in mainstream po-litical activities. By 1909, there were thirty-two affiliated clubs, from Rhode Island to California and from Michigan to Louisiana. The groups ranged in membership between thirty and one hundred, and they fo-cused on questions such as student sufferage, child labor, town im-provements, and the means of student participation in local, state, and national politics. While the ICL had little direct political orientation, it clearly fell in the stream of moderate progressivism which was a force in the American middle class at the time. The Cosmopolitan Clubs (CC) had roots and attitudes similar to the ICL, but it was concerned with promoting international understanding and good will.[22] The CC began in 1903, when an International Club was organized at the University of Wisconsin. In 1907, a National Association of Cosmopolitan Clubs was founded; by 1911 it had a national membership of 2,000 from sixty countries. The organization published a monthly journal, the *Cosmo-politan Student*, which informed members of activities around the world. The Cosmopolitan Clubs were one of the first American student organizations to affiliate with an international group when they joined the Federation Internationale des Etudiants. Like the ICL, the Cosmo-politan Clubs had no articulate philosophy and played no role in activ-ist politics. These organizations saw themselves as educational vehicles for college students. They provided a service to students and brought questions of social reform and international affairs to students who previously were unaware of them. If anything, these organizations are indicative of the optimistic, vaguely progressive, world view which pre-vailed in the middle classes during the early twentieth century.

Another, more political organization which flourished at this period was the Young Intellectuals (YI). This group was a precursor of the student movement of the twenties in that it was both politically and culturally radical. The Young Intellectuals attacked bourgeois culture as well as the institution of marriage and were active in both the feminist movement and in socialist groups. The Young Intellectuals supported the Industrial Workers of the World (IWW), anarchists Emma Goldman and Alexander Berkman, and was problably the most consciously radical group in American colleges at the time. For the most part, the Young Intellectuals were concentrated in Ivy League and Midwestern colleges, and they were largely from Protestant backgrounds. Many had participated in the "settlement house" movement and worked in urban slums. While there are no accurate figures concerning YI membership, it was probably smaller than the other groups mentioned above. Like its contemporaries, the Young Intellectuals were not interested in academic issues; rather, their orientation was toward the political and cultural ills of the society.

Members of the Young Intellectuals, as well as other socially concerned students—from the YMCA and ISS as well as independent students—were active during the 1914-1918 period in settlement house work. By 1911, there were 413 settlement houses which involved some 10,000 volunteers, many of whom were college students. Jane Addams felt that the students involved themselves in this work because they felt a lack in their own lives and wanted to do something constructive. [23] Settlement house work had a radical and sometimes socialist flavor, and exposed individuals like A. J. Muste and Norman Thomas to some of the country's social problems. Students who were engaged in this volunteer work felt that they were doing something both practical and political. Like YMCA-sponsored missionary work, the settlement houses provided middle-class students with an opportunity to "see how the other half lived" as well as to be "relevant" to social needs. In both cases, this kind of social service activity was often a radicalizing experience for those involved.

The final organizational focus for student social action in the pre-World War I period was the student Christian organizations, particularly the YMCA-YWCA. The YM-YW movement was started in the late nineteenth century, and reached major strength in the early twentieth century. By 1915, there were 778 YMCA groups serving students and thirty full-time staff.[24] Without any doubt, the YM-YWCAs were the largest student-serving organizations in the United States and were more influential than any other groups on campus, except perhaps for the ISS. Indeed, the 1915-1920 period was one of great growth and prominence for the YMCAs. In many of the larger state universities, YMCAs constructed their own buildings and were a major presence. Smaller denominational schools also often hosted active Ys which were the most socially concerned groups on campus.

The main thrust of YMCA activities was nonpolitical. The organization conceived of itself as a social and religious movement, and its approach had a strong element of evangelism. At the same time the Y movement was on the liberal side of American Protestantism in a period when the "social Gospel" was having an impact on American churches. Missionary work, both in the United States and abroad, was strongly urged by the YMCAs and also by the Student Christian Volunteer Movement, an offshoot of the Y which was responsible for coordinating missionary activities. YMCA programming included many national and regional conferences. These conferences provided communications among students and were active recruiting grounds for YMCA missionary and social service activities. Local campus programming differed greatly from college to college and included only a small part of social action content.

While there were many in the Student YMCA movement who opposed the First World War, the YMCA in general supported the war. It ran a $1.5 million fund drive for war-related activities and many Y groups participated in ROTC.[25] During the war period, even the fairly modest social action orientation of the Y movement abated and did not re-emerge until the early 1920s, when the YMCA was in the forefront of social action activity.

While the focus of this analysis is on national organizations and movements, local student activities should not be ignored. While this period did not see much militant activism, students in a number of universities were involved in politics often without belonging to national organizations. Many local activities were related to specific campus problems. For example, male medical students at an Iowa college protested against coeducation and bombarded female students with bricks.[26] In 1904, police and students battled at MIT over a nonpolitical matter and the number of police-induced injuries convinced the president to issue a formal protest against police brutality.[27] On a more political level, students at the University of California were involved in presidential politics and participated in local electoral campaigns. At the University of Pennsylvania, more than 500 students formed a free speech society to defend the student newspaper against administration censorship.[28] Harvard students, under the leadership of the Socialist Club, participated in both educational programs on campus and in local election campaigns in support of the Socialist Party. Harvard students were also active in social service activities through the Phillips Brooks House.[29]

While these are but a few examples of the kinds of student activism occurring locally at the time, nevertheless the campuses were generally marked by apathy. Only a very small minority of students were involved in any kind of social, academic, or political reform movements or activism. At most campuses this minority did not even exist. Student activism was limited geographically to the East coast and the large Midwestern state universities. There were isolated outposts at places such as the University of California and there were occasional outbursts at some smaller schools. Most of the activists of that period were from the middle and upper-middle classes. Radical students, however, were not without their critics, even in this period of moderate radicalism. Randolph Bourne, one of America's young radical intellectuals, had the following to say about student radicals:

> Youth can never think of itself as anything but the master of things. . . . Its enthusiasm for a noble cause is apt to be all mixed up with a picture of itself leading the cohorts of victory. . . . The youth of today are willful, selfish, heartless in their rebellion. They are changing the system blindly and blunderingly. They feel the pressure, and without stopping to ask questions or analyze the situation, they burst the doors and flee away.[30]

Bourne, in his various writings, attacked the undergraduate for his lack of interest in education and criticized higher education for its depersonalization and rapid growth.

An era of student involvement ended with the First World War. After the hiatus of the war, the activists and their adult supporters found that the campus atmosphere dramatically changed, as had the social milieu of which the campus was a part.

ORGANIZATIONAL DEVELOPMENT AND APATHY: THE TWENTIES

The period between 1919 and 1929 is a difficult one to understand—for American society at large as well as for student activism. While cultural conformity was the order of the day, there was also a significant "counter culture." In the midst of political conservatism and apathy, the American left was going through its birth pangs with the founding of the Communist Party. The educational system, particularly the universities, were experiencing unprecedented change and growth as a college degree became increasingly necessary for remunerative employment. All of these factors affected the campus, especially that minority of students who were concerned with political and cultural questions.

Since a substantial segment of student activism and concern during the twenties was focused on campus issues or stimulated by dissatisfaction with the university, it may be useful to discuss some of the concerns which were raised by students at this time. The protest and criticism aimed at higher education was unprecedented in that students had never before spoken out dramatically against the nature of their education. Journals such as the New Student carried numerous articles criticizing higher education, and local campus newspapers and journals, particularly at the prestigious schools, were actively demanding university reform.

The students questioned the expansion of higher education, the curriculum of the colleges, and the role of higher education in society. An editorial in the *New Student* (reprinted from the Amherst College student newspaper) was indicative of the type of criticism meted out:

> The schools and colleges of America are accused of standardizing men, of moulding and shaping them into a finished product of one set, definite type. If such accusations are true, America's educational institutions are simply an expression of a nationwide attempt to force people to think and feel alike on all subjects. The spirit of intolerance, supposedly a thing of the distant past, rules just as supreme in many places today as it ever has. Free thought and discussion are countenanced if they coincide with the opinions of the majority or the reigning minority. Any conflicting ideas, however, are termed pernicious or "bolshevistic", fit only to be outlawed and hunted down until eradicated from sight and hearing.[31]

One of the targets of the *New Student's* attacks was the "gigantism" which swept the universities. The *New Student* observed that higher education had become a major industry and that expansion on all fronts was proceeding unabated. This expansion, they argued, was adverse to students. The lecture, imperfect under the best of circumstances, became even more intolerable when professors had no personal contact at all with their students. Even university architecture had become "sterile and box like," while the curriculum was irrelevant and did not deal with social questions. The proliferation of courses on management exemplified the negative aspects of the changes in higher education. Finally links between the universities and corporations were attacked.[32]

Despite the barrages of criticism, the *New Student* and other voices of student dissent proposed few, if any, specific reforms for restructuring the university. The *New Student* did praise the tutorial system which had recently been introduced at Harvard and the independent study program at Stanford. Generally, the students demanded increased contact with their professors. A prominent student concern was protecting academic freedom on campus. The 1920s abounded with instances of censorship of student newspapers, firing of professors for their political and social views, and harsh discipline of students for political participation. Yet, despite the unprecedented interest in academic affairs, there were few student initiatives toward reform or change in university governance.

The campus press, which played an important role in student activism, is a good indicator of the tenor of the period. The censorship of campus newspapers and the sacking of student editors were common. The campus press was among the most liberal and socially conscious elements in the universities and often kept public issues before the student community. Many universities had daily newspapers which had "semi-official" status and, while most of these newspapers were not bastions of radicalism, they did cover both campus and national affairs.[33] Independent journals contributed to the ferment on campus. Among the journals founded at this time were the *Gadfly* at Harvard, the *Critic* at Oberlin, the *Proletarian* and *Scorpion* at Wisconsin, the *Tempest* at Michigan, the *Occident* at California, *Reveille* at Louisiana, and the *Saturday Evening Pest* at Yale. These journals were highly critical of both the university and society. Several national journals circulated on campus, notably the *New Student*, the *Socialist Review* of the LID, and the *Student Mirror* of the National Student Federation of America. The campus press incurred the animosity of university administrators. Student newspapers such as the *Michigan Daily* were often censored and their editors removed from their posts and occasionally expelled or suspended from the university. In many cases, this censorship was exercised over articles which administrators felt were detrimental to the university, such as exposés of university policy. The "underground" journals were seized by university officials on many occasions, usually for similar reasons. Thus, the student press contributed substantially to the ferment of the period.

Liberal Student Organizations

The first national student organizations devoted to liberal political thought and education were the Intercollegiate Liberal League (ILL) and the National Student Conference for the Limitation of Armaments (NSCLA). The ILL was founded in 1919 with the aim of "the cultivation of the open mind; the development of an informed student opinion on social, industrial, political, and international questions." A number of prominent educators lent their names to the organization and it quickly attracted 850 members. The ILL was moderate in its orientation and was vocally attacked from both right and left for its policies. Its emphasis was on raising political consciousness and interest among students, and its main activity was a speakers bureau of both students and prominent liberal adults who toured campuses. In 1921 ILL merged with the National Student Conference for the Limitation of Armaments, a single-issue conference of antiwar liberal students, to form the first major national organization, the National Student Forum (NSF).

The NSF, through its journal, the *New Student,* was one of the key voices of student liberalism and social concern in the twenties. The journal appeared continuously until 1928, when many of its staff joined the LID. Such a long life for a student journal is rare. Throughout this period, the *New Student* survived without major outside adult subvention, although it is likely that the journal did get adult support from members of its advisory editorial board. The journal soon became more important than the organization which founded it.[34] The NSF was devoted more to raising public issues than with pressing a particular ideology, although it had a consistent liberal approach. Its only stated policy was to favor free speech. The NSF grew rapidly and by 1922 had 1,000 members and several hundred graduate and faculty supporters.

By October, 1923, the NSF had twenty-five college branches and members at over three hundred colleges and universities. Among the institutions at which active NSF groups existed were Bryn Mawr, the University of Chicago, the University of Colorado, Dartmouth, Mount Holyoke, New York University Law School, George Washington University, Harvard, Howard, Hollins College, Hood, Miami University, Northwestern, Oberlin, Park College, Rockford, Radcliffe, Stanford, Swarthmore, Union Theological Seminary, Vassar, Wellesley, Western College, and Yale.[35]

The National Student Forum was run by an executive committee of thirty persons, including twenty undergraduates, five recent alumni, and five faculty members. The executive committee was elected by an annual national conference. The NSF's full-time staff, which at minimum consisted of an editor for the *New Student* and an executive secretary, received minimal salaries and usually were recent graduates or students who took off a year to work for the organization. Most of the staff and members of the executive committee were liberal and many had belonged to other student groups such as the YMCA. While radicals did not control the NSF, they did participate in NSF activities and attended conferences in order to present the radical viewpoint. It is very likely that radicals had more behind-the-scenes influence than was readily apparent. This might be indicated by the fact that when the NSF dissolved at the end of the decade, it became part of the League for Industrial Democracy.

The NSF, particularly in its early years, had an active program. A short discussion of some of its activities provides a clue to the orientation and scope of the group. In addition to its annual national conference, NSF sponsored regional meetings and NSF affiliates often sponsored local conferences. In 1922, a two-week "Liberal Summer School" was held on Nantucket at which many prominent liberals spoke to the student participants. Some conferences were aimed at special groups of students, such as a 1923 conference of liberal student leaders, attended by editors of liberal student journals from twenty-four campuses. Alexander Meikeljohn, then the president of Amherst College, spoke on "The Role of the Student in Administrative and Curricular Reform." Among the regional meetings were sessions at Swarthmore College on "Students and Workers" and a conference at Waukegan, Illinois, sponsored by NSF affiliates at the University of Chicago and Northwestern, on "Youth and the Warmakers." The NSF tried to facilitate the activities of its local groups, and its national office acted as a clearing house for information and coordination. The *New Student* printed reports of local activities and tried to support, for example, the many local student journals which were founded by NSF affiliates and independent liberal and radical student groups. The NSF tried to promote an understanding of international affairs among American students and not only sponsored conferences on this subject, but also arranged for a delegation of six foreign students to visit forty American college campuses. An American student delegation also visited Europe and was particularly active in studying the German youth movement. Numerous articles in the *New Student* dealt with youth and student movements in other countries.

Despite these moderate activities, the NSF was considered a radical organization by many college administrators and by the public. NSF leaders spent a good deal of time combating this image and tried to present themselves as concerned but essentially nonpolitical students. The NSF executive committee responded to attacks by the conservative National Civic Federation by expanding its advisory board of "respectable" adults and writing a pamphlet refuting the conservatives' charges.[36] They also restated that the only major goal of the NSF was to discuss contemporary issues seriously.

The most important of NSF's activities was the publication of the *New Student*. The *New Student* (*NS*) appeared without major interruption from April of 1922 until May of 1929. It was the most influential national student publication of the period, although its impact was limited to a fairly small number of the most active and politically conscious students in the more prestigious universities. The *NS* was affiliated throughout its history with the National Student Forum, but grew increasingly independent as time went on. Although the journal changed its emphasis several times, it generally featured articles on international affairs, particularly foreign news pertaining to student movements; current academic matters in the universities from a highly critical viewpoint; news of NSF and other liberal activity; and a potpourri of sports and other human interest news from the campuses. The *NS* publicized NSF activities as well as those of other social action groups and featured, for example, detailed reports of conferences of the YMCA and Student Volunteer Movements. The *New Student* is probably the most accurate available reflection of the "pulse" of the politically conscious student community during the twenties.[37]

The changes which took place in *New Student* editorial policy and in the journal's format over a period of time demonstrates the trends in the student movement. The magazine started out as a militantly liberal—at times even semiradical—biweekly in 1922. Articles constantly derided the Establishment both of the university and society at large. By 1923, the magazine modified its tone in order to appeal to more students and it became less militant in its approach. Under new editorial leadership, *New Student* focused less attention on the NSF as an organization and more on becoming a journal of wide student interest, with stories on international affairs and campus events unrelated to politics. Its tone remained fairly radical and propacifist at this time, and publication shifted to a weekly basis. Substantial attention was paid to problems in the university and sections of Upton Sinclair's controversial book, *The Goosestep*, were reprinted in *New Student's* monthly "magazine" supplement. The *New Student* considered itself something of a voice of its generation, stating in 1923, "Fellow students, we cannot escape the responsibility pressing upon us. The educated youth of today, of this generation, must be responsible for the future welfare of mankind. The future will be anything you command it."[38] In October of 1928, the journal editorialized, "With all respect to the older generation, some of us become more and more certain that they cannot feel the chaos as we do."[39]

The journal did not ignore the cultural ferment of the period or campus-related concerns. A series of *NS* articles on sex dealt with some of the social changes taking place among young people. Discussions of current literary trends were also printed from time to time. The *New Student* participated in the struggle to permit women to smoke on college campuses. Other campus-related issues which were featured in the pages of the *New Student* were the struggle against compulsory ROTC, which received major attention from the journal, and an end to compulsory class and chapel attendance. The *New Student* was especially active in conducting student "straw polls" concerning these issues, and most of them indicated that large majorities of students favored more liberal rules. *New Student* straw polls on the political preferences of students, however, did not show such a liberal orientation, since Republican presidential aspirants were invariably victorious during the twenties in the *NS* (and other) polls. The journal had a negative attitude toward fraternities and sororities, although this was modified as the *New Student* tried to become a bit more conservative. *New Student* favored a closer relationship between students and workers, favored the honor system on campus, and was consistently antimilitarist. Thus, the journal was firmly left-liberal and, indeed, was considered something of a beacon by the beleagured adult liberals of the period.

By the late twenties, the *New Student* staff felt that it was fighting a losing battle. The *New Student's* long-time editor Douglas Haskell (1922-1927), stated in an editorial that he was disillusioned by the lack of success of the various causes which the journal had championed during the years of his editorship.[40] He noted that even the campaign against ROTC, which had wide student support, was not very successful and that, in fact, a number of universities had added ROTC courses. With the departure of Haskell from the editorship and a financial crisis, the *New Student* again changed its format and editorial approach, and became a monthly "general magazine of opinion, with minor emphasis on intercollegiate affairs." Its politics became substantially less radical and more attention was given to such popular topics as sex. The *New Student* survived in this format until the end of the 1928-29 academic year, and then ceased publishing.

The *New Student*, in a way, reflects the moderate radicalism of the period and the effort by the minority of politically conscious students to instill a sense of political awareness and responsibility among larger segments of the student population. Its concerns were those of its generation, although phrased in intellectual and moderate tones. It presented criticism of almost all aspects of the current culture and echoed a disenchantment with the political system while providing no clear solutions. (Socialist alternatives were never articulated in the *New Student* or, for that matter, in NSF gatherings.) The educational system, perhaps as a part of "the system" was singled out for attack but no solutions of a radical nature were offered. Support was given to the tutorial system and other moderate reforms, but these proposed reforms did not really deal with the student critique of the university. Finally, the *New Student's* influence was limited to a tiny segment of the student population, although it was a large proportion of those who were politically active.

The *New Student* was a highly significant phenomenon. It was the first national student journal devoted in any way to political and social issues. It survived for seven years and helped to unite an inchoate and otherwise divided series of socially concerned groups. It provided a forum for liberal, moderately radical, and critical thought.

It is difficult to evaluate the impact of the National Student Forum. As has been pointed out, the *New Student* was the most important of its ventures and even its successes were limited. The other NSF activities had even less of an impact. The NSF's national, regional, and local conferences did include several hundred of the most active students each year and provided communication among liberals. These conferences did not result in any direct action, but were valuable for the participants. They may have promoted a sense of a national movement and a feeling that college liberals were not totally isolated. The NSF's speakers bureau no doubt exposed campuses to liberal speakers they might not otherwise have heard. While the NSF's membership figures are unavailable for its later years, it is unlikely that its membership rose above 3,000 nationally.

Another "mainstream" liberal student organization of the twenties was the National Student Federation of America (NSFA), which survived until 1946. The NSFA later became the model for the National Student Association, founded in 1947. It was the first federation of student governments and, as such, was something of a milestone in the development of the American student movement. The NSFA originated in liberal political and social concerns of the mid-twenties. It was less radical than the National Student Forum and certainly disappointed many radicals who attempted to push it in a more activist and critical direction.

The NSFA was organized as the result of two separate efforts in the mid-twenties. The first was an Intercollegiate World Court Conference held at Princeton in December of 1925. This conference included many student government leaders from East coast colleges and representatives of Christian associations and other campus groups. The issue of participation in the World Court was then a controversial topic and campus opinion was strongly in favor of American participation. The conference was held as a means of educating and mobilizing students behind a movement for joining the World Court. Delegates from 245 colleges and universities attended the Princeton conference and out of the meeting came a desire to organize a permanent organization that would be able to speak for the American student community. This desire was spurred by a number of American students who had visited European student unions, particularly the British National Union of Students.[41]

The other impetus for the formation of a national student organization came from the West coast. Students from seven Western universities had, in January of 1925, organized a National Student Federation of America. This group was built on the model of the European student unions and was supposed to "foster student cooperation, encourage travel, provide scholarships to students studying abroad, promote international cooperation, and promote interest in national and international affairs."[42] The new group claimed 50,000 members, since it counted the entire student enrollments of its member schools—the University of California at Berkeley, the University of California at Los Angeles, Stanford, Washington, Utah, Mills, Oakland, and Pomona. The West coast group expanded nationally in 1926, when representatives of the organization which stemmed from the World Court conference and those from the West coast NSFA met in Ann Arbor in December to found the National Student Federation of America. From the beginning, the NSFA was not a mass-membership organization but rather a federation of student governments. Groups like the NSFA, and later the United States National Student Association, claimed large memberships based on the numbers of students enrolled at affiliated universities. These figures are, of course, highly misleading since, in many instances, a very large number of students on the affiliated campuses had no contact with the NSFA or were even unaware of the organization's existence. In addition, because elections for student governments have traditionally been ignored by a majority of students at most universities, NSFA representatives often reflected the views of a relatively small minority of the students in affiliated colleges. Despite these limitations, the NSFA was the most representative student organization in the twenties and it reflected the views of more students than any other group. It was recognized by many adults, on and off campus, as the voice of the American student community. Thus, its statements received some attention and university administrators and others listened to these "legitimate" student leaders. The NSFA was, at least until 1932, the most important student organization in the United States.[43]

The founding convention of the NSFA, held in Ann Arbor, Michigan, in December of 1926, brought together student government officers from 200 colleges and universities. By 1928, the organization claimed to represent 400,000 students throughout the United States. By 1933, 150 student governments had affiliated. The NSFA started a journal in 1933, the *Student Mirror*, to facilitate communications among student groups, but by this time the organization had been overshadowed by the more radical national student groups of the thirties, such as the National Student League.[44] While NSFA was dedicated to the discussion of "controversial" issues and debates over such questions as the League of Nations, social reform, prohibition, and ROTC occurred at its conventions, the organization avoided political stands. Like its successor, the National Student Association, the NSFA spent a good deal of time discussing means of making local student governments more popular and effective. The organization did take stands on campus-related issues such as the honor system (support), smoking on campus (support), and freedom of the student press (support). It criticized fraternities and sororities for their attitidues of "artificial superiority," helped arrange for visits of foreign students, and encouraged American students to travel overseas. The organization was divided over campus ROTC and never took a position on it.

The basis of NSFA decision making was its annual convention, which usually attracted several hundred delegates and observers from affiliated student governments. Convention discussions ranged from critical national issues to campus-related questions. Workshops on how to make student governments effective were also part of the national meetings. The NSFA maintained a national office in New York City which helped coordinate activities of student governments, sponsor some speakers, and maintain relations with foreign student unions, particularly with the International Confederation of Students (CIE), to which it was affiliated. While the NSFA supported educational reform and its conventions seem to have been liberal in tone, the organization was by no means a beacon of radicalism on campus. Its desire to maintain a cross section of student governments prevented strong statements on most subjects. Even the *New Student*, by no means a militantly radical journal, stated that the NSFA's views were disappointly bland and indecisive.[45]

The NSFA did provide some valuable services to American students.

NSFA travel programs made it possible for many American students to visit Europe, either as tourists or as delegations. It provided an information center for student governments and a means of communication which otherwise would have been difficult. But the NSFA did not shape the consciousness of its generation, and had even less impact on students than did the NSF and the *New Student.* It was a "first" in that the NSFA was the first federation of student governments. It also provided something of a legitimate voice for American students.

Radical Organizations

The most striking thing about the radical student movement of this period was its weakness and lack of influence in comparison to the prewar periods and the 1930s. This is especially surprising given the cultural ferment on campus. Yet, the overall conservative political mood, on campus and off, partially explains the inability of radical students to establish any meaningful campus groups.

Student radicalism followed the general trends of the broader radical movement in America which had undergone substantial change as a result of World War I and its aftermath. The postwar repression inhibited the growth of any movement. Radicals, of necessity, focused increasingly on underground and semiclandestine activities. The Russian Revolution split the left. The Communist International, created in 1920 and dominated by the Russians, infused a new and, in the view of some observers, negative element into American radicalism. The factionalism that ensued resulted in the proliferation of radical groups, most of which spent more time fighting with one another than working for social change.[46] The once unified Socialist party became but one of many sects, the most important of which was the Communist party. All this had its effect on student groups.

The most important radical student organization of the prewar period, the Intercollegiate Socialist Society, suffered a sharp decline after the war and changed its focus in order to regain its popularity. In 1921, the ISS officially became the League for Industrial Democracy (LID) and shifted some of its emphasis away from the campus. During the twenties, many LID affiliates, formerly named "Socialist clubs" changed to "social problems clubs," "liberal clubs," or similar less ideological titles. The LID claimed around 2,500 campus members in the twenties and probably had campus affiliates at a minimum of forty colleges and universities. The organization's emphasis remained educational, although some activist campaigns occurred, notably the Sacco and Vanzetti case, in which Socialist students, particularly in New England, participated in efforts to save the two men. LID also played an active role in protests against campus ROTC.

The LID sponsored many conferences. Speakers were the mainstay of activities. Field Secretary Paul Blanchard spoke to 50,000 students all over the United States in 1924, according to an LID report, and at least three national or regional conferences were held each year on subjects ranging from educational reform to labor and union problems to foreign policy. LID programs attempted to forge ties between students and workers by bringing labor union officials to campus, involving students in labor activities. Students from the YMCA and other Christian groups were a target for LID educational efforts. While much LID educational work was on general topics, conferences also dealt with critiques of capitalism and with debates and discussions concerning the Soviet Union. LID educational conferences were not limited to centers of radical activity such as New York City, but were held in such places as Kansas City. The LID exercised some influence outside its own ranks. For example, many collegiate liberal clubs not formally affiliated with the LID were influenced by LID members or held broadly Socialist views. Since many college administrators prevented formal affiliation with such a radical organization as the LID, local groups had to be more informal in their contacts. In addition, LID leaders attended the conferences of such liberal groups as the NSFA, the YMCA, and Student Volunteer Movement and apparently found ready audiences in such organizations. Again, as in the prewar period, the LID was the best organized and most widely represented radical group on the campus scene. Its impact was more limited than in the prewar years, but this is probably due more to the political situation in the country than to any fault of the LID. The LID survived into the thirties and, in fact, beyond. In 1932 it added a specially student-oriented branch, which was called the Student League for Industrial Democracy from that time until it became the Students for a Democratic Society in 1962.

The radical political parties took some interest in campus affairs, although their attitude toward student organizing in the twenties was at best ambivalent. These parties, notably the Socialist party and the Communist party, felt, on the one hand, that the American "revolution" was not to come from the universities but rather from the industrial working class. On the other hand, they recognized that the colleges were a good place to recruit leftists since many adult radical leaders had been "converted" in college and were from middle-class backgrounds. Norman Thomas, A. J. Muste, and Jay Lovestone are among those who became radicals while in college.

By the Depression years, much of this ambivalence had disappeared and Socialists, Communists, and the various splinter groups all actively recruited among students and had a major impact on the student movement. Public support for radical political parties was at a relatively low ebb in the twenties and thus campus interest was probably quite limited. There were, nonetheless, efforts by these groups on campus.

The oldest Socialist youth organization is the Young Peoples' Socialist League (YPSL), which was founded in 1907 and received the official backing of the Socialist party in 1913. With major variations in strength, the YPSL has lasted to the present. In the beginning, YPSL was largely a "youth" organization and paid little attention to student organizing. The YPSL was consistently on the left wing of the Socialist party, and disputes were common between the adult Socialist party and its youth affiliate. By 1919, the YPSL claimed 10,000 members and strongly supported the Socialist party's antiwar position. Only a very small proportion of this number was college students, however. The YPSL was stronger and more active prior to World War I than in the years following it. The character of the organization and the nature of its activities, however, was similar during the twenty years under discussion in this chapter.

The YPSL's ambivalence concerning the organization of college students seems to have prevented the establishment of specifically college chapters of the group in the twenties. Nevertheless, in major cities, some students were involved in YPSL activities and in New York, the existence of the Rand School of Social Science, a Socialist educational enterprise, involved college students. The YPSL was not concerned with cultural questions, but rather with directly political issues. Strong stands were taken against militarism and in favor of various kinds of social reform. An educational emphasis was strongest in the YPSL and very little activism, with the exception of participation in Socialist electoral campaigns, was undertaken. In 1924, the YPSL established a journal, *Free Youth*, which had some students on its editorial board. By and large, however, the YPSL had little direct impact on the campus and did not try to involve itself in the interests and affairs of the student movement.

The Communist youth movement was similar to the Socialists concerning work on campus, but the Young Communist League (YCL) was not as well organized nor established as the YPSL. Indeed, the YCL in many ways emerged from the left wing of the YPSL. When the split in the Socialist party occurred in 1919, the YPSL was aligned with the left and many of its active members joined with the group which was to form the Workers Party (Communist) in 1921. The Young Workers League (later changed to Young Communist League) was organized in 1922 and functioned for some time under the difficult circumstances of political repression. The Communist youth movement remained fairly small during the twenties and did not orient itself to the campuses. Its various journals were not interested in student issues and strongly followed the lead of the Communist party. It was only in the early thirties that Communists took an active interest in student work. The student movement may have been even weaker than the nonradical orientation of society dictated, because of its lack of interest in university affairs. The adult groups, realizing that the campus was predominently middle class and following the traditional Marxist notion that revolutionary social change could not be initiated by bourgeois elements, had strong reasons for not paying attention to student groups. It is only in more recent periods that American Marxists have become more pragmatic in their thinking about the usefulness of student movements. Socialist and Communist student activity, where it existed in the 1920s, was concentrated in large cities and on campuses which had a continuing radical tradition. In particular, schools like the City College of New York, Temple University in Philadelphia, Hunter College in New York, and the Universities of Chicago and Wisconsin were centers of Socialist and Communist activity.[47]

Nonorganizational Activism

While the decade of the twenties was not one of militant activism, some issues were more important to students than others, and it is important to explore these nonorganizational efforts at radical activism. The question which aroused the most student interest and active concern was the peace issue. This has traditionally been true in the United States and contrasts with student activism in other countries. Because of the middle-class nature of the American student community, or the fairly strong internationalist orientation of the university culture, the campus has taken an active interest in foreign affairs, particularly in the prevention of war. This was evident in the nonactivist twenties, in the more radical period of the thirties, and again in the quiet fifties. The peace movement of the twenties is then an integral part of the ongoing campus political scene.

Student antiwar activity in the United States has generally been a combination of single issue ad hoc efforts—for example, against ROTC on campus—peace-oriented organizations such as the Fellowship of Youth for Peace in the twenties, and interest in peace-related issues by other organizations and movements, such as the YMCA and the National Student Federation of America. All three types of antiwar activity are considered as they apply to the twenties. Throughout this period there was substantial student support for antiwar positions of various kinds, if student opinion polls are any indication. Christian pacifism was strong and had active and articulate proponents in YMCA groups and denominational student organizations. ROTC was unpopular among many students, and the aftermath of World War I left a large number of Americans with a distaste for involvement in foreign military action. All of these elements contributed to the popularity of the antiwar movement on campus. Of course, there was substantial opposition from conservative elements, and a number of investigations of antiwar activists and pacifists occurred. These harassments were, however, not as serious as those against political radicals at the same time.

A number of antiwar groups existed in the 1900-1930 period. Prior to World War I, the Collegiate Anti-Militarist League, the Intercollegiate Peace Association, and other organizations functioned. In general, they had limited support and were overshadowed by groups like the Cosmopolitan Clubs and the ISS, whose activities had a strong antiwar component. The National Student Forum, whose parent organization was the National Committee for the Limitation of Armaments, was impelled from the beginning by antiwar sentiments. For all of its moderation, the *New Student* consistently opposed ROTC and arms expenditures and was pro peace throughout its existence. One of the earliest NSF projects was a campaign in favor of the Washington Disarmament Conference; 716 meetings were held on campuses during a period of three months during this campaign. A delegation of six regional campus representatives visited President Harding to urge that the United States make the conference a success.[48]

The Fellowship of Youth for Peace (FYP) was the first national student organization devoted solely to peace activity. Founded in 1922 at a national meeting of the Student Volunteer Movement (SVM), the FYP represented the strength of pacifist sentiment among the Protestant Christian activists of the SVM. At this national meeting, around 700 students indicated their unwillingness to participate in any way, and 300 joined the FYP. The FYP was an openly pacifist organization and its ideological basis was Christian.[49] With the help of adult pacifists, the FYP organized national educational programs, engaged in a series of speakers' tours, and supported local drives against ROTC and other military programs. While it was not as influential as the NSFA or the YMCA, the FYP affected many students and it clearly presented the pacifist position particularly to Christian students. In 1926 the FYP merged with the Fellowship of Reconciliation. The FOR is an adult pacifist organization with a Christian orientation. During various periods, it has been politically radical, especially when A. J. Muste was its secretary during the twenties. The FYP was the most successful and active peace organization of the twenties and represented the mainstream of peace sentiment. Most campus peace activism in the twenties was religiously oriented, hostile to fraternities, and by no means militantly radical.[50]

The FYP, aided by liberal and radical student groups, provided the vehicle for educating students on peace-related issues. Peace was one of the most prominent of radical issues of the period and had a greater degree of support among students than most of the other issues raised by radicals. The national peace organizations were instrumental in bringing speakers to campus, conducting opinion polls, and in circulating peace-oriented periodicals such as the *World Tomorrow*, a journal loosely associated with the Fellowship of Reconciliation but which had some influence among liberal students and faculty. *World Tomorrow* covered student affairs thoroughly and recognized the campus antiwar movement as an important aspect of the national antiwar effort. The major activism, however, was initiated locally and usually took the form of campaigns against ROTC; they were rarely impelled by national organizations.

The major campus antiwar issue during the 1920s was opposition to military training in the universities. At times, the opposition was directed against ROTC programs; at other times it was directed against compulsory participation in ROTC. The protest took many forms, including disruption of drill exercises, strikes against ROTC, petition campaigns, meetings, and lobbying of faculty and trustees. Demonstrations or other activities important enough to be noted in national periodicals occurred at no less than forty schools during the twenties.[51] The popularity of the antiwar movement led the *Kansas City Star* to editorialize that "pacifism is claiming the colleges for its own."[52]

One study conducted at the time indicated that a majority of American students opposed military training in colleges, although the survey indicated that dislike of regimentation and laziness played a substantial role in this majority. Among the important causes for anti-ROTC sentiment among nonpacifist students were religion, political liberalism, ROTC policy at the particular campus, repressive administration policy, internationalism, and the impact of outside speakers and peace groups. Antimilitary activities caused a good deal of administrative reaction and student demonstrators were disciplined or even expelled at a number of colleges.

The largest student movement of the twenties was not the antiwar movement or the various liberal organizations discussed previously. It was the student Christian movement. A series of organizations active on campus—the YM-YWCA, the Student Volunteer Movement, the denominational student organizations, and others combined to form a loosely organized, but nevertheless important aspect of the campus scene. The religious student movement was stronger in comparison to other influences on campus during the twenties than at any other time in the history of organized religious activity on campus. A YMCA document published in the 1940s looks back on the twenties as the most successful period of the campus Christian movement.[53] This success was due in part to an absence of other forces on campus, in part to the fact that religion was a more important aspect of American middle-class campus life than it was in later periods, and in part to the major efforts made by Christian organizations to mobilize support on campus. This aspect of the student movement has not been discussed, simply because the student Christian organizations were not primarily concerned with social issues. Their emphasis was a combination of religious, social, moral, and political concerns, of which social action was but a part. About 5 percent of the students were members of religious organizations and, of that number, perhaps one in ten participated in socially oriented activities.[54] Thus, the student Christian organizations were hardly a mass student movement, although they were clearly the largest in terms of members and the broadest in terms of geographical distribution group among students in the twenties.

Although the socially aware segment of the Christian student movement was only a small proportion of the total movement, it was important in convincing various official Christian student conferences to take radical positions on some issues. For example, the National Student Conference of the Student Christian Movement (mainly the YMCA and YWCA campus affiliates), attended by 2,500 students in 1927, went on record as opposed to the profit motive because it was unChristian. The same conference favored sending students to work in industry to promote collaboration between workers and students and it opposed military training. Strong support was expressed for an economic system based on cooperation rather than competition. Participants polled on war-peace questions replied as follows: 740 stated that they would be willing to support some wars but not others, 327 declared that they would support no wars at all, 95 stated that they would support any war in which the United States was involved, and 356 were undecided. The strength of antiwar and even completely pacifist sentiment was quite impressive.[55]

The student religious organizations grew substantially during the twenties. They were part of a general upsurge in extracurricular activities—for instance, there were 268 extracurricular student groups at the University of Illinois in the mid-twenties. The oldest national religious organization, the YMCA, continued to be quite active on campus and was probably the most radical of the religious groups. In addition, most Protestant denominations formed student groups at this time, and many of these were active from time to time in social action concerns. The Methodists, Unitarians, and to some extent the Disciples were the most prominent in this regard. Roman Catholic and Jewish groups were also active, but they were significantly less concerned with social action programs.

The YMCA had the largest organizational structure, with a number of full-time student secretaries and buildings on many college campuses. Generally, the Y took the lead in organizing social concern activities on campus. The Y movement was one of the earliest student groups of any kind to support interracial student programs. As early as 1901, the Southern field secretary mentioned this aspect of YMCA work. At the 1922 YMCA convention at Atlantic City white students stayed with Negro delegates in a Negro hotel as a means of protest. The YMCA also strongly supported the 1923 World Court conference at Princeton.[56] Pacifist sentiment was strong in the Y movement throughout this period, as it was in middle-class Protestant circles. The Y took a strongly internationalist stand and supported the World Student Christian Federation and World Student Relief programs after World War I.

The YMCA was one of the first campus groups to take an interest in the working class and the problems of industrialism. Beginning in the early twenties, the YMCA sponsored summer student industrial study groups in various cities. In the summer of 1922, for example, such groups were organized in seven cities for both men and women students and attracted a good deal of student participation. The fifty-two students who spent their summers working in factories and meeting regularly to discuss their experiences felt that this program deepened their understanding of American social problems.[57] Other YMCA-sponsored summer seminars and periodic conferences on many topics related to social problems, missionary work, and religious activities were held and involved many hundreds of students each year. YMCA groups were active in settlement-house work as well, bringing middle-class Christian students to urban slums in an experience that was important for many. The YMCA, unlike the more radical groups, was not limited entirely to the elite colleges but involved students from smaller schools which would otherwise have had no social-action programs at all.

The YMCA had a number of offshoots which also played a role in student social-action work. For example, the Student Volunteer Movement, which had been founded in 1886 out of YMCA concerns and activities, was primarily concerned with sponsoring missionary activities. It had a strong social action concern as well and its quadrennial conferences often attracted more than 7,000 students—probably the largest such gatherings in the United States at the time. At the 1923 SVM conference, held in Indianapolis, the 7,000 delegates voted by large majorities to sponsor antiwar educational programs in the universities. A resolution which states that "war is unChristian and the League of Nations is the best means of preventing it, but that we would resort to war in case an unavoidable dispute had been referred to the League of Nations or World Court without successful settlement" received 6,000 out of 7,000 votes.[58] The Indianapolis conference and YMCA conferences generally attracted radical and pacifist speakers such as Sherwood Eddy and Paul Blanchard, whose rhetoric was convincing to many of the students.

Like the YMCA and YWCA, the denominational student groups had the advantage of substantial amounts of money, trained professional staffs, imposing buildings on some of the large campuses, and an aura of respectability which legitimized social reform concerns. In addition, these groups were able to reach students who would not otherwise have been receptive to leftist politics. The growth of denominational groups after 1900 was quite dramatic. By 1920, for example, the Wesley Foundation (Methodist) had centers at 104 universities and the Baptists had 250 student centers. Eleven other Protestant denominations had a total of 314 campus groups on which more than $500,000 was spent. Roman Catholics were also active in the student area and had 262 student groups, of which thirty-four had their own buildings and dormitories. This growth was particularly evident immediately after World War I.

A black student movement slowly began to develop itself in the 1920s. The movement was confined to Southern black schools, mainly because higher education was largely segregated. One of the contributing factors to this growth of activism were the various currents which existed in the black community. For example, Marcus Garvey and his Universal Negro Improvement Association was symbolic of a sense of racial pride and organization among many blacks. While no national movement emerged at this time similar to the Student Nonviolent Coordinating Committee of the 1960s, there were many instances of unrest in black schools. Howard, Fisk, Shaw, Knoxville, Florida Agricultural and Industrial Institute, and Hampton Institute all experienced unrest during the twenties. The causes were varied and, in general, concerned local issues such as relaxed campus rules or improvement in the teaching staff or other reforms. If anything, administrators responded to demonstrations by even harsher disciplinary actions than was the case at white schools. Many students were expelled or severely disciplined in other ways. There is little indication that the small wave of unrest which occurred at black colleges at this time had much of an impact on developments in the thirties or is directly related to the black student movement of the sixties. Black students participated, although not in large numbers, in many of the liberal and radical student organizations of the twenties, as well as in groups like the YMCA. Instances of racism among white college students were common, even in groups like the National Student Forum, but blacks did find some acceptance and many of the first breaks in the color bar occurred in the student movement.

Conclusion

The period between 1900 and 1930 was neither as dramatic nor as militant as either the 1930s or 1960s; thus there has been a tendency to underemphasize its importance. It was during this period that the American student movement was formed. The kinds of organizations developed during that period—political, fraternal, religious, national co-ordinating groups—were reflected in later periods. Furthermore, the student movement, especially the Intercollegiate Socialist Society, was influential in shaping the political views and the lives of individuals who later became important in national political and intellectual life. This can be said of only a few other groups in the history of student activism.

The critiques of the student movement of the twenties are important to consider as well, since they reflect some of the concerns which students had in later periods as well as some of the key issues in society at the time. Many of the issues raised by student activists related to the broader society. Certainly the "cultural revolution" was a protest against the broader society and not the academic environment. The "disaffection" of the young, although limited to a minority, indicated a malaise in society at large which is reflected in the literature, politics, and social commentary of the time, as well as in the universities. A tiny minority of radical students participated in the shaping of the Socialist and Communist movements; this too was a reflection of some of the political scene which impinged on campus life. The concern for world peace which was the hallmark of the campus activist movement of the twenties marked America's emergence as a world power and was a result of the bitter aftermath of World War I. These same currents were important in the thirties, and contributed to the antiwar movement's impact then. Defiance of prohibition, new sexual styles, and new modes of dress were all important to the campus scene in the twenties and were all reflections of currents in society which have had lasting effects.

The student movement of this period was also concerned with academic life for the first time in the history of the American university. And the criticisms most often voiced at the time ring true in the sixties and seventies. Attacks on the university centered on its impersonality, its overexpansion, its ignoring the undergraduate, and its "gigantism." These criticisms are similar to those echoed recently and which contributed to the rise of student movement of the sixties. While these concerns were shared by many academics at the time, little was done to change the overall direction of American higher education, and during the period between 1920 and 1970, the American university system has grown tremendously in size, scope, and power. Little, however, has changed in the curriculum or in the increasing specialization of the faculty or the orientation toward graduate training and research in the most prestigious institutions. It is not surprising that the criticisms of the twenties which went unheeded again crop up to plague the academic community. If the academic community had listened to the students in the twenties and made some modifications in the universities, part of the crisis of the sixties would have been avoided.

Despite all this the twenties was not a time of great student movements. Student activists had virtually no impact on American society and very little influence on the universities. Student organizations were an educational force, at least in some universities, and the stage was set for later developments. But as a period of great influence by students on society, the twenties certainly do not qualify. In many respects, however, the movement of the twenties served as a prototype for later periods, and it is in that perspective that this period should be observed.

NOTES

1. It is impossible to discuss the political and cultural history of the twenties in any detailed way. Of social interest in this regard are Loren Baritz, ed., *The Culture of the Twenties*, (Indianapolis: Bobbs-Merrill, 1970), Frederick Lewis Allen, *Only Yesterday*, (New York: Harper, 1931), and Henry May, *The End*

*of American Innocence: A Study of the First Years of Our Own Time,
1912-1917,* (Chicago: Quadrangle, 1964).

2. S. M. Lipset has suggested this comparison in S. M. Lipset, *op. cit.,* pp.
160-161.

3. Quoted in S. M. Lipset, *op. cit.,* from Alfred Kinsey, *et al., Sexual Behavior
in the Human Female,* (Philadelphia: Saunders, 1953), pp. 298-302.

4. S. M. Lipset, *op. cit.,* p. 166. *New York Times,* October 22, 1920, p. 4, *New
York Times,* November 4, 1924, p. 6, *New York Times,* October 29, 1928, p.
14.

5. *New York Times,* August 22, 1922, p. 2, Section 2.

6. Adequate sociological data concerning the backgrounds and political attitudes of students during this period does not exist.

7. Allen F. Davis, *Spearheads for Reform: The Social Settlements and the Progressive Movement, 1890-1914,* (New York: Oxford University Press, 1967),
p. 183.

8. *Intercollegiate Socialist,* 1 (February-March, 1913), p. 13.

9. The alumni list of the early ISS reads like a guide to early twentieth-century
social reform. Among the ISS members who were active in politics were Paul
Douglas, Norman Thomas, Roger Baldwin, Stuart Chase, Paul Blanchard,
Randolph Bourne, Bruce Bliven, Alexander Meiklejohn, Robert Morse
Lovett, A. J. Muste, Jacob Potovsky, and many others. This number of
well-known alumni is especially impressive when it is recalled that the ISS
never had more than 1,300 members nationally prior to World War I. David
Shannon, *The Socialist Party of America,* (Chicago: Quadrangle, 1967), p.
56.

10. Bernard Johnpoll, *Pacifist's Progress: Norman Thomas and the Decline of
American Socialism,* (Chicago: Quadrangle, 1970), p. 38.

11. Ann Topham, "Light More Light: The Intercollegiate Socialist Society,
1905-1918," (Unpublished paper, University of Wisconsin, 1971), p. 15. Ms.
Topham has summarized data concerning membership and other statistics
from the *Intercollegiate Socialist.*

12. Harry Laidler, "Ten Years of ISS Progress," *Intercollegiate Socialist,* 4 (De-
cember-January, 1915-1916), pp. 16-22.

13. S. M. Lipset, *op. cit.,* p. 149.

14. A partial listing of ISS chapters will give an idea of the spread of the organiza-
tion: Alberta, Amherst, Barnard, Brown, California at Berkeley, Chicago,
City College of New York, Clark, Colgate, Colorado, Cooper Union, Cornell,
DePauw, George Washington, Hamline College, Harvard, Illinois, Indiana,
Kansas Agricultural College, Marietta, Massachusetts Agricultural College,
Meadville Theological Seminary, Miami, Michigan, Missouri, Montana, New
York Dental College, Ohio Northern, Ohio State, Ohio Wesleyan, Oklahoma,
Pennsylvania, Pennsylvania State, Princeton, Purdue, Richmond, Rochester,
Southern California, Springfield YMCA College, Swarthmore, Union, Union
Theological Seminary, Utah, Valpariso, Washington, Washington at St. Louis,
Wesleyan, Williams, Wisconsin, and Yale.

15. Frank Bohn, "A University Hunger Strike," *The Masses*, 5 (May, 1914), p. 10.
16. Norman F. Cantor, *The Age of Protest: Dissent and Rebellion in the Twentieth Century*, (New York: Hawthorn, 1969), p. 228.
17. *New York Times*, February 8, 1904, p. 5.
18. S. M. Lipset, *op. cit.*, p. 151.
19. Bernard Johnpoll, *op. cit.*, p. 38.
20. Thomas Neblett, "Youth Movements in the United States," *Annals of the American Academy of Social and Political Science*, 194 (November, 1937), p. 143.
21. Gerald C. Henderson, "The College and the Radical," *Harvard Graduates Magazine*, 20 (March, 1912), pp. 463-465.
22. Louis Lochner, "The Cosmopolitan Club Movement," in G. Spiller, ed., *Papers on Inter-Racial Problems*, (London: P. S. King, 1911), p. 439.
23. George Peterson, *The New England College in the Age of the University*, (Amherst: Amherst College Press, 1964), pp. 179-184, as quoted in S. M. Lipset, *op. cit.*, p. 152.
24. Commission on Student Work, YMCA, *op. cit.*, p. 14.
25. Clarence Shedd, *op. cit.*, p. 386.
26. *New York Times*, February 25, 1902, p. 8.
27. *New York Times*, November 4, 1902, p. 10.
28. *New York Times*, March 6, 1915, p. 11.
29. Francis B. Thwing, "Radicalism at Harvard," *Harvard Graduates Magazine*, 20 (December, 1911), pp. 260-263.
30. Randolph Bourne, *Youth and Life*, (Boston: Houghton Mifflin, 1913), pp. 23, 266, as quoted in S. M. Lipset, *op. cit.*, p. 118.
31. *New Student*, 2 (November 18, 1922), p. 4.
32. James Wechsler, *Revolt on the Campus*, (New York: Colvici, Friede, 1935), p. 34.
33. Richard H. Edwards, J. M. Artman, and G. Fisher, *Undergraduates: A Study of Morale in Twenty-three American Colleges and Universities*, (Garden City, New York: Doubleday, 1928), p. 91.
34. For additional information concerning the *New Student*, see Neil Katz, "The 1920's American Intellectual Revolt of Youth: Changing Attitudes and Issues in the *New Student*," (Unpublished paper, University of Maryland, 1970), see also MartinMcLaughlin, *Political Processes in American National Student Organizations*, (Unpublished Ph.D. Dissertation, Notre Dame, 1948), p. 16.
35. *New Student*, 3 (October 6, 1923), p. 23.
36. *New Student*, 2 (April 7, 1923), p. 5.
37. Martin McLaughlin, *op. cit.*, p. 17.
38. *New Student*, 2 (June 2, 1923), p. 00.
39. James Wechsler, *op. cit.*, p. 29.
40. Neil Katz, *op. cit.*, p. 17.
41. Marguerite Kehr, "The National Student Federation of America," *Student Government Bulletin*, 2 (April, 1954), p. 20.

42. *New Student*, 4 (February 7, 1925), p. 1.
43. Martin McLaughlin, *op. cit.,* p. 15.
44. Maurice Bore, *New Student*, (February, 1929), p. 00.
45. *New Student*, 6 (December 15, 1926), p. 1.
46. The literature on American radicalism in the twenties is quite extensive. For some of the best analyses, see Theodore Draper, *The Roots of American Communism*, (New York: Viking, 1957), Irving Howe and Lewis Coser, *The American Communist Party*, (New York: Praeger, 1957), and James Weinstein, *The Decline of Socialism in America, 1912-1925*, (New York: Monthly Review Press, 1967).
47. Irving Howe and Lewis Coser, *op. cit.,* p. 199.
48. *New Student*, 1 (April 19, 1922), p. 1.
49. *New Student*, 3 (March 15, 1924), p. 2.
50. Paul Porter, "Christian Students Scrutinize Life," *New Student*, 6 (1927), pp. 9-11.
51. Among the schools which had antimilitary activism are the following: Northwestern, Wisconsin, Pomona, Syracuse, Illinois, Pennsylvania State, Brown, Minnesota, City College of New York, Michigan, Columbia, Washington, California, Kansas, Nebraska, Georgia, Boston, Ohio State, DePauw, Howard, Cornell, Stanford, Missouri, Coe College, and Indiana.
52. *Kansas City Star*, (February 5, 1924).
53. Commission on Student Work, YMCA, *op. cit.*
54. W. H. Cowley, "Notes on Universities," (Unpublished manuscript) as quoted in S. M. Lipset, *op. cit.,* p. 166.
55. *New Student*, 6 (January 12, 1927), p. 1.
56. See Clarence Shedd, *The Church Follows Its Students, op. cit.*
57. *New Student*, 2 (January 13, 1923), p. 1.
58. Paul Porter, *op. cit.,* p. 101.

CHAPTER THREE

The Thirties:
A Movement
Comes of Age

The 1930s was the highpoint for student activism, at least until the emergence of the New Left in the mid-1960s. Compared to the 1920s there was a virtual revolution on campus. In the 1930s, proportionately more students participated in left-wing activism than during the New Left of the 1960s, and the student movement had an impact on the society at large through the antiwar movement of the period. The student movement of the thirties was not impelled by educational problems or changing cultural styles; rather it arose out of the massive social and economic crisis of the Depression and as a reaction to the rise of fascism in Europe. The massive social movements of the 1930s—the militancy of the labor unions and particularly the CIO, the growth of the radical political parties, including the Communists, and the growing radicalism in the middle class—helped to create an atmosphere in which student activism was accepted as a legitimate form of politics. This was one of the few times in American history when students were accepted as legitimate political actors, and were given a hearing, if not always a sympathetic one, at the centers of political power. Student activism, although based largely in the middle class and focusing on middle-class issues, such as the antiwar question, fit neatly into a society which had a fairly high degree of political mobilization.

The thirties was not marked either by cultural conflict or by student alienation from the values of adult society so characteristic of the twenties. Radical student organizations were, for the most part, tied to adult groups. The lack of cultural conflict in the thirties was due in part to the overwhelming importance of political questions and in part to changes in American culture that caused young people to perceive it as more open. Prohibition, for example, was ended in 1932 and avant-garde cultural forms became more popular. The forces motivating student activism were the threat of war, the economic depression, ideological politics, and, infrequently, questions of academic freedom and university reform. Student protest was concentrated, as in earlier periods, on the more prestigious campuses and in urban schools, especially those in the New York City area. Despite the intense activity of the 1930s, most American students were uninvolved in politics, although they were probably more aware of social issues than ever before.

THE CAMPUS SCENE

The campus of the 1930s was a place of many contradictions. While the colleges and universities had grown substantially during the twenties, administrators continued in their paternalism toward students and perceived of the university as it had been in earlier and less complex and troubled times. By the early 1930s, the student population had grown to about 1.2 million. During the decade, only modest growth occurred due to economic conditions; by 1940 the college student population reached only 1.5 million. Most colleges and universities were still far from the mainstream of social and political life. Few at the time saw the universities as crucial to society, although their importance as a means of social mobility and a "certification agency" for the elite had grown. The research function of higher education, while growing modestly, was not a major national resource and few young people felt strong pressures to attend college. Faculty members, except at the most prestigious universities and in urban schools, had a fairly conservative view of the university and did not press for either institutional or personal involvement in social or political issues. Some faculty members, notably those active in the fairly radical college division of the American Federation of Teachers, were politically involved on campus and supportive of student activism, but by and large, the faculty was notable in its silence during the thirties.

While the university was not in the forefront of society, economic pressures bore heavily on it. Students, with good reason, worried about obtaining jobs after graduation. In the period between 1929 and 1934 between 50 percent and 85 percent of male graduates were unemployed.[1] Stories of students living on milk and crackers were common during the period. In addition, the economic and social crisis facing the nation impinged directly on the student community, as it did eventually on the faculty and administrators. Payless pay days, faculty layoffs, loss of jobs by the parents of students, and other economic disasters were commonplace.

During the 1930s political attitudes in the United States began to move toward the left. Students also became more liberal and numbers involved in political dissent grew. This trend became evident as the thirties moved on. In a 1932 poll students supported Herbert Hoover in his presidential bid by a vote of 28,000 for Hoover to 18,000 for Roosevelt, and a surprisingly large 10,000 for Norman Thomas, the Socialist party candidate.[2] The move toward liberalism began after 1933, when students became more seriously affected by the Depression and Hitler's rise to power in Germany. After 1933 students found part-time jobs increasingly difficult to obtain, and the Columbia *Spectator* estimated that 75 percent of graduates had difficulty finding any type of employment.[3]

By 1933 a poll of 1,000 representative students in nine Eastern colleges demonstrated the leftward trend: half the students were willing to "try socialism;" 77 percent saw politics as a "tool of wealth" and 40 percent were opposed to the free enterprise system while 13 percent declared themselves in favor of "communism and revolution."[4] The most significant finding of the poll was that 52 percent did not know whether the American form of government would continue to work. Other polls showed similar shifts in attitudes in a liberal or radical direction; another student poll showed that 24 percent of students considered socialism positively.[5] This widespread liberalism, however, did not necessarily translate itself into large numbers of students engaging in militant activism; only 2 percent of the student population became activist.[6]

College students, while leaning toward liberalism, tended to resist activism of any sort. *Fortune* magazine, which conducted a student survey in 1936, indicated that "the present day college generation is fatalistic. . . . The investigator is struck by the dominant and pervasive color of a generation that will not stick its neck out. . . . If we take the average to be the truth, it is a cautious, subdued, unadventurous generation. . . . Security is the *summum bonum* of the present college generation."[7] The *New Republic*, a liberal journal, also commented that while students showed greater social concern, they expressed it with little imagination. In sum, students in the thirties tended to be more left politically than any other generation of students. While the student population's concern with social and political issues was unprecedented and an articulate and active group of radicals emerged, the campus as a whole was not politicized or militant.

While society and students began to move toward liberalism, academic administrators did not. They repressed student activists without hesitation. For example, many universities refused to allow chapters of the Young Communist League or the Young Peoples' Socialist League on campus, claiming that they were not solely student groups. While students often protested these decisions, they were seldom successful in changing administration policy. Students were regularly expelled or suspended from colleges simply because of their politics or their participation in demonstrations or other activism. One case occurred at the University of California at Los Angeles in 1934 where five radical students were expelled for organizing activities. This particular incident caused a student strike and the provost of the university was forced to reinstate the students when he could not produce any evidence of wrongdoing.[8]

But such capitulation by university officials was rare. Campus disciplinary rules remained harsh, and administrators retained substantial control over extracurricular life. More daring college presidents felt obligated to berate student radicals when students disagreed with their views. One of the most famous cases of this kind was when President Frederick Robinson of the City College of New York objected to the behavior of radical students by flailing them with an umbrella and calling them "guttersnipes." Robinson tried to keep the lid on one of the nation's most radical campuses by summarily firing faculty and disciplining students. His efforts were less than successful since CCNY continued to play an important role in national student politics as one of the most "radical" schools in the United States. President Robinson, in a sense, provided a useful rallying cry for the student left since he was an easy target on which to focus activities.

Student newspapers also were subjected to administrative discipline, especially when they took a liberal or radical position. Publication was often suspended and editors fired by the campus administration. For example, in 1932 the editor of the Columbia *Spectator* was expelled for publishing an article condemning the operation of the dining halls. His expulsion precipitated a series of major campus disruptions including an unprecedented one-day strike and rally which 4,000 students attended.[9] The university was forced to reinstate the editor. This event, which received national publicity and gave the National Student League (a Communist student organization) its start, served as a model for later action.[10]

Professors and students found themselves in difficulty because of their political beliefs and actions. Radical student journals as well as the mass media include many incidents of professors being disciplined or fired because of their political activities. Incidents of the firing of radical faculty were widespread, occurring at institutions like Yale, Harvard, and the University of California. At the University of Omaha, the liberal president of the school committed suicide after having been hounded out of office by conservatives. The fairly repressive atmosphere on campus meant that liberals and radicals had to spend much of their time fighting for academic freedom and free speech. While concerned students and faculty lost most of the time, the free speech campaigns did mobilize students, helped to build political consciousness on campus, and involved large numbers of otherwise uncommitted students. Loyalty oaths for teachers were instituted in several states, including Massachusetts, in an effort to drive radicals from the universities.

Military training on campus was an inflammatory issue throughout the thirties. Radical student organizations such as the American Student Union raised the ROTC issue on a number of campuses and built substantial movements. The issue was particularly explosive at many of the large state universities, where military training was often mandatory for all male students. In addition, local ad hoc groups opposed ROTC. Practically all liberal and radical student organizations, from the Young Communist League to the YMCA, opposed compulsory ROTC and many opposed any military programs on campus. The ROTC question conveniently raised both a local issue, which affected many male students, and an international one, and was thus particularly attractive to radical and pacifist groups.

Anti-ROTC agitation took a variety of courses. At several universities, such as Ohio State and Cornell, the faculty, with strong student support, petitioned the trustees to abolish compulsory ROTC. At others, such as California, the students demanded the abolition of compulsory ROTC without faculty support. More militant tactics were used on a number of occasions. University of Minnesota students sponsored a "Jingo Day" and 1,500 demonstrated despite threats of administrative repression.[11] While the anti-ROTC campaigns mobilized many students, they seldom yielded results. For the most part, universities retained their requirements.

Despite radical student concern over ROTC and free speech, radicals focused their energies on political issues in the broader society. The organization of a student labor union at the University of Michigan was an exception to the mainstream of student activities. In this case, a Student Workers' Federation was formed which successfully bargained for higher wages, seniority rights, and payment for overtime for student workers.[12]

The most important issue of the decade was the war-peace question. By the mid-1930s, this issue was the major question on campus and antiwar sentiments were held by large numbers of students. Many Christian student organizations, motivated in part by traditional Christian pacifism which was rather strong at the time, in part by isolationism, and in part by radical social concern, opposed war in general and helped shape the consciousness of many of their members. Radical student groups opposed American foreign policy from a Marxist perspective or because such opposition reflected the interests of the Soviet Union. Regardless of motivation, however, many students were antiwar and leaned toward pacifism. So large was the peace movement that the mass media expressed concern that American youth would not defend the country in time of need. These fears proved to be unfounded; very few students opposed American entry into World War II in December 1941.

Student pacifist sentiment has been documented by various polls taken in the thirties. The poll taken in 1935 by the *Literary Digest*, a liberal journal, while justifiably criticized for its methodology, shows the extent of antiwar sentiment; 65,000 students were questioned. Of this number 68 percent felt that the United States should stay out of another war and 81 percent said that they would not fight if the United States were the invader; 90 percent favored government control of munitions manufacturers.[13] The Brown University *Daily Herald* surveyed sixty-five colleges in twenty-seven states and found that 39 percent of the respondents took an absolute pacifist stand and only 33 percent said that they would fight if the United States was invaded.[14] A majority of Columbia University students said that they would fight only if the United States were invaded. Such pacifist sentiments were not limited to large cosmopolitan schools. A psychologist found that one-third of the students at a small Ohio college considered themselves conscientious objectors to war and another 25 percent thought that they might be objectors. A poll of 22,000 students conducted by the Intercollegiate Disarmament Council indicated that 39 percent would not participate in any hostilities and another 33 percent said that they would fight only if the United States were invaded.[15]

While the twenties were marked by student opposition to the culture of the period, the thirties were notable for the lack of such concerns. Even among the most radical students, there was little disaffection from the dominant social norms. Indeed, Communist literature stressed the fact that Communist students were like all other students—they were interested in dating, sports, and campus affairs and differed only in that they believed in dialectical materialism.[16] Major cultural nonconformity was absent as students, regardless of their political views, were preoccupied with securing jobs.

The only glint of a counterculture was the Communist party's espousal of a "proletarian culture." Despite this, radicals accepted middle-class values and tried to avoid being considered "offbeat." There was little disaffection with adults either; most of the major student political groups were linked to adult political parties and organizations, either formally or informally. The student organizations often followed the orders of adult advisors and several, like the YCL, slavishly mimicked the political line of the Communist party. The general lack of cultural nonconformity and willingness of student groups to follow the lead of adult organizations is distinct to the thirties and is an important element in understanding the nature of that era's activism.

In most respects the student movement of the thirties did not differ dramatically from activism at other periods. The centers of the movement were at the prestigious universities and colleges and, to some extent, in metropolitan areas, particularly New York City. Members of student groups came predominantly from the social sciences and humanities, few came from the professional and technical fields. Many activists were among the brighter students. They came mostly from middle-class backgrounds, reflecting the general nature of higher education at the time, and there were proportionately more Jews among activists than any other religious group.

The issues which aroused student concern in the 1930s were similar to those which have been important at other times. As an overall concern, the antiwar issue has been one of the questions which has aroused major interest among students in all periods of student activism. The antiwar movement of the thirties was more influential than at other periods (except perhaps the mid-1960s), and it differed in motivation from the twenties. In the thirties, radical students were more interested in the antiwar movement from a socialist viewpoint than from a liberal or pacifist stance, and this shaped the nature of the movement. Thus, while opposition to war and particularly to American involvement in foreign conflicts was a major thrust of student activism in the twentieth century, the motivations behind this antiwar sentiment differed from decade to decade. Issues which related both to local campus questions and national developments, such as civil liberties and free speech, have been recurrent themes in American student activism. However, the thirties were unique in several respects also. The close ties between student organizations and the adult radical movement were characteristic of that decade, as was the impact of adult politics and ideologies on students. The movement of the thirties was unconcerned with several issues which have motivated later student organizations; campus questions, for example, were of only minor concern and few students were interested in educational reform or related issues. The emphasis of the twenties on educating the student community itself was diminished as the larger student organizations of the thirties tried to influence society at large. Civil rights for blacks and other minorities, which was so important a motivation for the early New Left in the sixties, was a muted issue in the 1930s. The emphasis of student activism in the thirties on foreign affairs, and on European developments particularly, is striking since the United States was in a period of unprecedented social upheaval. This stress on foreign policy in the midst of domestic social crisis is indicative of the middle-class nature of the student movement and, indeed, of the student population as a whole. Foreign policy has traditionally been a concern of the American middle class, and this is reflected in the student activist movement. Furthermore, the student community was not as hard hit by the Depression as other segments of the population (although stories of destitute students were common) and thus economic issues did not strike so close to the lives of the students.

ANTIWAR STUDENT ACTIVISM

The antiwar movement was the most important element of student activism in the 1930s. The antiwar movement managed to combine elements of other segments of the broader student movement, ranging from religious students to those involved in ideological organizations and parties. The height of antiwar activism on campus was from about 1935 to 1940, the period when the rise and expansion of European fascism and Naziism was a burning issue. The European left, to which American radicals had strong political and emotional ties, was concerned with foreign policy issues primarily during this period. The Spanish Civil War, a highly emotional and critically important issue to radicals, was fought at this time as well. And in the United States, the government, along with articulate public opinion and the radical movement itself, was trying to come to grips with America's proper role in the deepening European crisis. There is no question but that foreign policy, and the broader ideological and moral issues which were related to foreign questions, was the key political question at this time. Antiwar student groups had more than their share of factional disputes and splits, and the movement was eventually destroyed in large part by internal dissention and American involvement in World War II. Nevertheless, it was the one element of the student movement which involved a broad sector of activist-minded students and was the one issue on which students had a good deal of independent influence.

Concern with international issues and peace did not, of course, begin in the 1930s. As has been noted in Chapter 2, the National Student Federation of America was founded out of a conference on the World Court, and the League of Nations was an important campus issue during the twenties. Foreign affairs and the war-peace question also had been prominent issues among student radicals. The thirties saw the height of the campus antiwar movement and in a sense is comparable to the movement against the Vietnam war in the 1960s. Nonpolitical middle-

class students, as well as liberal and radical students, were deeply concerned with these issues. This made organizing around foreign policy
questions effective. Several factors account for this concern; isolationism and the tradition of Christian pacifism was strong, especially among
many middle-class Protestant students. Because of the threat of fascism
in Europe and the devotion of the Communists to the foreign policy of
the Soviet Union, the radical movement also emphasized international
affairs.[17]

The student antiwar movement of the 1930s had two organizational
forms: the first and most important was ad hoc committees and antiwar
conferences; the other was the direct involvement of liberal and radical
organizations. The entire range of the student movement—from the
Communists and Socialists to religious groups such as the YMCA and
strict pacifists like the Fellowship of Reconciliation—was involved in
antiwar activity. The ideological battles which were evident in groups
like the American Student Union were also played out in the antiwar
movement.

One of the first antiwar conferences in the thirties was the Student
Congress Against War, held in Chicago in December of 1932. Organized
by Communist students, particularly by the NSL, to coincide with an
international antiwar meeting in Amsterdam, the Chicago meeting attracted 600 college students from fifty-three colleges.[18] Conflicts between absolute pacifists such as Jane Addams (who participated actively in the meetings) and those such as James Wechsler and J. B.
Matthews (who held that international conflicts were caused by the
capitalist system and distinctions had to be made between "imperialist"
and other wars) were evident at this meeting and were characteristic of
the antiwar movement of the thirties. While the organizers hoped that a
permanent organization would emerge from this meeting, none did,
although the seeds of the broad student antiwar campaigns of the following years were planted. The significance of the Chicago meeting was
that it brought together elements from a variety of persuasions on a
common basis. This means of organizing proved very successful later.

One of the key antiwar campaigns of the thirties was the *Oxford
Pledge* movement. The Oxford Pledge originated in February of 1933,
when the Oxford University Student Union in England voted by a large
majority that it would under no circumstances fight for king and country (257 in favor, 153 against). This unprecedented event attracted

immediate international attention and was considered an example of the "problem" of youth at the time. The student newspaper at Brown University, as well as other local campus groups, adapted the pledge to American circumstances by rewording it to read that the signer would refuse to "support the United States Government in any war it may conduct."[19] It is significant that the American version was directed against wars that the United States government might conduct but not necessarily against all wars. This was deliberate on the part of radical leaders who supported revolutionary wars. Almost immediately, some ninety colleges in thirty states held debates on the Oxford Pledge, and a number of student polls indicated that a very large majority of American students opposed war. A spate of local and regional meetings were held when it was clear just how widespread antiwar feeling was on campus.

The radical student organizations moved quickly to take advantage of antiwar feeling and the SLID called for an April, 1934 national "peace strike," centered around the Oxford Pledge, to commemorate America's entry into the First World War. The NSL joined in sponsoring the "strike" and about 25,000 students (15,000 of them in New York City) participated in the demonstrations, which had received almost no prior national publicity and were hastily prepared.[20] Although the "strike" often took the form of a one-hour abstention from normal campus activities and a rally (and was, on most campuses, not a strike in the traditional sense), it was nevertheless an impressive demonstration of student opinion and received widespread publicity. For the first time, the student antiwar movement became a subject of national attention and began to take itself seriously.[21]

The radical movement repeated its strike in 1935, again with the focus on the Oxford Pledge, but this time with the support of many liberal and religious organizations and a great deal more national publicity. The National Student Federation of America, the American Youth Congress, and the Methodist students were all active in the preparations, as were the NSL and the SLID. The results were even more impressive, with 150,000 students participating nationally. Again, this "participation" should not be exaggerated, since many students simply attended campus meetings, which were often cosponsored by the school's administration. Nevertheless, it was an unprecedented success for the student movement and an indication of the popularity of the antiwar cause. Some 18 percent of the American student population participated in some way in the strike.[22] Local figures are also impressive and indicate that participation was national in scope and not limited to the larger universities. Students came out by the thousands at institutions like Columbia, Wisconsin, CCNY, Stanford, Minnesota, Temple, Western Reserve, Chicago, and Berkeley; but students also participated at smaller schools such as Connecticut State College, Smith, Virginia, Texas Christian, Howard, Idaho, and Wyoming.[23] Thousands of students took the Oxford Pledge, which infuriated much of the Establishment press.

The 1936 strike, the most successful of all, marked the end of this type of demonstration. After 1936, the tactic became "worn out," and the antiwar movement, engaged in internecine disputes, was less able to mount a concerted national effort. Some 500,000 students demonstrated nationally in 1936. The main organizer was the ASU, which was supported by a number of other groups. The official sponsor was the United Student Peace Committee, which had at least ten national groups affiliated to it. College classes were dismissed by administrators at such institutions as Alfred University; the Universities of North Dakota, Idaho, Oklahoma, and Pennsylvania; and Vassar College.[24] A questionnaire sent to college presidents by the ASU elicited forty replies. Nine college presidents fully supported both the strike and the peace movement, twenty-three had reservations about the strike but supported the peace movement, and eight rejected both the strike and the movement.[25] A strike was attempted in 1938, but splits in the ASU and a general fragmentation of the peace movement limited its impact. In 1937, the Socialists supported the Oxford Pledge while the Communists did not, and this led to differing approaches to antiwar strategy. While it lasted, the peace "strike" was an effective tool in that large numbers of students were mobilized and substantial national attention was attracted.

In addition to these nationally coordinated events, many local and regional antiwar activities took place during the decade. The Veterans of Future Wars was formed in 1936 by some Princeton students who demanded their war bonuses in advance. Four hundred college students picketed the home of J. P. Morgan in New York as a show of antiwar sentiment. Religious and liberal student groups actively debated antiwar issues and votes in meetings of denominational student organizations, the Interseminary Movement, and other groups indicating that the movement had strong support among nonpolitical students.

By 1939, the discord within the radical movement had affected the antiwar movement and limited its impact. In addition, many Americans became more and more convinced that rearmament was a wise policy, given the outbreak of World War II in Europe. And by Pearl Harbor, there were few who supported the antiwar movement. The United Student Peace Committee, under the leadership of the Communists by 1939, called the traditional April antiwar strikes which were held in some parts of the country, particularly in New York City. The split in the peace movement, however, had become irrevocable. The Youth Committee Against War (YCAW) was formed by Socialists, pacifists, and some religious students to oppose the Communists. YCAW maintained support for the Oxford Pledge and advocated complete American neutrality. The ASU and the UPSC, on the other hand, favored collective security.[26]

The Youth Committee Against War (YCAW), which was one of the last surviving student peace organizations active through the attack on Pearl Harbor, was an amalgam of Socialist, pacifist, and religious organizations. The main participants were the Student Peace Service of the American Friends Service Committee, the National Council of Methodist Youth, the Young Peoples' Socialist League, the War Resisters' League, and the Fellowship of Reconciliation. While the YCAW cooperated with conservative and isolationist groups on a few specific activities, it was the most radical of the antiwar groups, especially after the Communists had abandoned peace as an issue. The YCAW opposed conscription and increased armaments budgets and sponsored a national march on Washington, D.C. to fight against Lend-Lease when it was introduced in 1941. Their program never influenced national policy and YCAW demonstrations were much smaller than those called earlier by the united front peace movement. The YCAW continued its activities right up to the entry of the United States into the war on December 7, 1941 and the organization's policies remained consistent.

Pacifist students, while few in number, were active in the peace movement of the 1930s although their impact was limited. Pacifists participated in a number of denominational youth and student organizations and in broader Protestant organizations such as the Student Volunteer Movement. Through the decade, they pressed for the adoption of strong "peace" positions in these organizations and were quite successful in such groups as the National Council of Methodist Youth and at times in the YMCA.[27] Pacifists were behind many ad hoc attempts to build a strong campus peace movement. For example, in 1932, pacifist students organized a conference at the University of Chicago to discuss the establishment of a peace movement which attracted 600 participants. By the mid-thirties, however, the antiwar activities overshadowed the pacifists' efforts and most pacifists ended up in the broader ASU-run movements, often through their affiliations with Protestant student organizations.

Pacifist publications such as the *World Tomorrow*, which expressed the pacifist point of view, had some influence on liberals and politically-minded Protestants on campus. The *Christian Century*, an influential weekly journal, while not overtly pacifist, gave pacifist activities and ideology a good deal of attention.

With the withdrawal of the ASU and some other political groups from the antiwar movement in the late thirties, the pacifists became more important because of their continued commitment to peace action. The Fellowship of Reconciliation, a Christian pacifist organization with strong support among Protestant intellectuals, took a leading role. The FOR appointed a student secretary and greatly expanded its campus programs. FOR initiated a committee to coordinate peace action on campus. This committee consisted of representatives of the Interseminary Movement, the Student Volunteer Movement, the FOR itself, and the American Friends Service Committee. FOR members were active in the YCAW and locally sponsored pacifist discussion groups. Pacifist activists never numbered more than 1,000 in the thirties, but they were energetic and influential in other student groups, particularly in the religious student organizations. FOR members were especially active in attending summer conferences of other student organizations and distributing literature and engaging in discussions on pacifism. The FOR's journal, *Fellowship*, while it had a small circulation, was read by many pacifists and religious activists.

As war broke out in Europe and Asia, the constituency for the peace movement declined. As noted, the Communists and their allies abandoned it in 1939, and many liberals supported President Roosevelt's preparedness programs. The worsening international situation convinced many that American involvement in the hostilities was only a matter of time. By 1940 and 1941, the peace movement, along with some anti-Communist Socialists such as Norman Thomas and the Young Peoples' Socialist League, had been reduced to its pacifist and isolationist core. This situation brought the pacifists into the foreground of the movement, if only because they were one of the few remaining in it. When the Selective Service System was introduced in 1940, the FOR opposed it, and a number of young pacifists were jailed for their refusal to register. During the war years, pacifists were jailed in fairly large numbers for their refusal to serve in the armed forces.

While the student pacifist movement was a small adjunct of a much larger peace movement for most of the decade, it assumed larger importance as the peace movement declined. During the war years, the pacifists, particularly those in the FOR, were one of the few groups either on or off campus which took an active role in social action. Groups like the FOR retained a fairly steady membership through the decade, although they grew after 1940 as a result of their being one of the few viable organizations left.

The net result of the student peace movement was, of course, very small. The United States did enter the war and with the exception of the small radical pacifist wing which continued to function throughout the war years, the peace movement immediately collapsed. The fact that only 49,000 draftees out of a total of more than 10 million registered as conscientious objectors is indicative of the demise of the peace movement and the fact that it had little lasting effect on the many thousands of students who had participated in it during the 1930s. The antiwar movement indicates, as does the history of the American Student Union, that many factors contributed to the ultimate failure not only to influence events, but also to build a viable, lasting movement. Certainly outside political manipulation, particularly by the Communists, disillusioned many students and made it difficult for groups to function effectively. But the main element of failure was the world situation, particularly the rise of fascism in Europe and the outbreak of World War II. The very large numbers of students who expressed strong antiwar or even pacifist sentiments in the late 1930s completely changed their minds by 1941, and most had changed as early as 1939 or 1940. The antiwar students of 1937 were effective soldiers in 1942.

The peace movement was also the last major effort of the student movement of the thirties, and with the collapse of the ASU and the YCAW, the student movement of the period came to an end.

RADICAL STUDENT ACTIVISM

The student movement of the thirties was predominantly leftist. Its ideology ranged from the liberalism of the left wing of the Roosevelt administration and the Democratic party to the Marxism and Stalinism of the Communist party. Radicals were not in the majority in the universities, but when activism arose, they were usually the most influential elements. The radicals were active in student groups politically to the right of them, thereby extending their political views. The radicals, in short, set the tone for the student movement of the thirties.

The oldest radical student group was the Intercollegiate Socialist Society (ISS). The ISS had changed its name to the League for Industrial Democracy (LID) in the 1920s and in 1932 its youth section adopted the name Student League for Industrial Democracy (SLID) to emphasize campus organizing. The LID, as an adult organization, continued to exist and was active during the thirties, as it is today. It published a weekly newspaper, the *New Leader*, which represented the views of the social democratic wing of the radical movement, and it substantially influenced its student affiliate, the SLID. LID financial and administrative assistance to SLID was necessary for its survival. In general, relations between the LID and its campus groups were fairly harmonious and open splits did not occur in this era. Before 1932, the LID was an "umbrella" organization for Socialist students. After 1932, when other, more radical student organizations emerged, it became more ideological and therefore excluded many leftists, particularly those who considered themselves "revolutionary" or "Marxist." Until 1935, it refused to work with Communist students and was strongly opposed to Communist groups.

The SLID was one of the more important student groups of the thirties, although it did not play the dominant role that it had in earlier periods. It had a strong historical tradition which gave it some legitimacy, and it maintained a social democratic position on campus while engaging in a range of moderate radical activities. Its fairly moderate position shifted somewhat to the left as the decade wore on, but perhaps not fast enough to satisfy many students who demanded a more clearly revolutionary student organization. SLID, significantly, was able to maintain contacts with more conservative student groups, thus providing a basis for the unity of the student movement which took place in the mid-thirties. The fact that the SLID (along with the LID and the Socialist party) was critical of the Soviet Union, at a time when many radicals felt that it represented a struggling socialist state, somewhat limited its growth potential among leftists. Although it remained a force on campus throughout the thirties, SLID was clearly eclipsed by the American Student Union, into which it merged in the mid-thirties, and never regained its position of prominence when the ASU broke up and SLID reestablished its own identity.

SLID was born officially in December, 1932. The student division of the LID had grown so rapidly after 1930 that a separate student organization, tied to the adult LID, seemed logical. In 1930, the LID student division had 3,000 members. The 1931 LID conference, which laid the groundwork for an autonomous SLID, was held at Union Theological Seminary in New York and was attended by 200 student representatives from forty-four campuses.[28] The founding of the SLID was more than the formation of a student branch of the LID. It marked a change in orientation, away from an educational perspective to activism, as SLID became involved in joining labor unions on picket lines, protesting cuts in college budgets, and the like. SLID retained an educational program, and its activities remained geared to the student community. It began a journal, first called *Revolt*, but later changed to *Student Outlook* in an effort to gain respectability. It was not published until the SLID merged with the NSL to form the American Student Union in 1935 and covered campus issues, such as ROTC, and national and international politics from a Socialist perspective.

SLID had chapters on at least fifty campuses by 1933. It was well organized at prestigious universities like Harvard and Wisconsin, as well as at such urban schools as CCNY and Wayne State which had large working-class populations. SLID attracted many people who later became prominent in left and liberal causes. Walter and Victor Reuther (who were SLID organizers at Wayne State University), William Shirer, Daniel Bell, Sidney Hook, Talcott Parsons, Max Lerner, Gus Tyler, Will Rogers, Irving Stone, and James Wechsler, are among SLID alumni of this or somewhat earlier periods.

SLID actively participated in the factional politics of the decade. It worked closely with the Young Peoples' Socialist League with whom it had an overlapping membership. SLID, until 1935, devoted much of its energy fighting the National Student League and engaged in bitter ideological debates with Communist students on the local level. So volatile was the rivalry between the SLID and Communists that physical disruption of meetings occurred in New York and Chicago. While SLID fought the Communists, it effectively cooperated with liberal student organizations on specific issues, and close campus relationships between SLID and Social Problems Clubs (and similar less radical groups) existed at many universities.

While the leadership of SLID was strongly and consistently Socialist, much of the membership was less ideological. Despite the hardening of the student movement in the thirties SLID was open to students of varying persuasions. As the domestic and international political crisis of the decade pushed much of the Socialist movement to the left, SLID joined Communists for specific demonstrations and actions. The (Communist) National Student League was moving somewhat to the right in accord with Communisty party policy in 1935 and thus made a united front attractive to the SLID. The period of ad hoc cooperation between Socialists, Communists, some elements of the liberal student community, and others began around 1934 in the antiwar movement. By 1936, the American Student Union was established as a "united front." Perhaps the main factor uniting otherwise opposing student organizations was the rise of fascism in Europe, the economic crisis at home and the desire to present an effective left-wing response to the New Deal. Most radical groups agreed that the left must unite against fascism, and the united front attempted to effectively forge such a union.

The Young Peoples' Socialist League (YPSL) was the other major non-Communist democratic Socialist campus group during the thirties. Like SLID, the YPSL had a long historical tradition and was guided by the Socialist party's (SP) ideological positions. Because the YPSL was the youth affiliate of the SP, it was even more closely tied to the party line than the SLID. Throughout the decade, the YPSL was hindered by its ambivalence toward campus oranizing; it never emphasized student work. In accordance with traditional Marxist thinking, the YPSL focused on working-class and noncollege youth, despite the fact that much of its leadership were college students. The YPSL's internal journal, the *Young Socialist Review*, deemphasized college work and instead stressed high school organizing. The YPSL was active from time to time in campus affairs, mainly through individual members who joined campus groups like the ASU and the SLID. It was always a small organization, ranging from 2,000 to 6,000 members, most of whom were not students.

Like SLID, the YPSL was involved in the internal factionalism of the left. It was even more strongly affected by them, since at various times major ideological splits occurred within the YPSL, some of which changed its political direction. For example, in the mid-thirties, a group of Trotskyist students entered the YPSL and succeeded in temporarily taking it over and changing its ideological direction. When they were finally expelled, the organization was substantially weakened and many of the most militant and active members were lost to the Trotskyists. [29]

The YPSL was consistently to the left of the Socialist party, thus causing continous friction between them. The YPSL was also more ideologically diverse than the SP; Trotskyist groups were strong within the YPSL and successfully pushed the organization leftward. YPSL policies were in harmony with the student movement. The 1936 convention supported the Oxford Pledge, the CIO, and the American Youth Act, and declared itself against imperialist wars, stating that the struggles against war and for socialism were linked. These positions were very similar to the American Student Union and other radical groups. However, the YPSL differed in style from most other groups; ideological positions always seemed more important than action. The ideological nit-picking they brought to campus bored and usually alienated most students, even those politically aware.

In 1936, the YPSL began to turn toward the campus and formed a National Student Committee. Despite this, it was never able to establish itself, due perhaps to its late start, its close ties to the Socialist party and its policies, and to its intense factionalism. The only strength the YPSL had within the student movement was through the active and politically sophisticated YPSLs who became key elements of other student organizations and were able to influence them to adopt YPSL political positions. For example, in the late thirties, the Methodist youth movement was consistently close to the YPSL because of the work of one individual. YPSL members in organizations like the American Student Union and the American Youth Congress were vocal although, in the last analysis, they were outmaneuvered by the Communists. When the peace movement was dominated by the Communists in the late thirties, YPSL members and pacifists helped create the Youth Committee Against War (YCAW). YCAW was an arena in which the YPSL voiced its politics in the peace movement. Besides YCAW, on campus, the YPSL actively promoted the electoral campaigns of Socialist candidates, especially Norman Thomas's campaign in 1940.

The YPSL represented one political trend in the thirties, anti-Stalinist socialism emphasizing ideological purity. The ideological infighting within the YPSL and the Socialist party is part of the reason why the Socialist movement never attracted mass support in the period. The YPSL's ambivalence about organizing students prevented it from becoming a force on campus. Given its socialist goals, the real failure of the YPSL of the 1930s was its inability to gain support among working youth. Nevertheless, the YPSL and the political views which it represented did reach the campus. Communist student groups had a wider appeal to the student politics of the period than did the social democratic, probably because they, unlike the Socialists, were able to adjust their campus tactics to the major concerns of the students. In addition, for part of this period, the Communists advocated a more moderate political line that appealed to many liberals. They also offered, to those who were more radical, an ideology which had the support of a major foreign power, the Soviet Union. The Socialists offered no such foreign support.

There were two Communist organizations which were concerned with youth and students. One, the National Student League (NSL), was exclusively oriented toward the students; the other, the Young Communist League (YCL), had both student and nonstudent members and was not as important as the NSL in the student movement. Communists were a critical element in the student movement of the thirties, particularly between 1934 and 1940. They exercised influence through organizations which were openly Communist, such as the YCL and the NSL, and through nominally non-Communist groups in which they exercised dominant political control, such as the American Student Union (ASU) and the American Youth Congress (AYC).

The role of the Communists in the student movement has been hotly debated by activists, scholars, and journalists for a number of years. Some have argued that the semiclandestine role of Communists in groups like the ASU had, in the long run, a damaging effect on the movement as a whole because the Communists tried, with a good deal of success, to manipulate the organization according to the shifts in Communist party policy. The ASU, and other organizations influenced by the Communists, were subjected to factionalism which resulted in the disillusionment of many of its members.[30]

Communist youth and student groups were the largest groups on the left; the YCL claimed 11,000 members in 1936 as compared to the 4,000 that SLID claimed. Their influence was greater than their numbers indicated: many joined the Communist youth movement for only a short time. The disciplined nature of the Communist movement gave it a substantial advantage over its more anarchistic Socialist and liberal opposition. A fairly small number of Communist cadres could, without much difficulty, have a substantial influence on large groups through the use of parliamentary procedure and strict discipline. Finally, the Communists, for at least part of the thirties, offered a political alternative which many left-leaning Americans found convincing. During the "united front" period, Communists stressed opposition to fascism abroad and oppression and injustice at home, as well as a willingness to work peacefully with any anti-fascist and democratic groups. This combination of a nonthreatening domestic stance, which was hardly revolutionary in nature, and a long-range radical perspective was attractive to many who wanted social change but were unwilling to join a small factional group.

There were other forces, as well, that accounted both for the attitudes and tactics of the Communists, and for their attraction. The Communists remembered well the repression of the 1920s, and therefore tried to protect themselves during the thirties from easy infiltration by the FBI and possible repression. The thirties, it must be recalled, was a period of unprecedented instability in the United States as well as overseas, and many liberals and radicals felt that capitalism was in irreversible decay and that revolution was a distinct possibility. The Communists naturally tried to prepare themselves for this potentially revolutionary situation by careful internal organization according to Marxist-Leninist models and at the same time to extend their potential control over other organizations. This strategy fit well into the "united front" of the period. The Soviet Union played an important part in the thinking of radicals and Communists at this period. The Soviet Union was in great danger at the time, and it was natural for Communists around the world to help to defend it. Many independent liberals and radicals felt a sympathy toward the Soviet Union, since it was felt to be a functioning "socialist" state. Although the Stalin purges of the thirties weakened this attraction, it was still strong and an element of opinion which the Communists would use to gain domestic support. Thus, Communist actions in the 1930s were not without consistency, and it is not surprising that Communists had a good deal of support during the turmoil of the period.

The impact of the Communists in student activism should not be overestimated. Their period of major power was relatively short—1936 to 1939—and the large majority of students who were members of Communist-dominated groups like the ASU or the AYC were not influenced by communism. Indeed, a large majority of ASU members quit the organization when it became clear that it was controlled by Communists. In a sense, Communists wielded influence as long as their politics were moderate and hardly distinguishable from the "mainstream" of the liberal-radical student movement.

One of the important Communist student organizations was the National Student League (NSL). The NSL was founded in 1931 in New York City as the New York Student League. Most of its original members were formerly active in the League for Industrial Democracy but were more militant both ideologically and tactically than the LID. Many early NSL activists felt that the LID was too closely tied to the Socialist party. From its beginning, the NSL was controlled by the Communists and echoed Communist policy on both campus and national issues, although it never openly acknowledged its Communist leadership. During the first year of its existence NSL was able to expand rapidly because of several events which brought it national publicity and attention and helped it grow beyond its New York City base.

The first of these dramatic efforts was a trip by a busload of Eastern college students to the coal fields of Harlan County, Kentucky, the scene of a bitter strike and one of the most depressed areas in the United States at the time. The students wanted to investigate the situation and see what could be done to help the miners. The authorities in Harlan County did not welcome them and the students were turned back by the local sheriff with some violence and a good deal of national publicity. This trip was a brilliant publicity stroke for the NSL, since it focused national attention not only on the miners of Harlan County but on the NSL itself. The students involved in the trip (mostly from New York City) were able to use it to organize on campus.

The other events which helped the NSL organize were local campus issues at several New York City colleges. NSL activists organized a protest against tuition increases in the New York City colleges in June of 1922. Further, the NSL was instrumental in protesting the dismissals of several radical professors in New York, particularly Donald Henderson at Columbia University, who was a prominent NSL organizer and a Communist. The expulsion of the editor of the Columbia University student newspaper for printing articles critical of the university's administration led to an NSL-organized student stike. These local issues helped the NSL establish itself on campuses. They all built the image of the NSL as a major national student organization unafraid to speak up and act for its beliefs. This activist approach was much more appealing than the educational orientation of the SLID.[31]

The NSL expanded quickly. By 1933, it had 129 local chapters. Its membership was diverse and few of the rank and file were Communists, although the leadership was unquestionably Communist. The NSL published a journal, the *Student Review*, regularly from 1931 to December, 1933, when it failed for lack of financial support. The *Review* combined the NSL's concern for university issues and broader political questions and emphasized nonacademic political issues and the activities of NSL chapters. The NSL took militant stands on many issues. Because of this, many college administrators refused to allow NSL chapters on campus, and the organization was often involved in struggles to defend a local group's right to exist.

NSL policy, as stated at its annual conventions, covered a broad range of political and social issues. The NSL emphasized worker-student cooperation in its early years and urged student involvement in workers' struggles. The Harlan County trip reflected this, as did several other campaigns supporting strikes like the UMW strike in the Illinois coal fields. NSL took stands on a variety of educational questions. It opposed increased college fees and reduction in teachers' salaries and favored federal aid to education and equality of education regardless of race, religion, or national origin. The NSL stressed academic freedom on campus, particularly the right to freedom of expression in student newspapers, and attacked the firing of faculty for political reasons.

The NSL expended most of its energies on national and international politics. From the outset, the NSL was antiwar, but it distinguished between imperalist wars and "progressive" wars (anti-imperialistic or class wars). Correctly noting the strength of the antiwar movement on campus, the NSL took a strong stand against ROTC.[32] It condemned fascism and racism and was a proponent of civil liberties. Generally, the NSL pledged itself to work for "socialism" and passed several resolutions, notably at the 1932 convention, committing itself to popularizing the Soviet Union.

The NSL was not solely oriented to the colleges. In 1932 it established a high school section and organized in the New York City high schools. On campus, it repeatedly urged cooperation among all student groups and consistenly, from 1932 on, pushed for a single, united student left. It was somewhat successful in this endeavor when the SLID joined it in forming the American Student Union. NSL activities were a combination of national policy and local initiative. Despite the efforts of the national office to build a unified and disciplined student organization, this proved to be impossible. There are some common elements in the activities of NSL groups, but differences between local chapters are more striking. NSL activities most often concentrated on antiwar work, student-worker collaboration, and campus and educational issues. Of these, the antiwar activities received the most attention. From its beginning, NSL groups were active in anti-ROTC campaigns. In December, 1933, the NSL cosponsored a national antiwar conference in Chicago to build a broad national antiwar movement under Communist guidance. The Chicago conference also called for the abolition of ROTC and for the end of the Morrill Act which provided state universities with funds and pressured them to allow campus military programs.[33] Local NSL groups were active in campaigns to abolish compulsory ROTC. For example, the Social Problems Club at the University of California, an NSL affiliate, sponsored anti-ROTC activities, as did groups at Yale and George Washington University. The issue of peace in general was critical to both local and national programs. In 1934, the NSL successfully organized the first national antiwar strike, in which 25,000 students, mostly in the New York area, participated.

Worker-student collaboration and campus issues were also integral on the national and local levels. In 1932, an NSL team made a survey of Ohio coal fields and were harassed by local authorities. Local magazines were founded by a number of NSL groups at such schools as Harvard and at Commonwealth College in Mena, Arkansas, where the journal was called the *Red Menace*. The NSL was involved in the defense of Scottsboro Boys (one of the key Communist efforts of the early thirties) which involved defending several Negroes accused of a rape in the South. In New York City, NSL groups were involved in academic freedom efforts at a number of colleges and high schools. They started their own school featuring courses on modern economics, fascism, imperialism, philosophy, and poetry.[34]

The NSL was active on both prestigious campuses and at smaller liberal arts and normal schools such as LaCrosse State Teachers College in Wisconsin. By 1934, it had a fairly wide distribution of affiliated groups around the nation. The NSL had fifty active affiliates in 1934, and another forty-four groups, not officially affiliated, were dominated by the NSL. Without doubt, the NSL was one of the largest national student groups in 1934, and it was certainly one of the most active. Its growth in several years to this position was quite impressive and reflected several factors. The organizational abilities and dedication of the NSL's Communist leadership helped. Perhaps more important, however, was the organization's combination of a relatively moderate program with a substantial degree of activism. This combination took advantage of the growing radicalism on campus, but did not place the NSL firmly in the camp of the "sectarian" left. The NSL, no doubt, provided a key means of recruiting students to the Communist party in the early thirties. With the founding of the American Student Union in 1935, the NSL lost its individual identity. The basic political approach of the NSL remained a strong force in the student movement and continued in various organizational forms throughout the thirties and, for that matter, to the present time.

Communism appeared openly on the American campus through the Young Communist League (YCL). Although not primarily a student organization, the YCL did play an important role on campus, especially after the Communist party began to orient itself to the campus. As Murray Kempton noted:

> The Communists set the tone for the movement of the Thirties. . . . because they had the advantage of numbers, because they offered the weak the impression of strength and because they had a church which no one else could match. They offered in short an available escape from reality. Most students, of course, managed to bear reality quite well enough to be apathetic about any avenues for escaping it. The Communists were a tiny fragment of the whole, but they were a majority of the committed. To reject them meant to surrender even the illusion of strength and condemn yourself anew to that alienation which had moved you to commitment in the first place.[35]

As radical organizations went in the campus situation of the 1930s, the Communists were strong and maintained the important advantage of a disciplined membership often capable of carrying out directions.[36] This contrasted sharply with many of the other radical groups, which had to deal continually with internal factionalism and were unable to control either their own members or the campus political climate. The Communists were especially strong in New York City, Chicago, and several other large cities. YCL groups existed in many universities, but some were not as influential as those in the cities. While in absolute numbers the YCL and other Communist groups were not very large, they were important in the campus radical community. For example, at Brooklyn College, one of the strongholds of the Communist student movement, only 3 percent of the students voted for a Communist candidate in a presidential straw poll, although one-third of the politically active students were Communists.[37]

The "behind the scenes" role of the YCL was more critical than its direct involvement in campus affairs. The YCL on campus often functioned as a semi-underground study group limited to providing political education to its members and coordination of Communist activities in other campus organizations. YCL members, for example, were the leaders of the NSL and were the major force behind the American Student Union. Communist students were active in local campus movements at schools where they were strong. In short, the YCL is important not so much because it was a visible and vocal student organization but because it was a disciplined organization capable of exercising leadership in other organizations. Other ideological student groups also played an indirect role in broader student movement, and this was not limited to a "Communist conspiracy." Socialist and Trotskyist students actively involved themselves in nonideological groups. As has been mentioned, the YPSL influence in the Methodist student organization was quite strong.

The YCL was very attractive to serious campus radicals. It claimed 3,000 and grew to 22,000 by 1939, but most of these were not students. For much of the thirties, YCL policy did not differ much from that of other groups like the NSL or, for that matter, non-Communist radical organizations, and this in part accounted for its appeal. The YCL, for example, favored the National Youth Act and worked hard to assure its passage. In this area it worked through the NSL and the American Youth Congress (AYC), a mass organization under Communist leadership. YCL favored the eighteen-year-old vote, unemployment insurance regardless of age, full rights for Negroes, and was in favor of a "Soviet America."[38] On the surface, its approach was not especially revolutionary. Through much of the decade, the YCL rejected violent revolution and stated that its desire was to win members through educational programs.

The YCL, like the other ideologically based student and youth groups of the period, was very much involved in leftist factionalism. In part, this factionalism was caused by organizational rivalries, but it was also based on ideological differences. One's analysis of the Soviet Union—whether it was truly "socialist" or not—was the subject of great controversy. The role of Leon Trotsky and the "purge" trials in the Soviet Union caused heated debates. Tactics within the United States—for example, debates concerning pacifism, the solution to the "Negro problem," and other issues—also were a source of controversy. YCL journals devoted much space to attacking "Trotskyists" and the YPSL, among others. The American Student Union and the American Youth Congress were scenes of major battles between the YCL and social democrats and most of them were won by the Communists. This factionalism, often over issues which were irrelevant to the campus, bored and alienated less ideologically committed students and ultimately damaged the student movement. Further, the reliance of the YCL on the changing position of the Communist party and the foreign policy position of the Soviet Union caused both the YCL and the student groups in which it worked many problems. This was especially true in the pro-collective security stance taken before the Stalin-Hitler pact, the antiwar position taken after it, and the final abandonment of the anti-war position when Germany invaded the Soviet Union. Mass disaffections occurred not only within the YCL, but also in organizations which the YCL had dominated and had forced policy changes in, namely the ASU and the AYC.

LIBERAL STUDENT ORGANIZATIONS

Although radical student organizations dominated the thirties, liberal groups were plentiful on campus and probably more accurately reflected the student mood than their radical allies. Many radical groups, particularly during the "united front" period, actively courted the liberals. Liberal student organizations, such as the National Student Federation of America (NSFA), moved substantially to the left during the thirties, pushed by the political currents in society and the pressure of the radicals. The most important liberal organization of the 1930s (as well as of the 1920s) was the National Student Federation of America. The NSFA, a federation of student governments, was more representative of broad American student opinion than the more radical groups, although it had less of an impact on campus because of its educational orientation and tactical moderation. The NSFA had affiliates on campuses which the radical organizations seldom, if ever, reached—small colleges and Midwestern and Southern schools with more conservative traditions. Thus, the NSFA, a "middle of the road" group at the University of Wisconsin or at the City College of New York, became a radical organization at the University of Oklahoma.

Throughout the thirties, the NSFA carried on an active program. Annual conventions discussed key issues related both to the practical problems of student governments and campus-related concerns as well as national politics. The emphasis, however, was generally on the campus. For example, the 1933 NSFA convention, held in Washington, D.C., attracted more than 200 delegates. It considered a range of student-related issues and took liberal stands on political issues; among other things, it supported the NRA and equal rights for Negroes. At the same convention, a motion to oppose ROTC was defeated. One observer noted that the level of political consciousness was not very high.[39]

A survey of NSFA activities provides an idea of the scope of the organization. The NSFA put out magazines on a regular basis. The

National Student Mirror began publication in 1933 and appeared for three years. Later a weekly *NSFA Reporter* was published. The NSFA held a series of educational conferences. In 1934, the organization established a National Institute for Public Affairs in an effort to involve students in discussions and conferences on topics of national importance. They were helped in this endeavor by the United States Office of Education.

In 1935, the NSFA produced a series of radio programs broadcast nationally on the CBS network. These programs dealt with controversial issues such as the peace movement and unemployment as well as student-related concerns. Finally, the NSFA ran a travel service which successfully arranged tours for American students in Europe and the Soviet Union.

As the decade grew more turbulent and the student movement more radical, the NSFA responded by moving to the left. Although in 1936 its major activities were sponsoring a national campaign for highway safety and setting up athletic commissions, the NSFA took more political stands. It came close to supporting the American Youth Act, which was sponsored by the radical American Youth Congress. The tone of the *Mirror*, which reflected the NSFA leadership if not the bulk of its members, became more radical and focused on issues such as the Spanish Civil War, the peace movement, and unemployment. The NSFA was careful to avoid committing its member schools to activism and limited its resolutions to paper support. The NSFA developed friendly relations with such groups as the United Student Peace Committee, the American Youth Congress, and other activist groups and raised funds for student refugees in foreign countries. In short, it came close to participating directly in the radical student movement but stopped short of active involvement.[40]

The relationship of the NSFA to the other radical student organizations was ambivalent and it tried to keep some distance from groups like the American Student Union. The ASU tried to push the NSFA in a more radical direction, and also attempted to attract some of the NSFA's supporters. ASU commented favorably on the NSFA's gradual shift to the left.[41] On at least one occasion the ASU openly requested closer cooperation with the United Front. The NSFA denounced this effort as an attempt to interfere in its internal affairs, and nothing came of the overture.

The NSFA's importance as a national student organization came at the end of the 1930s and the early 1940s, when the radical student movement collapsed following the Nazi-Soviet pact and some formerly activist students joined the NSFA in a more active but anti-Communist program. At this time, the NSFA merged with the International Student Service. The 1940 convention of the NSFA reflected this trend. With the coming of the war however, the NSFA became mainly concerned with student service activities and support for the American war effort.[42]

The NSFA survived because it served a stable element of the American student community: college student governments, which were regularly in need of services such as speakers, publications, and travel bureaus. Its radical political stance was a temporary response to the leftward trend of the campus at the time, and probably reflected its constituency. For the most part, NSFA affiliates engaged in traditional student government educational and service activities, and its leadership was far from being committed social activists. The revival of the NSFA's importance at the end of the decade was due more to the collapse of other elements of the student movement than to the vitality of the NSFA itself.

THE UNITED FRONTS

The American student movement had its greatest success both in terms of numbers and in impact as measured by attention paid to student activism in the national press and influence among students between 1934 and 1938, the period of the "united front." During this time, a union of Communist, Socialist, and many liberal elements in several organizations, most notably the American Student Union (ASU), created a unified force on campus which could mobilize substantial numbers of students. In a sense, this period is one of the most difficult to analyze, since it entails a complicated set of groups engaged in intermittant ideological struggle and involved in a wide range of activities. The united fronts were effective in increasing student concern for foreign policy, particularly student opposition to American rearmament and entanglement in European problems. During this period, the radical movement as a whole was antiwar, but elements within it had varying reasons for their positions. Socialists saw war as inimical to socialism, but they were not absolutists in opposing all wars, as were the pacifists. The Communists shifted their antiwar position several times, coincidental with changes in Soviet foreign policy. Many liberals and nonpolitical students opposed American rearmament and involvement on purely isolationist grounds. Thus, the peace movement—the most important thrust of the student movement at this time—was a curious combination of independent radicals, Communists, liberals, and some isolationists united around a specific issue on which they could tentatively agree. It is not surprising that the "unity" expressed in the ASU was fragile; when the issue became more complicated, the various participating groups began fighting among themselves.

The United Front was possible only in the context of the 1930s. Americans generally, and the educated middle classes in particular, were concerned about the turn of events in Europe and the danger of another European war. Memories of the "betrayal" of World War I were still strong, and many Americans wanted nothing to do with another European war. At the same time, the rise of fascism in Germany and Italy was abhorrent to many Americans. At home, the depth of the Depression had passed by 1934, but full economic recovery was still a long way off. The New Deal itself introduced many measures which only a few years before would have been considered wild-eyed radicalism. The leftist political parties grew in strength, although they never became a national force of any significance. Midwestern populism and regional radicalism had bursts of strength in some parts of the country and Upton Sinclair came close to winning the governorship of California on a semi-Socialist program. The militant tactics of the CIO brought substantial change to the trade union movement and industrial unionism grew. Within the trade union movement radicals assumed some positions of leadership. In short, American society at large moved to the left in the thirties in the sense that social planning became more acceptable, and this shift, and the accompanying willingness to accept radical social change as a normal event, had implications for the campus scene. Perhaps at no other time in American history was the student movement able to function in a context which accepted its goals and criticisms as a legitimate part of the American scene.

Within the left, the mid-thirties was a particularly propitious time for a unified and effective student movement. For different reasons, various segments of the American left were converging on goals and tactics, despite the fact that they were divided on ideological questions. Many, but by no means all, socialists, feeling that their success in winning widespread support was limited and that foreign policy issues were of increasing importance as Europe moved toward war, began to participate in united fronts on specific issues. This represents a remarkable shift in policy, especially given the intense anticommunism and unwillingness to compromise ideological purity characteristic of most socialist groups in the early 1930s. The Communists were willing to move to a united front for quite different reasons. As the Soviet Union found itself isolated in Europe and confronted with the real possibility of a military invasion by Nazi Germany, Communists throughout the world mobilized to oppose fascism and isolate Germany politically. Unity with other antifascist elements, most notably Socialists and liberals, who had been previously attacked by the Communists, became party policy. The American Communist party, following the Soviet lead, modified its political position to make itself acceptable to moderate elements in the radical movement and violent attacks on opposition leftists ceased. Liberals also desired a united front. Impelled largely by the impending international crisis, they were willing to accept support from radicals, whom they saw moving in their direction on foreign policy questions.

Just as the unity was created by forces outside the campus, it was destroyed by these same elements. The Communists were responsible for the demise of the united front, for their strict adherence to the changing Soviet line made it impossible for other groups to work with them. From 1935 to 1939, the united front stood for "collective security" against fascism, aid to Spain, and antifascism at home and abroad. When the Soviet Union signed its nonaggression treaty with Germany in 1939, the Communist position changed literally overnight and the CP and its allies became almost isolationist in their policies. These shifts divided groups like the ASU. Socialists and liberals alike were more consistent in their policies and refused to go along with this sudden change. The final break came when the Soviet Union was invaded by Germany in 1940. At this time, the Communists again reversed themselves and vigorously advocated immediate American entry into the war and massive American aid for the allies, particularly for the Soviet Union. Liberals and socialists involved in the peace movement continued to support a noninterventionist party and an irreparable split occurred. The rank and file of the student movement felt betrayed and disillusioned by the ASU's changes in tactics which mirrored the Communist line. By the time the United States entered the war in December, 1941, the student movement for all intents and purposes had died.[43]

The American Student Union is the major united front antiwar organization of the 1930s and is, therefore, of great importance to this analysis. The ASU, however, had some predecessors which set the stage for the united front. One of these forerunners was the National Conference on Students in Politics, a conference which was held in Washington, D.C., in December, 1933, and which was sponsored by a range of student organizations. It was planned by the National Student Federation of America, the Student League for Industrial Democracy, the National Student League, the Young Men's and Women's Christian Associations, International Student Service, League of Nations Associations, and other groups. The bulk of the participants were liberals, although the proceedings were controlled from behind the scenes by radicals.[44] The Conference attracted students from around the country, and was keynoted by Eleanor Roosevelt. Subjects such as pacifism and revolution, trade unions, tariffs, fascism, armaments, racial discrimination, and education were discussed.[45] Some of the debates were heated and the resolutions which emerged were moderately radical in nature, reflecting many of the concerns of the united front student movement which came a few years later. According to some observers, the conference was a battleground for the various political factions, and in this respect reflected broader trends in the student movement. As George Rawick put it:

> The Conference was a harbinger of the youth politics of the decade, as represented in the American Student Union and the American Youth Congress. The rhetoric was vague and collectivist, the Socialists and Communists dominated the discussion, the liberals were youth of good will, and just a bit confused by it all.[46]

The conference was an example of how liberal students from organizations like the NSFA and the YMCA, with relatively limited political sophistication, were led by more ideologically committed and organizationally astute members of the radical student organizations. A permanent consultative organization was to emerge from the conference, but none did and in this regard the meeting was a failure. On the positive side, it did attract major national attention in the press and other media and involved leading members of the Roosevelt administration, informing them of the concerns of the radical student movement.

The American Student Union deserves some detailed attention, not only because it was the largest student political organization of the decade, but also because it reflected many of the trends evident in the student movement and in American liberal and radical politics at the time. Without question, the major issue of concern to students was peace, and the ASU was intimately involved in the peace movement.

The origins of the ASU go back at least a year before the founding convention in December, 1935. The National Student League was particularly interested in convincing other student groups, particularly the Student League for Industrial Democracy, to join in a broad, united student movement to work for common aims. SLID, after initial opposition and unwillingness to work with Communists, changed its position, and the stage was set for the emergence of the American Student Union. Indeed, the NSL and the SLID had participated in several joint activities in 1934 and 1935, which had been fairly successful. The founding convention of the ASU took place in Columbus, Ohio, in late December, 1935, and attracted around 500 delegates, only half of whom were affiliated with either the NSL or the SLID (although these two groups dominated the proceedings and the later organization). More than 200 colleges were represented at this initial meeting. The administration of Ohio State University refused to permit the ASU to hold its convention on campus and the campus YMCA hosted the meeting. The convention attracted national publicity, and both liberals and radicals hailed it as the beginning of a new era for the student movement. Following this convention, ASU membership rose to approximately 6,000 persons.[47]

The ASU was a national membership organization with campus chapters as well as more loosely affiliated groups. Unlike the NSFA, the national ASU had authority to commit the organization to specific policies, to initiate programs, and to sponsor demonstrations and various actions. The highest governing authority in the organization was the annual convention, which was controlled by locally elected delegates. The National Executive Committee had very broad powers; it made policy and tactical decisions between conventions, set the time and place of the convention, determined relations with other organizations, and appointed the administrative staff. The National Executive Committee had twenty-one members, about equally divided between NSL and SLID members, and some seats were allotted to unaffiliated liberals. Due to some defections from the Socialist ranks, notably that of Joseph Lash (who became editor of the ASU's journal, the *Student Advocate*) and the pro-Communist stance of some of the liberals, the NSL had effective control of the Executive Committee from the outset and never lost this control. The ASU's national staff, usually consisting of four or five individuals, also had substantial power in the organization, if only because the staff was, in most cases, the national "voice" of the organization. It often took national speaking tours and prepared press statements and other publicity. While the ASU had a formal democratic structure, the control of the organization in practice rested with the Executive Committee and national staff.

The Columbus convention set the stage for future ASU policy and indicated the organization's direction. The major stress was on antimilitarism. ROTC was denounced by a large majority, and after a close vote (193 to 155), the liberals and Communists succeeded in getting the ASU to favor "collective security" against fascism over the Socialists' "purist" position of equating capitalism and fascism. The stand enabled the ASU to support united action by all powers against Germany and Italy while opposing American rearmament. The Oxford Pledge was strongly supported by the delegates (244 to 49) at the 1935 convention, placing the ASU in the militant wing of the peace movement. [48] The Oxford Pledge, which has already been discussed, was a pledge not to participate in any armed conflict initiated by the American government. The ASU also took a strong stand in defense of academic freedom, and placed particular emphasis on the right of professors and students to express radical positions without fear of recrimination. The 1935 convention called for an alliance with labor and urged a more meaningful National Youth Administration. It opposed racial discrimination and supported curriculum changes in higher education, although this concern with educational reform was never a major focus of the organization.

There were some disputes which marred the convention and were perhaps indicative of tensions within the ASU. Socialists and Communists differed on whether to support the USSR, and this conflict was resolved by ASU's lack of any clear position on the issue. Later ASU policies, however, reflected the Communists' view more accurately than the Socialists'. The question of whether the ASU should affiliate with the League Against War and Fascism, a Communist-dominated organization, was also hotly debated. In the end, the ASU did not join. While collective security was endorsed by the convention, the ASU also supported the Oxford Pledge, which was by implication critical of collective security. In short, compromises between Socialists and Communists were worked out in the context of the convention, although only after long and often acrimonious debate, much of which was probably of limited interest to many delegates. The Columbus meeting ended in a spirit of general unity and a feeling that the American student movement had taken a substantial step forward.

The ASU immediately initiated a series of programs aimed at increasing its influence on the campus and stressing the programs and political concerns. One of the ASU's most effective vehicles was its journal, the *Student Advocate*, which appeared from 1936 until 1938, when ASU policy abruptly changed. The *Advocate* combined SLID's *Student Outlook* and the NSL's *Student Review*. Its circulation quickly reached 30,000 with two editions, one for college campuses and the other for high schools. The journal was published monthly, and featured reports of ASU activities, stories on international affairs of relevance to ASU members, articles on campus events and issues, and occasionally analyses of educational questions. Joseph Lash, editor of the *Advocate* for most of its history, noted that its pages were remarkably bland given the political and social turmoil of the times and the internal dissention within the ASU.[49] While many of the ASU's leaders were Communists, they were willing to let the *Advocate* reflect a much more moderate tone in order to gain acceptance on campus. None of the differences within the ASU are reflected in the journal and thus the rank and file of ASU members were uninformed of the debates over tactics and policy. From 1936 until 1938, the height of the united front, the *Advocate* read like a New Deal publicity organ. Many of the issues raised in the journal were similar to those of concern to the student movement of the sixties—war and peace, social justice, race relations, ROTC on campus, in loco parentis, and popular culture.

Unlike most other student organizations, the ASU was successful in organizing high school students. By 1936, at least 110 high schools had

ASU affiliates and numerous special publications for high school students were issued by the ASU. Much of this activity was due to an energetic high school secretary.

The ASU took a leading role in academic freedom cases in various parts of the country. It tried to help a radical English instructor who was dismissed from CCNY, a student who was expelled from Columbia for political participation, several Washington University students who lost their scholarships because of their politics, and a college newspaper in Texas which was censored by the administration. The *Advocate* provided a national publicity for these incidents. Nationally, this was all the ASU could do. The ASU actively supported Republican Spain in the Civil War, and a number of ASU members, as well as other radical activists, volunteered to fight with the antifascist forces in Spain. The ASU favored the National Negro Congress and assisted in a number of labor struggles such as the Milwaukee journalists' strike, an Akron rubber workers' strike, and a national strike of office workers. In most of these situations, local ASU chapters gave concrete aid, while the national ASU provided publicity.

Nationally, the ASU devoted most of its energies to the peace movement. The 1936 antiwar strikes, sponsored by the ASU, and a number of other student organizations were highly successful, and probably brought the ASU its most valuable support and publicity. On many campuses, local ASU chapters were the leading elements in the antiwar movement and gained a good deal of support and prestige from their involvement.

Most of ASU's activities were on the local and regional levels. The hub of ASU's strength was in the New York City area, where the national office was located and which was the center of radical politics in the nation. ASU won student council elections in the five New York City colleges, and 800 students turned out for the initial ASU meeting at CCNY. ASU also had regional offices in its most active areas which helped to coordinate programs. Other strong ASU affiliates were at Harvard, Vassar, Berkeley, Wisconsin, Ohio State, Michigan, Temple, Minnesota, Reed, Smith, and Swarthmore. Local groups differed from one another, and many did not even use the ASU name. For example, the Harvard Student Union, an ASU affiliate, had strong ties to the National ASU while other chapters, located on smaller campuses, were less open about their national affiliation. The "clandestine" affiliations occurred because many college administrations did not permit campus groups to be tied to national organizations. Thus, a number of local organizations, while not formally tied to the ASU, were informally allied with it. The political composition of local groups varied substantially.[50] Some were under militant and politically sophisticated leadership, usually either Socialist or Communist, and were outspoken on campus and international affairs within both the ASU structure and locally. Others were liberal discussion groups, and many had little political awareness and were in the ASU because of vague antiwar feelings or because the ASU represented dissenting opinion on campus. The national ASU and its internal political feuds had little impact on these latter groups.

The changes in ASU politics are illustrated in the organization's conventions. For example, its 1936 meetings, which were held in Chicago in December, were characterized by unity; 384 delegates from twenty-four states attended. At the 1936 convention the Communists found themselves in the curious position of supporting moderate stands on most issues, particularly on antiwar and foreign policy questions, in order to broaden the base of the ASU and attract more liberals.[51] The Socialists, who opposed collective security, took a more radical stance and almost got their resolution passed. But this marked the height of Socialist power in the ASU. By 1937, the Communists managed to secure control over the organization and kept tight reins throughout the remainder of its history.[52]

The 1938 ASU convention, held at Vassar College, saw a dramatic shift in policy. The Oxford Pledge was dropped in favor of a position fully favoring collective security. Opposed by Socialists and pacifists and supported by liberals and Communists, the Pledge was dropped by a vote of 382 to 108.[53] The convention received national attention and messages from President Roosevelt and other national leaders were sent to the ASU. Part of the reason for this attention was the fact that the ASU strongly supported the New Deal's foreign and most domestic policies. The 1938 convention passed resolutions favoring campus cooperatives and student participation in "progressive" political campaigns. It also took positions on Spain and China. As in the past, the major debate was over foreign policy. The moderation of the organization, under Communist leadership, was best illustrated by the dropping of opposition to ROTC. The convention placed stress on the "collegiate" nature of the ASU and its link with traditional campus activities. All of this was very much in line with Communist strategy.

After 1938, the ASU began a slow decline, which was culminated by its dramatic policy shifts over the Nazi-Soviet pact of 1939. Socialists and some liberals in 1938 were publically very critical of the ASU, and growing numbers of non-Communist ASU members and chapters began to realize that the organization was closely tied to the Communists. With some organized opposition, many ASU local groups disaffiliated or became inactive. An example of Communist domination of the ASU can be seen at its 1939 convention, held at the University of Wisconsin. The meeting, which took place shortly after the Soviet invasion of Finland (an event which was roundly condemned by most Americans, regardless of political persuasion, although defended by Communists), refused by a vote of 322 to 49 to condemn the Soviet Union. The ASU's policy changed from one of collective security to one of total neutrality after the Soviet Union signed its nonaggression treaty with Germany.[54]

In 1940, Joseph P. Lash, who had been general secretary of the ASU for four years, resigned from the organization over his frustration with the ASU's slavish adherence to Communist policy. His departure, and that of most of the remaining liberals, signaled the end of the ASU as an effective student organization. Lash went on to work with the National Student Federation of America and with other groups and was instrumental in forging an anti-Communist alliance of student organizations.[55] The ASU declined in membership from a high of around 20,000 in 1938 to 2,000 in 1940.[56] It continued to function through 1941 and held a convention in December of 1941, which was attended by 250 delegates from twenty-five colleges and high schools.[57] At that time the organization placed itself at the service of the nation and the war effort. Little was heard from the ASU after that.

While the American Student Union was the major united front campus organization, another national group, the American Youth Congress (AYC), deserves brief mention here, since it was similar to the ASU in its politics and was influential during the mid-thirties.[58] Organized by liberals, the AYC was quickly taken over by more radical elements, notably by Communists, at its first conference in 1934. The AYC was an amalgam of other national youth and student organizations and served for a time as the major national "spokesman" for American youth. It supported the Roosevelt administration, and Eleanor Roosevelt took a strong interest in AYC and helped it gain national attention. Shortly after its founding, the AYC claimed that it represented 1.7 million youths in organizations ranging from the Young Communist League to the Boy Scouts. (Some of the more conservative groups, such as the Scouts, quit the AYC at a later date.) By 1935, 500 clubs and 846 organizations, including 157 unions, forty-eight churches, 202 cultural associations, and many antiwar and student organizations were affiliated with it.

The major goal of the AYC was to pressure Congress into passing a National Youth Act guaranteeing rights, such as a minimum wage and education. The AYC was also active in the antiwar movement. Despite its large membership and its ability to speak for youths, the AYC had relatively little impact on campus and, for that matter, on American youth generally. It was to a large extent a "paper" organization, and the very large majority of its membership had little knowledge of its activities or commitment to its program. The student movement was strongly represented in AYC. In 1939, when the AYC claimed 4.7 million affiliated members, of the student groups, the National Student Federation of America belonged. Communists maintained their control over the organization by holding key posts in the administration, through the use of disciplined tactics, and by obtaining the support of a number of liberals. As with the ASU, the twists and turns of the Soviet Union in the late thirties, plus a good deal of "red baiting" by conservative elements meant the end of the AYC by mid-1940.

OTHER STUDENT ACTIVISM —
CONSERVATIVE AND RELIGIOUS GROUPS

Two secondary, but important, elements of the campus political scene were the conservative and religious student groups. Such organizations, while not in the mainstream of campus politics in the 1930s, were nonetheless active and, in some areas and on some campuses, constituted an important part of the student movement. Conservative student organizations, where they existed, were active mainly on the local level. No national conservative student movement emerged in the thirties, and there is little evidence of national coordination of conservative organizations. There was an undercurrent of conservative opinion on campus in the thirties. Student opinion polls, which were often conducted by liberal groups and therefore subject to some bias, consistently reported a strong conservative minority. Occasional expressions of anti-Semitism or racism appeared in campus newspapers. The fraternities and sororities, which were quite strong at many of the large universities, represented conservative values when they represented anything at all, and fraternity members participated in many of the antiradical incidents reported through the decade. Because liberal and radical organizations clearly were so active and because campus conservatism was fragmented and usually unorganized, right-wing student groups in the thirties have received little attention.

Much of the conservative activism was of a sporadic and unorganized nature. Students served, for example, as strike breakers in the San Francisco waterfront strike of 1934, with the support of the President of the University of California.[59] Student governments were often conservative. At the University of California, a bastion of liberalism even in the thirties, the student government investigated radicalism on campus in such a manner that the President of the University, Robert Sproul, called them "brutal vigilantes."[60]

Right-wing students were engaged at various times in efforts to break up leftist or liberal meetings or demonstrations. The University of California was the scene of such conflicts during this period. One of the most famous incidents occurred at the University of Wisconsin, where right-wing students threw a number of radicals into the lake following a demonstration. An article in the *Student Advocate* pointed to the increase of right-wing activism in 1937, but mentioned only a few specific cases.[61] John Spivak wrote a series of articles in the *New Masses* in which he claimed that right-wing professors and administrators, as well as students, were trying to dominate the campus. Spivak claimed that a secret right-wing and anti-Semitic society called the Paul Reveres existed on many campuses.[62]

Local conservative groups existed at a number of universities. At Michigan State, Indiana, and other schools affiliates of the KKK existed on campus. Radical students were beaten up not only at Wisconsin, but at MIT and at the University of Oregon.[63] The American Liberty League, a large conservative organization, made some efforts to organize on campus and was successful, particularly in the South. For example, when the NSL tried to organize a chapter at the University of

North Carolina, the Liberty League quickly started a group which was much larger and more effective than the small NSL affiliate.[64]

As in other periods of American student activism, the religious student movement was influential in the thirties. It is very often ignored because of the overwhelming influence of groups like the ASU and AYC. But, as in the twenties, a number of religious organizations were actively involved in social concerns. Some organizations were more active than others. For example, the National Federation of Methodist Youth (NFMY) was closely allied to the Young Peoples' Socialist League and the peace movement through its members. The YM-YWCA and the Interseminary Movement also participated in radical and liberal politics. These organizations, along with other religious groups, were affiliated to the AYC and later were active in the YCAW. As in previous periods, the liberal wings of the Protestant churches were the most involved while Roman Catholics and fundamentalist Protestants usually abstained from any political activities. Jewish youth and student groups, perhaps for the first time, became organizationally committed to the peace movement. The Protestant groups were most influential in smaller liberal arts schools and church-related colleges where groups like the ASU and NSL did not exist. Thus, because of their geographical position, their role was quite important during the thirties. Jewish student groups tended to be strong in the larger urban universities where radical groups existed.

The oldest and largest campus religious movement was the YM-YWCA. With large budget and staff, the student Ys claimed 68,500 members at 1,409 institutions in 1930 and had more than 100 staff members. However, the student Y had declined: in 1920, it claimed that 15.6 percent of the student population were members; by 1930, only 6.2 percent belonged to the Y despite a rise in absolute numbers.[65] The reason for this decline is twofold. First, the various Protestant denominations took an increasingly active role on campus, and by the 1930s had at least 200 college chaplains and religious workers serving the student community. In addition, the campus religious movement declined as a motivating force on campus at the beginning of the thirties. America was becoming secularized, and this was especially true among the educated middle classes. Furthermore, as most colleges abolished compulsory chapel attendance and other outward manifestations of religiosity, the direct impact of religion declined. The YMCA, while concerned with social issues and allied in some cases with political student groups, was by no means a primarily political organization in the thirties. It retained its religious approach, and the large majority of its members continued to use its facilities for religious or social purposes. Indeed, more conservative YMCA members felt that political involvement was inappropriate for a religious organization.

The Y movement was particularly active in race relations and in the peace movement. It focused on educational programs aimed at both its own membership and the broader student community. A number of pamphlets on social issues were published, including one entitled "Toward a New Economic Society" which advocated collective ownership of natural resources and public utilities. This pamphlet aroused much criticism in the press, and the YM-YWCA had to formally disavow a socialist program. The Y movement, although consistently close to pacifist organizations, such as the Fellowship of Reconciliation, was forced, after heated debate in the councils of the Y movement over official endorsement of the peace strikes of the mid-1930s, to modify its support for them.

The Y's liberal position on race relations was a continuation of the tradition it had begun early in the twenties. The Y sponsored a conference in Atlanta in 1930 to bring together an interracial group of 200 students and staff from ten states to discuss common problems. National Y meetings reaffirmed their commitment to equality throughout the decade.[66] Like other student groups, the Y was not free of factional discontent. The most important problem in the thirties was the continuing opposition of the adult YMCA movement, which felt that the student Y was moving too far to the left on political questions and was taking too many political stands. These disputes were not sufficiently serious to cause permanent splits in the Y movement.

The YMCA-YWCA were not the only student religious groups to take political stands and participate in the student activism of the thirties. As noted, the denominational youth and student affiliates were also involved in politics. Some denominations were more radical than others, with Methodists, Quakers, and Unitarians becoming the most politically committed. The Student Volunteer Movement (SVM) continued to take social action stands, although it did not move far enough for some of its more activist members. An SVM meeting in Indianapolis in the mid-thirties indicates this move toward social concern. The convention placed a good deal less stress on missionary work, its traditional emphasis, and devoted more time to discussion of social issues. Conservative leadership and adult manipulation prevented the adoption of a strong radical program, but the organization did move substantially to the left.[67]

There were other efforts to get Christian students involved in social action concerns. A 1934 meeting of leaders of forty-one Protestant denominations formed the Christian Youth Council of North America and adopted the following statement, so typical of stands taken by Protestant youth and student groups in the 1930s.

> We declare our purpose to join with those who would bring this strife and suffering to an end, and build a world of brotherhood, where God-given resources are used to serve all minkind, where cooperation replaces competition, where peace abides in place of war and where special privilege gives way to justice and equal opportunity for all.[68]

There were other attempts to unite the various denominational groups during the thirties. A National Assembly of Student Christian Associations met at Oxford, Ohio, in 1937 and focused on social action issues. This meeting was attended by 1,350 student leaders from 300 colleges in forty-two states. The meetings took a number of radical stands and agreed to cooperate with the LID in several summer institutes.

Large summer conferences of Protestant students from around the nation met under the auspices of groups like the YMCA, SVM, and various Student Christian Movement federations, which dealt seriously with social and political questions. Many of these conferences were addressed by radical speakers, and groups like the ASU, the FOR, and the YPSL sent representatives to them. The overall impact of the religious student movement on Protestant students is difficult to assess. It is certainly true that the movement brought social issues to students who might have otherwise not been exposed so directly to them. The large numbers of Protestant students, who lent their names to the peace strikes and other radical activities, enhanced the prestige of these activities and of organizations like the American Youth Congress. Certainly, the level of political sophistication of the religious student movement was not very great, particularly when compared to the cadres of the ASU or the YCAW. Yet, Protestant students did take an increasingly active role in the political ferment of the decade, and there is little doubt that the role of the religious student movement in advocating such activism played an important role.

As World War II approached, a new phenomenon emerged on the campus scene—a prowar student movement. Impelled by the deteriorating international situation and by a growing feeling that America must be rearmed to meet any overseas threat, a number of student organizations developed which favored rearmament and increasing American aid to the Allies. The Communists, as has been noted, by mid-1940, after the German attack on the Soviet Union, fully supported American rearmament and aid to the Soviet Union. The "imperialist" war had turned into a "people's" war, and the previously militant Communist students became superpatriots. The nature of this change in the American Student Union has already been discussed.

Probably the largest prowar student organization of the 1940-1941 period was the Student Defenders of Democracy (SDD), which was founded in January of 1941. It started a journal, *SOS* (Sweethearts of Servicemen), and rapidly achieved a membership of around 5,000 within a year.[69] The SDD, while strongly favoring lend-lease and increasing aid to the Allies, was liberal on domestic questions, supporting the labor movement, civil rights and civil liberties. Another organization, the Student League for Progressive Action, was formed of dissident (anti-Communist) former ASU members in early 1941. These two organizations, with several others, formed a Student Merger Committee in October, 1941, and planned to hold a conference to create a large, liberal, prowar organization. This conference was postponed when war broke out. In December of 1941, however, these organizations merged into the Student League of America (SLA), a broad-based organization which participated actively in the war effort. Its founding convention focused on ways in which students could aid in the war effort. Organizations, such as the National Student Federation of America, were also involved in SLA.

The prowar student organizations played no important role in preparing America for participation in World War II. International events took care of that. These groups rather reflected how the campus followed political currents in the broader society. In part, the prowar, anti-Communist, and domestically liberal student organizations were a reaction to the role played by Communists in the student movement of the thirties. In a sense, they are the precursors of groups like the United States National Student Association in the fifties, which continued this anti-Communist but liberal tendency.

CONCLUSION

Was the student movement of the 1930s a failure, or was it the high-point of American student activism, at least prior to the mid-1960s? It was probably both. There is no question but that more students were involved in activism as a percentage of the total student population than at any other time in American history, including the 1960s. The organized student groups of the period, most notably the ASU, were the largest and best organized up to that time, and they were in some respects more impressive than the organizations of the 1960s. What, then, is the balance sheet of the 1930s?

For the first time in American history, student activist groups succeeded in making their presence felt on the national political scene. Students, with their allies in the adult pacifist movement, to some extent in radical political parties, and in other groups, kept foreign policy issues before the nation. The nationwide peace strikes of the mid-thirties were particularly successful in focusing national attention on the antiwar position and crystalized segments of public opinion against American rearmament and involvement in European affairs. A few years later, student organizations were among the most active groups in pressing for aid to the Spanish Republic in its fight against fascism and, while the students were unsuccessful in changing the policy of American "neutrality" in that conflict, the Spanish question was a key national issue. The national meetings of groups like the American Student Union and the American Youth Congress received national attention. The Roosevelt administration, for a period, accepted the voice of the activist student and youth movements as the legitimate expression of American youth, thus increasing the prestige of the movement.

The organized political groups, most of which were tied in some way to adult political parties of the left, were also successful in involving unprecedented numbers of students in ideologically oriented political activism as well as in activst demonstrations of various kinds. Local units of the American Student Union, for example, involved thousands of students, particularly in the prestigious universities, in active programs of discussion, direct action, and outreach to uncommitted students. The scope of student activism also increased, with students at colleges which had never been involved politically active for the first time. The impact of radical ideas on more established student organizations, such as the YMCA and many religious student organizations, was also unprecedented and a key element of student activism and its impact in the 1930s. Student newspapers and other periodicals, local student governments, and other parts of the student community became involved in activist politics or at least aware of campus political currents for the first time.

Despite these unprecedented successes, the activist movement failed in many respects. Indeed, a careful analysis of the 1930s by perceptive elements of the New Left of the 1960s might have helped the New Left to achieve greater success. While it can be claimed that the student movement failed to influence national policy on foreign affairs in the long run, this is not a serious criticism. International events were, in large part, responsible for dictating America's response to the deepening crisis, and it is likely that the antiwar movement succeeded in delaying America rearmament to some extent. A more serious criticism is that the student movement of the thirties failed to build the basis for a continuing activist thrust on campus. The reasons for this failure have been discussed in this chapter—internal factionalism on the left, slavish adherence to the changing ideological and tactical positions of adult radical organizations, ignoring campus-based issues, and a degree of deception and dishonesty by the leadership on a less sophisticated following. The ASU had, by 1940, alienated so many students, among the ideologically sophisticated as well as among the masses of American students, that student activism in general was probably set back a few years. Continuing tactical and ideological shifts discredited the major radical student groups, and particularly the ASU, among many politically conscious students. In a sense, the student movement of the 1930s may have retarded the growth of a distinctive student movement and of a distinctive student counterculture. Links to the adult left during the thirties prevented such an independent, and perhaps in the long run, more effective movement from developing.

In some, more indirect and subtle respects the student activism of the 1930s was effective. A number of researchers have recently pointed out that many of the parents of the current generation of student activists were involved as young people in radical politics.[70] It is possible that the political socialization of the student movement of the 1930s had an impact on participants later in their lives, and indirectly on their children. The student movement of the thirties also proved that it was possible to create a large and active campus-based social action movement. And at least some of the organizational lessons of the 1930s (for example, that swerving obedience to adult political parties, may not be in the best interests of the student movement) may have been learned by later student generations.

The question of the nature of "radicalism" in the student movement of the 1930s is an important one. It is the burden of the data presented in this chapter that the main thrust of student activism during the decade was foreign policy and a general sense of a social system in crisis. It was not any specific ideological program, or even the broader concept of a socialist society. The leadership of the student movement was, for the most part, specifically socialist (or Communist), but the ideological convictions of the leadership does not seem to have had a deep impact on the rank and file of the movement despite some of the official statements of groups like the American Student Union. Opinion polls and other indicators show that a substantial minority of the student population had little confidence in American capitalism during the 1930s. This is not surprising considering the economic and social crisis of the period. But this lack of faith in the "system," which seems to have been more widely shared among students than similar alienation during the 1960s, was not translated into a coherent mass-student organization committed to the overthrow of capitalism. The ASU based its appeal on a single issue basically—foreign affairs, and other elements were less popular among the ASU's constituency.

Why did a student movement of unprecedented strength arise in the 1930s and not in an earlier period? It is only possible to speculate on some of the reasons. Without question, the apparent social, economic, and political crisis in the society was the main factor. Even the middle class was affected by the Depression, and deep apprehension concerning the European crisis and the rise of fascism was apparent among the middle classes. The existence of other militant social movements, particularly the labor movement and to a lesser extent the larger radical parties such as the Communists, indicated to students that radical social action was possible and at least minimally accepted in society. Very different social conditions in the periods before and after the thirties go a long way toward explaining why similar activist student movements did not flourish at these times. Thus, it seems that a combination of growing dissatisfaction with major elements of the political system among increasing numbers of students, the existence of a visible radical movement and of ideological leadership from this movement, a massive social and economic crisis in the society, and an academic system at least somewhat involved with this crisis were all contributing factors to the rise of a student movement of major proportions in the 1930s.

That the student movement of the thirties failed to maintain its momentum in a very much altered campus, social and economic, and international situation is not surprising in the light of the foregoing explanation. It is to these changes that we shall turn in the next chapter.

NOTES

1. Calvin B. T. Lee, *The Campus Scene: 1900-1970*, (New York: David McKay, 1970), p. 49.
2. "Hoover Far in Lead in Poll of Colleges," *New York Times* (October 28, 1932), p. 1.
3. Neil Katz, "The 1930's American Radical Student Movement and its Pacifist Impulse," (Unpublished paper, University of Maryland, 1970), p. 4.
4. *New York Times*, (December 10, 1934), p. 23.
5. S. M. Lipset, *op. cit.*, p. 184.
6. *Time*, (October 24, 1938), p. 40. It should be noted that these surveys must be examined quite critically and are probably less than totally accurate. Sampling methods were fairly unsophisticated and different procedures were used in the various surveys. The data may also be weighted somewhat toward a radical direction because most studies were done at the more prestigious schools, which are usually more liberal.
7. Quoted from *Fortune* in Calvin B. T. Lee, *op. cit.*, p. 71.
8. C. Michael Otten, *op. cit.*, p. 110.
9. Calvin B. T. Lee, *op. cit.*, p. 62.
10. James Wechsler, *op. cit.*, p. 108.
11. James Wechsler, *op. cit.*, p. 123.
12. "A Campus Labor Union," *New Masses*, 23 (May 4, 1937), p. 28.
13. *Literary Digest*, 119 (February 2, 1935), p. 35.
14. Neil Katz, *op. cit.*, p. 7.
15. John T. Smith, "What One College Thinks Concerning War and Peace," *Journal of Applied Psychology*, 17 (No. 1, 1933), pp. 17-20.

16. Cited in Hal Draper, "The Student Movement of the Thirties: A Political History," in R. J. Simon, ed., *As We Saw The Thirties*, (Urbana, Illinois: University of Illinois Press, 1967), p. 181.

17. A summary of student concerns in the *New York Times*, published in 1932, reflected this concern among American students. The article stated that students have been most active in peace and disarmament activities, both from a political and religious perspective, and that ROTC was a major thrust of student activism. J. F. Green, "Youth in World Causes," *New York Times*, (June 12, 1932), p. 8.

18. *New York Times*, (December 29, 1932), p. 8.

19. Hal Draper, *op. cit.*, p. 169.

20. *Ibid.*, pp. 168-174, C. Michael Stanton, "Student Protest: Youth Response to Depression and Affluence," (Unpublished manuscript, Boston College, no date), Chapter 2, p. 30, and George Rawick, "The New Deal and Youth," (Unpublished dissertation, Department of History, University of Wisconsin, 1957), p. 202.

21. Eunice Barnard, "Students Lay a Barrage Against War," *New York Times Magazine*, (April 29, 1934), pp. 5ff.

22. C. Michael Stanton, *op. cit.*, Chapter 2, p. 31.

23. James Wechsler, ' Strike Sweeps the Campus," *New Masses*, 15 (April 23, 1935), pp. 19-20.

24. *Student Advocate*, (May, 1936), p. 3.

25. *Student Advocate*, (April, 1936), p. 14.

26. *New York Times*, (April 21, 1939), p. 10. For a detailed analysis of the student-peace movement, see Patti Peterson, "Student Organizations and the Anti-war Movement in America, 1900-1939," *American Studies*, 13 (Spring, 1972), pp. 131-148.

27. Jeffrey W. Campbell, "Youth, Religion, and Peace," *Socialist Review*, 6 (July-August, 1938), p. 11.

28. George Rawick, *op. cit.*, p. 274. Rawick's dissertation is probably the best single source for a discussion of the youth and student movements of the thirties.

29. See Hal Draper, *op. cit.*, for a more detailed discussion of this incident.

30. The Communist student movement has had a good deal of analysis by scholars and others, although a full survey of this important segment of the student movement remains to be done. George Rawick, *op. cit.*, in his dissertation deals at length with the American Youth Congress, a key "front" organization of the period. James Wechsler, *op. cit.*, also discusses the student movement from the perspective of a participant. Hal Draper, an activist from the period, has written cogently of his experiences in his essay, *op. cit.*, pp. 151-189. Other analyses include Robert Iverson, *The Communists and the Schools*, (New York: Harcourt Brace and World, 1959), Lewis Feuer, *op. cit.*, pp. 318-384, S. M. Lipset, *op. cit.*, pp. 175-195.

31. George Rawick, *op. cit.*, p. 276.

32. *Student Review*, 3 (December, 1933), pp. 11-13.

33. *Student Review*, 2 (February, 1933), pp. 12-13.
34. Edward Alexander, Jr., "The N.S.L. School," *New Masses*, 14 (March 12, 1935), p. 21.
35. Murray Kempton, *Part of Our Time*, (New York: Simon and Schuster, 1955), pp. 320-321.
36. This discipline was made possibly by the concept of "democratic centralism," which permitted free discussion within the ranks of the party, but bound members to a unified position when interacting with others.
37. Robert Iverson, *op. cit.*, p. 146.
38. Dora Zucker, *Young Communists at Work*, (New York: New Age Publishers, 1934).
39. *New York Times*, (December 25, 1933), p. 41. See also Selden Rodman, "Youth Meets in Washington," *Nation*, 138 (January 17, 1934), pp. 70-71.
40. Marguerite Kehr, *op. cit.*, p. 21.
41. *Student Advocate*, (February, 1936), p. 19.
42. See Martin McLaughlin, *op. cit.*, p. 21, for further commentary on this point.
43. Curiously, no full-scale discussion of the American Student Union has appeared. Among the best partial discussions are Hal Draper, *op. cit.*, George Rawick, *op. cit.*, Lewis Feuer, *op. cit.*, pp. 318-384, and various articles in the ASU's journal *Student Advocate*, the Communist journal *New Masses*, and the Socialist journal *New Leader*.
44. George Rawick, *op. cit.*, p. 278.
45. Eunice Clark, "Lo, the Poor Student," *The New Republic*, 77 (February 17, 1934), pp. 277-278.
46. George Rawick, *op. cit.*, p. 281.
47. Martin McLaughlin, *op. cit.*, p. 23.
48. George Rawick, *op. cit.*, p. 299.
49. Joseph P. Lash, "Do the Thirties Have Anything to Tell the Sixties?" in *Student Advocate*, (New York: Greenwood Reprint Corporation, 1968), pp. 1-3. [Reprint introduction to the *Student Advocate*].
50. American Student Union, *Student Almanac, 1936*, (New York: American Student Union, 1936).
51. Joseph P. Lash, "Another View of the American Student Union," *American Socialist Monthly*, 5 (May, 1936), p. 29.
52. George Rawick, *op. cit.*, p. 314.
53. *Student Advocate*, (March, 1938), p. 30.
54. George Rawick, *op. cit.*, p. 360.
55. Martin McLaughlin, *op. cit.*, p. 20.
56. C. Michael Stanton, *op. cit.*, Chapter 2, p. 19.
57. *New York Times*, (December 29, 1941), p. 29.
58. The best discussion of the origins, role, and politics of the American Youth Congress can be found in George Rawick, *op. cit.* There is, indeed, no other comprehensive view of this organization.
59. C. Michael Otten, *op. cit.*, p. 106.
60. *Ibid.*, p. 117.

61. *Student Advocate*, (October, 1937), p. 19.
62. John Spivak, "Plotting the American Pogroms: 8—The 'Hate the Jew' Campaign in the Colleges," *New Masses*, 13 (November 20, 1934), pp. 9-13.
63. James Wechsler has a somewhat more detailed discussion of right-wing activism in his book, *op. cit.*, pp. 232ff.
64. Maxine Davis, *The Lost Generation: A Portrait of American Youth Today*, (New York: Macmillan, 1936), p. 45.
65. York Lucci, *The YMCA on the Campus*, (New York: Bureau of Applied Social Research, Columbia University, 1960), p. 13.
66. Clarence Shedd, *op. cit.*, p. 397.
67. "Is There to be a Student Christian Movement?" *Christian Century*, 53 (January 15, 1936).
68. Thomas Neblett, *op. cit.* p. 149.
69. See Patti M. Peterson, *op. cit.*, for a detailed discussion of this and other organizations related to war-peace questions.
70. See especially Richard Flacks, "The Liberated Generation: An Exploration of the Roots of Student Protest," *Journal of Social Issues*, 23 (July, 1967), pp. 52-75, and Kenneth Keniston, "The Sources of Student Dissent," *Journal of Social Issues*, 23 (July, 1967), pp. 108-137.

CHAPTER FOUR

The Postwar Years:
Liberal Currents
Amidst Apathy

An era in the American student movement ended with the outbreak of the Second World War. For all practical purposes, protests so typical of the student movement of the 1930s ceased and winning the war became the critical national issue. Further, the questions around which students had organized earlier were no longer relevant. The antiwar movement ended as war broke out; economic issues were, for the most part, resolved by full employment stimulated by the war (the student movement was not much concerned with economic questions in the thirties in any case) and most liberals and radicals ardently supported the struggle against Naziism and fascism. In short, the war brought a sense of national unity rare in American history.

A NOTE ON ACTIVISM DURING WORLD WAR II

While student organizations concerned with politics and social action continued to function during the war, there was almost no activism opposing either government policies or university regulations. The campus was devoted to winning the war and other matters were temporarily put aside until it ended. The student population declined somewhat during the war years, from 1,500,000 in 1940 to 1,155,000 in 1944. Many universities were taken over by various military training programs and academics put themselves at the disposal of the military. Many students were drafted and forced to interrupt their academic careers while others volunteered for military service. In short, there was a moratorium on activist and radical politics during the war.

The thrust of the radical student movement was also blunted by the war. The ASU and other Communist-supported groups were no longer interested in the peace issue, and this had been the main mass organizing tool of the student movement of the prewar years. Those groups which had continued the antiwar struggle, such as the Youth Committee Against War and the YPSL, found that when war finally came, there was almost no peace sentiment on campus. World War II was popular both on campus and off, and few Americans opposed the government's activities. Sacrifices were willingly made on the "home front" without complaint. The most powerful element of the student movement, the Communists, strongly supported America's war efforts, particularly American aid to the Soviet Union. Communists applauded efforts to increase production and were, if anything, superpatriotic. Communist campus efforts were aimed at increasing the involvement of students in the war effort and were notably nonpolitical. Other radical groups, while retaining more independent political concerns during the war, were not basically opposed to the war effort and were, in any case, in no position to organize militant demonstrations at the time. Religious student groups continued to take some interest in social action and in foreign affairs, but they were staunchly loyal to the government and the war effort and were not a party to any oppositional activities.

The pacifists were the only element in the student community which did not support the war. The Fellowship of Reconciliation (FOR) was particularly active in supporting conscientious objectors, hardly a popular cause at the time, and tried to focus campus attention on such questions as the shape of international relations after the war. Direct organizing against the war was impossible, but such indirect activities as conscientious objection and foreign affairs were accepted as legitimate, even if there were relatively few involved. The FOR also helped organize the Congress of Racial Equality (CORE), which was founded in 1943 by students at Chicago Theological Seminary, many of whom were active in the FOR, including James Farmer. Involvement at this time in civil rights work indicates the broad concerns of campus pacifists. CORE, and later SNCC and SCLC, which were influenced by pacifists and used nonviolent direct action, were, to some extent, indebted to the FOR and the War Resisters' League for their staff and their orientation. The role of pacifists, many of whom were from the campuses, in the Civilian Public Service camps, and in prison for their conscientious objection to military service is an important aspect of the social action movement of the war years, but one which is beyond the scope of this volume.[1]

A number of national student organizations functioned during the war, and these groups contributed to the postwar organization of the United States National Student Association. The United States Student Assembly, which was a confederation of various anti-Communist and liberal student groups, was formed just prior to the war and continued to function throughout the war. It devoted itself to coordinating non-political student activities and supporting the war effort. The USSA was dominated by a number of ex-leftists active in student politics in the thirties.

The involvement of American students in assisting students in war-ravaged countries, and later in developing areas, received substantial impetus during the war, largely because the needs of refugee students were so great. The main vehicle of such assistance, International Student Service (ISS), had much campus support and provided funds and technical assistance to overseas students. Again, these relief efforts were linked to liberal activists and became one of the concerns of the NSA when it was organized in 1947. The importance of such confederations of student groups should not be overemphasized—only a small fraction of the students on American campuses was even cursorily involved in them. Nevertheless, they were, by and large, the major existing groups and were recognized by the government and by many university officials as the "spokesmen" for the American student community. The Communists' student efforts during the war, as noted, were largely nonpolitical. They too tried, with only minimal success, to organize a "liberal" group which might later take a more militant position. This group was called the American Youth for Democracy (AYD), which had some campus support, notably in the New York area, during the war and attracted larger numbers after hostilities ended. It never was able to achieve the prominence of the ASU.

By the end of the war, most of the roots of the prewar student movement had been destroyed, and political activity, by and large, had to start anew. The concerns of the prewar movement were, for the most part, no longer relevant to either students or the broader society. The credibility of the ASU and its successor groups was shattered by its prewar performance, and students were notably wary of the political student groups. Most of the individuals who had been involved in the movement before the war were no longer active, and a new generation of students was on campus, a generation which was unused to militant oppositional student organizations. Many of them were veterans who wished to finish with their educations as quickly as possible. It is in this political, demographic, psychological, and social situation that the student organizations of the postwar period had to function.

THE IMMEDIATE POSTWAR PERIOD

While a full-scale discussion of American society and broader developments in higher education is beyond the scope of this volume, it is necessary to deal with some of the general elements of the postwar era which had a key impact on shaping student activism, basically until the growth of the New Left in the early sixties.[2]

It is possible to summarize some of the important trends which had a major impact on campus life and on student activism. The most overwhelming social force in the late forties and early fifties was a pervasive conservatism in American society. The era of good feeling and international cooperation evident during the war was quickly dissipated as the Cold War gained momentum. The informal alliance with the Soviet Union abruptly ended with the Soviet intervention in Czechoslovakia and the Greek Civil War. The spectre of the atomic bomb hung over the world, and particularly in the consciousness of Americans. And when the Soviet Union developed nuclear weapons, it was a blow to the self-assurance of the American people and a scapegoat was sought. Internal "subversion" and particularly the Communists became a convenient scapegoat, and political repression on a scale not seen in America since the early 1920s became the order of the day. The promise of the United Nations as a preserver of the peace and molder of international harmony faded quickly and, in the process, disillusioned many liberals.

America's conservative phase had an impact on campus as well as in society. Except for the end of the decade, when the largely apolitical "beat generation" was born and had some impact on campus, most of this period was one of general cultural conformity and stabilization. The bohemianism, pervasive on campus in the twenties and later in the sixties, was not evident. The fraternity-sorority system was a powerful element on most campuses, although it was severely weakened at the end of the decade. The cultural ethos symbolized by the fraternities was evident during most of this period both on campus and off.

The desire for a return to "normalcy" cannot be overestimated, particularly in the early years of the decade. The war literally interrupted the youth of a whole generation of Americans, and people returned from the armed forces with a great desire to proceed with the business of life. Many wanted nothing better than to obtain quickly needed college or professional degrees and get a job.

Radical groups declined seriously during this period for a number of reasons. Among them was the general conservative shift which has already been noted. In addition, the repressive actions taken against many radicals, and particularly against Communists, during this period had a particularly damaging effect. Not only were many of the most active radicals jailed or kept busy with legal defenses, but much of the constituency of the radical movement was effectively intimidated. The legacy of the political splits and infighting of the thirties also made the recreation of a radical movement more difficult. For much of the fifties, as will be seen later, small radical sects, which looked back to the ideological wars of the thirties rather than to contemporary affairs, were engaged in internecine warfare which accomplished little.

Finally, American higher education underwent unprecedented changes in the fifties, and these changes greatly affected the campus scene. Clark Kerr, in writing about the "multiversity" was, in fact, describing an institution which reached its apogee in the late 1950s. Universities grew in enrollments, finance, and influence during the fifties as never before. University research budgets expanded particularly fast at this time, and the emphasis on graduate training became the prime concern for many of the most prestigious institutions. Undergraduate students somehow got lost in the shuffle, and the impact of undergraduate dissatisfaction on student activism has been recognized ever since.[3] Faculty salaries rose impressively, and there was a shortage of qualified professors in many disciplines. The student population grew from 1,600,000 in 1945 to 2,650,000 in 1950, and continued to rise at an unprecedented rate to 3,215,000 in 1960. The immediate postwar period saw a tremendous overcrowding of the institutions as a result of the crush of returning servicemen, and the following years were ones of frenzied construction of new libraries, dormitories, and classrooms. In short, the fifties and, for that matter, most of the sixties were years of unprecedented growth and prosperity for higher education. The university moved from its traditional ivory tower to the very center of American political, intellectual, and economic life. And the impact of this move was very significant, both for the institutions themselves and for students.

The university of the fifties was focused on professionalism as much as anything else. Stress on graduate training and research, combined with a residual fear of expressing political opinions, meant that the professoriate retreated to kind of "professional" orientation which permitted them to act as "experts" without becoming greatly involved or responsible for the subjects of their expertise. Thus, the overall campus image was one of apoliticism and withdrawal from the controversial affairs of society. Students, however motivated initially, were influenced by this atmosphere.

The decline of activist student organizations in the fifties was quite dramatic and is demonstrable statistically. After the small upsurge at the end of the war, the liberal Students for Democratic Action (SDA) had a membership of 3,500; by 1952, it had shrunk to 325 nationally. The Communist student group, the Labor Youth League (LYL), dropped from 6,000 in 1948 to 400 in 1952.[4] By the mid-fifties, radical student groups had no influence or impact whatsoever outside a few of the large and prestigious universities. Even there such organizations were very small and on the fringe of campus life. Nationally, student activism in the fifties played absolutely no role at all.

While student political organizations and movements which existed during the thirties declined dramatically, changes were occurring on campus. Unprecedented numbers were attending college and increasing proportions went on to graduate school. Universities were prospering as never before. Extracurricular life was active and, unlike earlier periods, most activities and groups were nonpolitical or only peripherally related to politics. Despite this, students did not totally revert to privatism. Student governments were very important in this period, if only because there were few other organizations of even a semipolitical nature functioning. The growth and role of the National Student Association

(NSA) reflects this trend. The NSA was, without question, the largest politically oriented organization in the United States during most of the fifties. Religious student organizations also were critical in alerting students to social concerns. The Quakers, through the American Friends Service Committee, the YMCA, and the Unitarians stand out as groups in the Protestant community, which were particularly concerned with social problems during this rather nonpolitical decade.

The roots of the New Left of the sixties were developed during the fifties. As will be seen later in this volume, organizations like the Student Peace Union (SPU), the ad hoc civil liberties groups, and a bit later the Student Nonviolent Coordinating Committee (SNCC) helped to lay the groundwork for what became, in the mid-sixties, a student movement of major proportions. In a sense, the peace movement of the late fifties was a precursor of the antiwar movement of the sixties, and the civil rights movement tested its philosophy of nonviolent direct action in the fifties. SNCC, SCLC, and other organizations focused in the fifties on both an issue and a tactic that was to prove volatile later. The civil liberties movement helped to persuade Americans, particularly the campus community, that it was again possible to speak out on political or other controversial issues without fear of reprisals. Even the beat generation provided a background for the hippies. The "cultural revolution" of the sixties went far beyond the beat generation, both in size and scope, but it can trace its origins to the beats.

THE CAMPUS SCENE IN THE EARLY FIFTIES

Many commentators called the students of the fifties a "silent generation," and hoped for a resurgence of social concern and activism. Indeed, some of the same individuals, who were decrying the silence of that decade, were calling for more restraint as the activism of the sixties exceeded their sense of propriety. Symposia in the *Nation, American Scholar*, and other liberal intellectual publications repeatedly commented on the apolitical campus situation. Indeed, a yearly series of articles, published around graduation time, in the *Nation*, is a particularly good commentary on this situation.[5]

It is perhaps significant that Kenneth Keniston, one of the most acute observers of American youth, wrote his first book dealing with students in 1960 and entitled it *The Uncommitted: Alienated Youth in*

American Society. This volume dealt with the directionlessness of a sample of students and made almost no mention of politics. Keniston's second book, published in 1968, was entitled *The Young Radicals*, and dealt with case studies of activists involved with the antiwar movement. Keniston himself has remarked on the dramatic shift in the cutting edge of a generation of young people between the fifties and early sixties. While activists remained a minority even in the heyday of the New Left, the thrust of the student community changed from an aggressive apoliticism to a concern with social and political affairs and a underlying dissatisfaction with the direction of American society.

What, then, was the campus mood of the fifties? Surveys of student attitudes are an indication of the campus mood and the orientation of the student generation. Most observers indicate that students were, in general, conformist, fairly conservative, and simply uninvolved in social issues. David Riesmen, analyzing a *Time* magazine survey of college students in 1955, noted that there was very little discontent among students over impending military service, that students emphasized family life and values, had no major concern with work as a fulfilling part of life, and accepted the "married, suburban life style" as a positive goal.[6] Students tended to be politically conservative during the fifties. A student opinion poll conducted in 1948, for example, noted that 73.9 percent of a sample of students favored Republican Thomas E. Dewey for president.[7] A survey of college student opinion in 1954 showed that freshmen in college were "mature and realistic" but made little mention of social awareness.[8] One interesting exception to this trend of overwhelming conservatism was student opposition to the Korean War; 33 percent of students in a national sample opposed outright American policy in Korea while only 48 percent fully supported it. Another poll corroborated this finding in 1953.[9] Thus, student attitudes toward the Korean War did not differ much from attitudes toward Vietnam a decade later. Yet, the student response to Korea was apathetic, no protest movement of any proportions developed against it, and no effective opposition to the draft occurred. However unpopular the war was, young people still served in the military without major opposition.

While the data is not extremely clear, student opinions gradually liberalized during the decade and began to change appreciably toward its end, when the Supreme Court decision on school desegregation had made an impact, the repressive atmosphere of McCarthyism had worn off a bit, and the peace movement was at least moderately active. But through most of the 1946-1958 period, student opinions were moderate to conservative and strikingly apolitical.

Commentators on the campus mood, mostly liberal, were almost unanimous in their pessimism concerning the campus scene and the prospects for political change. A survey of "communism on campus," conducted by *Newsweek*, in 1949, could turn up with only a half-dozen campuses on which any Communist activity was taking place (California, Harvard, Chicago, Washington, Wisconsin, North Carolina, Ohio State, and Oregon). In most of these schools, the number of individuals involved was very small, generally under twenty.[10] Another commentator noted that the Communists were the strongest group at UCLA in the mid-fifties but that they had "several hundred" supporters and that a few other leftist groups had much less support but did exist.[11] A sense of political inefficacy was universal among all activists, and serious discussions were held on the prospects of fleeing to Mexico to avoid the coming nuclear war.

The University of California at Berkeley, one of the nation's most active campuses, was called "repressive and apathetic" in the fifties. The number of political speakers on campus indicates the level of activity and consciousness. In 1954, there had been seven political speakers on campus all year; by 1958 the number had risen to thirty-one. In contrast, there were 188 such speakers in 1965.[12] Similar trends have been noted at the University of Wisconsin and Harvard.[13] Much of the activism that did exist on these campuses was led by student government and was very moderate in nature. At the University of Wisconsin, the student newspaper, the *Daily Cardinal*, was one of the key sources of controversy during the period.

The fifties were a period of repression on campus, and much of the activism of the decade was aimed at restoring the elementary rights of free speech. A survey of seventy-two campuses indicated that students were fearful and that loyalty oaths and suppression of radical and liberal speakers were common. "Broadly speaking the study showed that caution, weariness, and inhibition induced by current pressures live side by side with free scholarship and independent inquiry."[14] Demands for membership lists of radical organizations by academic administrators forced groups at the University of Wisconsin out of existence. Students were afraid to sign petitions of any kind. While many of the best universities tried hard to protect freedom for faculty members to do research, some were not always successful. The nationally publicized loyalty oath fight at the University of California resulted in 1950 in the firing of thirty-two professors. Loyalty oaths were also instituted in Illinois, Massachusetts, and other states. Similar, although generally less publicized struggles went on at other universities. These events had an impact on both students and faculty, and resulted inevitably in a growing and pervasive fear of public expression. At one college in California, tape recordings were made of classroom discussions of the "Communist Manifesto" in order to protect students against subversive influences. The pervasiveness of such repression can hardly be exaggerated in discussing the fifties and its politics. While few were actually fired from academic jobs or expelled from colleges for "radicalism," (probably less than a few hundred nationally) the atmosphere was sufficient to stifle all but the most committed of activists.

For many reasons, students in the fifties were not interested in activist politics. One student radical, writing in 1956, cogently describes the two kinds of students she perceived on the campus: the managerial type, interested in professional advancement and careerism and oriented toward business; and the intellectual, characterized by a research orientation and ivory tower interests divorced from politics.[15] The intellectual was often headed for an academic job. Both of these "styles" on campus had common elements in that they divorced values from goals, shunned social responsibility, and distrusted social change. The writer was particularly surprised at the lack of other forms of intellectualism on campus, a marked change from the situation in the thirties. Careerism and conservatism went together. A recruiting pamphlet prepared by the Socony Vacuum Oil Company stated that "personal views can cause a lot of trouble. Remember then to keep them always conservative. The 'isms' are out. Business being what it is, it naturally looks with distaste on the wide-eyed radical or even the moderate pink. . . ."

There was some activism in the fifties, and its nature reflects the atmosphere of the decade. There was a resurgence of panty raids and other traditional kinds of boisterous campus behavior. The *New York Times* carried items about a riot of 2,500 at Yale of undetermined origins, a raid on a Barnard dormitory by 1,000 Columbia University students, and other similar actions. The largest demonstration at Berkeley in the fifties was a panty raid which took place in 1956. The Greek system, which was still strong (although by the end of the decade it was in some decline), was not conducive to political activism and the fraternities and sororities dominated the extracurricular scenes at many universities. The dominant trend was a nonpolitical activism which did some property damage but was accepted by university authorities and the public as a "natural" aspect of collegiate life.

By the end of the decade, there were signs of change. Opinion surveys noted a growing liberalization of student attitudes, and the pervasive fear of the McCarthy period gradually diminished. The increasing freedom was indicated by the civil liberties movement on campus and the willingness of students to sign petitions again. At Berkeley, SLATE, a liberal-radical student political party which helped to create the atmosphere which made the 1964 "revolt" possible, was founded in 1957, the year of Joseph McCarthy's death. Students at the University of Wisconsin demanded in 1958 that courses become more relevant, and University of Chicago students tried, unsuccessfully, to save the general education program. A growing movement against the House Committee on Un-American Activities developed. Finally, the peace movement emerged with the founding of the Student Peace Union in 1959 and student support in some areas for the National Committee for a Sane Nuclear Policy, a liberal disarmament group.

These brief notes provide some context for the largely organizational discussion which follows. The anti-Communist posture of the National Student Association is understandable, given the climate of opinion on campus. Even the NSA was branded as a Communist front and conservative students succeeded in having their schools disaffiliate with the NSA because of its "radical" proclivities. Indeed, the links, only publicly disclosed in 1967, between the NSA and the CIA and other government agencies are much more comprehensible in the political context of the fifties. It is, therefore, important to keep in mind the campus climate, trend of student attitudes, and intellectual orientations of the fifties when considering the student organizations and their fates during this decade.

THE LIBERAL STUDENT MOVEMENT: FROM WORLD BROTHERHOOD TO ANTICOMMUNISM

To the extent that the campus was political in the fifties, it was dominated by liberal student organizations. the U.S. National Student Association epitomizes the liberal student groups that became influential in the decade. NSA reflected many of the concepts of the decade. It was reformist on domestic politics, favoring desegregation, higher minimum wages, and similar policies, but took a pro-Cold War stance on international questions and was strongly anti-Communist on both foreign and domestic issues. While the NSA had a large "paper" membership, its impact on campus was modest. And the revelations, in 1967, that much of NSA's budget had been coming from the CIA through "dummy" foundations and other conduits, was not very surprising, given the spirit of the period and the overall direction of American liberalism in the fifties. This section examines several of the more important liberal national student organizations, focusing on how they functioned and their effect on campus.

As has been noted, the end of the war saw a resurgence of idealistic concern for the future of the postwar world. A number of organizations grew up at that time which reflected this, the most important of which was the United World Federalists (UWF), whose strength was impressive among middle-class Americans and students for several years following the war. The adult UWF was formed in 1947 in part because of a request from loosely federated student groups interested in forming a broad national movement to press for world government. The first student chapter of the UWF had been formed in 1942 and by 1945 there were chapters in twenty-five states. In 1946 a national conference was called and a national organization formed with around 2,500 members and a newspaper, *The Student Federalist.* The adult organization claimed some 40,000 members soon after its establishment, most of whom were fairly wealthy professionals with a degree of local influence. The federalist movement was important during the first postwar years. It was based on the notion that there should be a world government which could limit arms and could press for social advancement. The United Nations was seen as the framework for world government. Ideologically, the movement had little firm basis, and the increasing tension between the United States and the U.S.S.R., beginning in 1947, made it apparent that effective world government would be very difficult to achieve. The UWF declined from its position of some importance, although it still survives as a small organization.

The Student Federalists (SF) had a short period of strength as well. From around 5,800 national members in 1949, the organization declined to some 3,500 in 1950.[16] The activities of the Student Federalists consisted largely of educational efforts to convince students of the need for world governments through its publications, travelling speakers, and local meetings. SF chapters existed on most large university campuses in the mid-forties, but seldom made a major impact on campus or organized large numbers of students.

The decline in SF membership in 1950 led to an organizational split between those who wanted the group to continue on its fairly conservative path and come increasingly under the control of the adult UWF organization, and those who wanted to continue to emphasize campus organizing. In 1951, there was an official split and a new organization, WORLD (World Order Realized under Law and Democracy), was formed. The new group emphasized the needs of the developing countries, anticolonialism, and stressed the importance of civil liberties. WORLD, perhaps typical for the period, had only a short period of growth and its second national conference, held in September of 1952, attracted only twenty-two delegates. The fact that a number of Socialists were very active in WORLD may have helped lead to its demise, in that "leftist" manipulation of student groups was greatly distrusted at the time. The more conservative wing of the Student Federalists continued to function under the tutelage of the UWF national office but lost any viability it had on campus.

The Student Federalists were not the only expression of student idealism and concern for foreign policy during the early postwar years. Several other organizations, mainly emphasizing "single issues," cropped up at the time. One group which had survived the war years was the U.S. Student Assembly, a predominantly liberal organization which was a federation of local and regional student groups. At its fourth annual convention, which was attended by 300 students from seventy-five colleges, major emphasis was given to student efforts to aid war-ravaged foreign countries. The convention, for example, called for a "wheatless day" per week in order to provide overseas assistance. The convention also voted to abolish compulsory ROTC in universities.

Similar concerns were echoed in groups such as the Committee for the Marshall Plan, which existed in 1947-1948. This group, which apparently had the support of some government officials, was aimed at creating support for the Marshall Plan and for humanitarian aid to Europe. There is no evidence that it had much widespread campus support. A Committee for the Placement of Displaced Students was formed in 1948 in New York, with the purpose of finding campus locations for the 10,000 or so refugee students from Europe. A number of other national organizations, including NSA, and Catholic, Protestant, and Jewish groups supported this effort.

Foreign policy concerns and a generally moderate-to-liberal approach can be seen in the Association of International Relations Clubs and in the Collegiate Council for the United Nations (CCUN). Both of these groups were active in a variety of universities and in 1953, the CCUN claimed affiliates on 300 campuses. The IRC group, which was founded shortly after the war, also had many campus affiliates, and its main activity was sponsoring conferences and meetings on events of international concern. It abstained from taking positions on issues. The CCUN was a bit more political in that its main goal was to convince students that the United Nations was an important agency worthy of strong American support. During the fifties, this was, in some places, a radical position. Both groups had publications and tried to keep their members informed of activities and educate them on substantive questions.

The major thrust of semipolitical concern on campus during this period was related to foreign affairs. Other groups had some temporary strength too, and some of these will be discussed in some detail later. For example, the American Veterans Committee (AVC), the liberal veterans organization, had a short period of great strength among the thousands of veterans who streamed onto the campuses taking advantage of the GI Bill of Rights. The AVC was liberal in its orientation but more concerned with student living conditions and relations with the United States government with regard to veterans rights than with anything else. Few American students were overly concerned with domestic political questions and such issues rarely, if ever, aroused militant activism. The 1948 presidential campaign attracted some interest, particularly among radicals who supported Henry Wallace, but, as noted before, a majority of the student population supported Thomas Dewey, the Republican candidate.

The National Student Association (NSA)

One of the most important student organizations of the fifties was the U.S. National Student Association. This group is important not only for what it did on campus, but for what it symbolizes about this period of American liberalism and the American campus.[17] While the NSA was never effective in organizing the American campus—it was to a substantial extent a "paper" organization since most of its one million or so affiliated members knew little about its activities and had little, if any, loyalty to the organization—it was nevertheless able to act as the "spokesman" for American students for twenty years and was the most widely representative national student organization for much of this period. The NSA was not a membership organization. It was, rather, a federation of student governments. Individual students, by virtue of their (often mandatory) membership in campus student governments, were automatically members of NSA. Communications took place between elected local student leaders and the national organization. Delegates to the annual NSA congress, the highest policy-making body in the organization, were elected by students on the local campuses, although the interest on campuses in such elections was often not very great and the delegates who attended the national congresses often did not report back in any detail to their local constituencies. Thus, over the years, the NSA became something of a national bureaucratic structure, subject annually to scrutiny by local representatives but, in general, functioning in a rather autonomous manner.

The focus of this discussion is on NSA's organizational structure, role on campuses, and its views on matters of importance to both national politics and the campus. The NSA's important international role, which developed after 1951 and continued actively until 1967, is not the primary focus. In a sense, the international program of NSA, financed by the CIA, was the tail that wagged the dog. While only a small part of the total emphasis of the organization, the international program spent a large proportion of the NSA's annual budget and had a lion's share of the staff. Although the International Affairs Vice President (IAVP) was elected annually by the congress, the international section functioned autonomously and its appointed staff was basically responsible only to the vice president and had little or no contact with the member campuses. Financially, the international program was able to attract "foundation" funds, at least some of which were channeled into operating the national office and into domestic programs. In reality, something between half and 80 percent of the NSA's total budget came from "foundations" between the early 1950s and 1967. And, as it turned out, these "foundations" were conduits for the Central Intelligence Agency. Thus, without CIA funding during the fifties, the NSA would not have survived at all.[18]

The origins of the NSA go back to the immediate postwar idealistic phase of the student movement and are linked to the development of the International Union of Students (IUS). A group of American students, representing a range of political views from Communists to fairly conservative Catholics, attended the founding congress of the IUS in Prague in 1946. While visiting postwar Europe, they were impressed with the effectiveness of the powerful student unions and vowed to organize such a union in the United States. The emphasis of European student unions was on student services and coordination of their functions. They rejected a purely political role for student unions. In the United States, there was a tradition of coordinating student organizations. The National Student Federation of America, the oldest such group, was still remembered by some student leaders, and the U.S. Student Assembly was already functioning as an effective organization. The new organization was to be much larger and more effective than any of these groups, encompassing both local campus student governments and wider regional and national student groups of various kinds.

The returning activists took the initiative to call a national meeting, held in Chicago in 1946 and attended by 500 delegates, to discuss the creation of a viable national student union in the United States. [19] Liberals dominated the Chicago meeting, although all political persuasions were represented, with strong delegations of Catholic and Communist students playing major roles. The Chicago gathering indicated that there was widespread support for the creation of a national student union, and a founding convention was planned for September of 1947, to take place at the University of Wisconsin in Madison.

Eight hundred delegates from 351 colleges and universities and twenty national organizations attended the meetings, which succeeded in drafting a constitution, a Student Bill of Rights, elected officers, and set broad policies for the operation of the new organization, called the U.S. National Student Association. The constitution set up a complicated organizational structure which left basic policy making and supervision to the annual student congresses. Officers were to be elected by the congress, and a National Supervisory Board was created, with virtually unlimited powers to interpret policy mandates given to them by the congress. The Student Bill of Rights, which was one of the most highly publicized creations of the founding convention, stressed academic freedom, freedom for students to organize and bring speakers to campuses, emphasized the right of every young person to a college education, stressed equal opportunity for all, and opposed discrimination because of political or racial criteria. The policies and statements made by this congress, as well as most of the following congresses, not only represented a strong liberal orientation, but also intended to compromise the often divergent opinions of conservative delegates from small church-related schools and more radical (and occasionally ideologically sophisticated) delegates from large urban universities. Despite some lengthy and acrimonious debates—for example over whether to take a strong or weak position (a moderate compromise was hammered out) on racial discrimination, most of the delegates felt that a good beginning had been made.[20]

The political alignments which were evident at the founding congress were to remain unchanged for most of the NSA's history. The major force was a rather amorphous alliance of liberals from the Northern and Western universities. This alliance was based in part on personal contacts among its leaders and was close to the views of the Students for Democratic Action (SDA). The liberals were willing to compromise on many issues and succeeded, by a combination of numerical strength, skill, and a fairly pragmatic position, in holding the NSA together. On the right was a well organized group of Catholic delegates opposed to communism and exhibiting a generally moderate approach. The Southern regional caucus also exerted a conservative influence, particularly on race relations, although the Southern delegates were, by and large, "liberal" in the context of Southern higher education at the time. On the left, there was a small Communist group which had a minimal impact and a shifting group of Socialists and independent radicals who, from time to time, attended NSA congresses. Most NSA presidents and vice presidents, who were the key elements in the organization's functioning, remained strongly rooted in the broad, "liberal" center of the NSA.

The NSA emerged from its founding congress as the nation's largest student organization and an important force in national student life. Its challenge was to create an impact at the local and regional levels and to provide both services and leadership to some of the colleges and universities affiliated with the organization. From the beginning, NSA officers and active participants recognized this challenge and tried hard to make NSA programs both relevant and accepted on campus. They recognized that, in the past, federations of students had taken too political a stance and that this had cut them off from the mainstream of the student population. NSA tried to avoid this by stressing its service and coordinating functions, and during the 1950s maintained a fairly low level political tenor.[21] NSA aimed to educate the university community—administrators as well as students—concerning issues which it felt important. Pamphlets and study papers on a range of issues, from in loco parentis and civil liberties to methods of conducting meetings of student governments, were published. In addition, the organization attempted to stimulate the growth of democratically elected student governments on campuses, and sponsored a travel service which provided assistance to students travelling abroad. In its early period, the NSA was particularly interested in providing services to its member student governments, and indirectly to the students affilated with it. Student filmmakers were encouraged to submit films to an annual NSA sponsored festival, a *Student Government Bulletin* was published, and other services, such as those provided for campus newspapers, were fostered by the national NSA office.

NSA did not completely ignore political issues, even in the conservative early 1950s. From its birth, NSA focused on ending racial and religious discrimination on campus and actively fought against quotas and other overt discriminatory practices of universities and campus fraternities. Academic freedom and civil liberties attracted much attention from the NSA. Strong statements were made by NSA congresses in these areas, and it should be noted that the NSA opposed the anti-Communist "witchhunts" of the 1950s on civil libertarian grounds—that Senator McCarthy was using unconstitutional means for a "good cause." These positions were not taken without substantial opposition from moderate and conservative elements within the NSA, but the liberals won the important battles, and indeed moderated their own position in order to placate the more conservative.

By the end of the 1950s, the NSA was taking an increasingly vocal part in the emerging political questions on campus. It was particularly involved in civil rights activities. Many hundreds of Northern white students went to the South to engage in direct action as part of NSA programs, and funds were channelled to Southern student protestors. With the financial assistance of the Field Foundation, the civil rights desk at the NSA national office provided coordinated Northern support, conducted research, and otherwise helped in the early period of the civil rights movement. Despite this new activism, the NSA was not in the forefront of any movement; it never took the initiative in pushing student activism further in a left or more action-oriented direction. Rather, NSA followed the lead of groups like SNCC, SDS, or the Student Peace Union.

During the fifties, the NSA was the most important political forum for American students. Its annual congresses were attended by 500 or more delegates and representatives from a range of student and adult organizations. The deliberations of the congresses were reported in the mass media and were even occasionally considered by students on local campuses. It is a tribute to the liberal leadership of the NSA that it was able to maintain its influence and control of the organization during the 1950s, since the moderate liberalism of the NSA was much to the left of the campus mainstream at the time. Rhetorical skill, organizational sophistication, control of the national office (and finances through CIA connections), and a good deal of behind-the-scenes maneuvering were responsible for the maintenance of this control. The liberals did not, however, go unchallenged. On several occasions, conservative students tried to take control of the NSA by putting up their own candidates for president and pressing for conservative resolutions at the congresses. These efforts were so unsuccessful, however, that conservatives made several attempts to destroy the NSA either by urging that schools withdraw from the organization or set a rival federation of student governments. This latter tactic achieved some success in the 1960s, when a number of student governments who felt that the NSA had moved in too political a direction withdrew from the organization and formed their own group, the Associated Student Governments, which still exists and had a good deal of strength, mainly from Southern universities and smaller schools with more conservative student bodies. None of these efforts, however, seriously damaged the NSA, although they forced the liberal leadership to move slowly for fear of alienating even larger numbers of their constituents.

In a sense, the National Student Association was pushed during much of its history by currents on the campus. It was radicalized to some extent by the changing leftward mood among students. During the fifties, the NSA was very cautious about taking stands on political questions, although throughout the decade it remained on the liberal side of things. NSA's development in the sixties did not differ much from the basic patterns which have been mentioned here. Organizationally, it remained stable. Behind the scenes, a small group of NSA leaders, who maintained strong interest in the organization, advised the incumbent leadership and helped perceive a sense of organizational conformity. Through training in regional groups, participation in the International Student Relations Seminars, and interaction with the "old boy" NSA network, most of the organization's officers and national staff members had been well "socialized" into their roles. With this relative stability and the financial security that came with the secret subsidies from the CIA, the NSA was able to shift its orientation to meet changing times without major dislocation.

What kind of individual became an NSA officer? This question is difficult to answer, since there have been no studies of officers. Martin McLaughlin, who was an activist in the NSA, noted that the officers tended to be articulate, somewhat to the left of center, and concerned with social issues.[22] NSA officers also tended to be basically moderate in their view of the political system, since they were willing to engage in the "sandlot" politics of the local campus in order to rise to the top of the NSA bureaucracy. And this combination of pragmatic politics and sober idealism marked the historical development. It is not at all surprising that a number of NSA ex-officers were involved in the presidential campaigns of Eugene McCarthy in 1968 and George McGovern in 1972.

Between 1960 and 1967, the NSA assumed a more militant rhetoric and increasingly became involved in broader political issues. Its open and relatively radical support for the student civil rights movement and strong stands on poverty, civil liberties, and race issues demonstrated this move to the left. Only on the question of Vietnam did NSA part with the left—not until after its break with the CIA did NSA take a militant antiwar position. Prior to 1967, the NSA called for negotiations and was critical of continued escalation. It did not call for American withdrawal. The shift to the left did bring a degree of trauma. While most of the NSA's constituency moved along with the organization to the left, or even moved ahead of it, some were critical. Since 1967, the year of the NSA-CIA ties and the subsequent ending of those ties, NSA has become much more radical. (It also has been plagued by financial crisis.) While remaining out of the mainstream of the New Left, the NSA has adopted militant antiwar positions, was instrumental in the "People's Peace Treaty" of 1970, and was directly involved in the radical wing of the educational reform movement. With modest help from the Ford Foundation, the NSA established a Center for Educational Reform, which takes a militant position on many issues and is devoted to the thoughts of reformers such as Ivan Illich and Edgar Z. Friedenberg.

Despite the fact that NSA's international program was of little relevance to most American students and did not contribute significantly either to NSA's own strength on campus or to the political awareness of American students, it was important in that it was a key element of NSA's orientation and the source for most of its funds. Moreover, the international program can tell us something about the nature of student politics in the Cold War.

One of the most important aspects of the NSA's foreign program was the annual International Student Relations Seminars (ISRS), started in 1952 and continued until 1967. The ISRS seminars were held during the summer for around six weeks and were "invitation only," intensive sessions aimed at giving the dozen or so participants a thorough knowledge not only of NSA and its functioning, but also of the affairs of the international student world. The ISRS was particularly significant because it provided the NSA's leadership, and presumably its CIA mentors, with an opportunity to "screen" potential national officers and to train a cadre of able individuals to effectively participate in NSA activities. ISRS staff included former NSA leaders, representatives of the State Department and other government agencies, and some professors. ISRS members went directly from the seminar to the annual congress and were often able to substantially influence the congress because of their organizational sophistication and their detailed knowledge of NSA policy and procedures. A very large proportion of NSA officers, particularly international affairs vice presidents, were alumni of ISRS seminars.

Why was the CIA interested in the NSA and willing to spend millions of dollars on the organization over a fifteen-year period? The converse, why the NSA turned in the first place to the CIA and was willing over a long period to accept funds and some guidance from the CIA, is also significant. Only some tentative answers to these questions can be suggested here. From the CIA's viewpoint, the NSA offered a useful tool for presenting the more liberal side of American life to foreigners. NSA also was a means of collecting data on the future elites of some developing countries, and it occasionally could influence foreign student unions or individual student leaders. Further, the NSA represented firm opposition to the Communist-dominated student unions of Eastern Europe and the IUS. Given the unremittingly conservative stance of United States foreign policy at the time, it was impossible for official United States government agencies to have cordial relations with intellectuals and students in developing areas. But an "independent" student group like the NSA could engage in such relations and was not hindered by United States government policies. Thus, the NSA permitted Americans to interact with, and occasionally influence, foreigners on a variety of issues in a way which would have been impossible for government functionaries. And there is evidence that the NSA was fairly effective in this area. It attracted student leaders, sometimes quite radical in their politics, to the United States and permitted American students to get to know their counterparts quite well. NSA, through the International Student Conference which had its headquarters in Holland, helped to create an effective counterweight to the Communist-dominated International Union of Students.[23]

While the primary goal of the NSA's international program was not espionage, there is no doubt that some of the rather impressive amount of data collected by NSA officers and staff was useful to the United States government in analyzing foreign policy questions and in understanding future elites in developing areas. NSA officials wrote very detailed, confidential reports on aspects of their work, including information on the personal and political predilections of leaders of student unions in many countries, as well as on the orientations and views of student unions. Finally, the NSA permitted the CIA, which was probably more liberally oriented on foreign policy questions than was the mainstream of the United States government in the fifties, to express its views, albeit indirectly. It is signficant that a number of former NSA officials went into the CIA as full-time employees after the end of their tenure in the student movement and this kept the ties between the NSA and the CIA fairly strong. Thus, the NSA may have served as a recruiting ground for CIA and other government officials.

The NSA's reasons for entering into a relationship with the CIA are clearer. For one thing, the NSA faced a severe financial crisis during its early years, and despite debates in congresses concerning the dangers of accepting funds from outside sources, it turned increasingly toward attracting funds from foundations and other agencies, although, in the early fifties, with little success. Somehow, the CIA became involved in NSA funding and remained heavily involved. And once the NSA was dependent financially on the CIA, it was difficult to get out from under this burden, even when substantial efforts were made to find other sources of money. It was clear that the member schools of the NSA either could not or would not provide money in sufficiently large amounts to run an effective national organization.

Given the state of the Cold War and American intellectual community in the early fifties, it is not surprising that the NSA leadership would not think that involvement with the CIA was particularly distasteful or dishonorable. Indeed, the reactions of many former NSA officers to the NSA-CIA involvement after the 1967 "exposé" reflected the attitude that there was nothing dishonorable about the relationship in the context of the Cold War. NSA leaders felt that they were supporting the broad interests of the United States, were intelligently opposing communism, and were pressing for their own liberal values, both at home and abroad. The fact that funds were secretly obtained and that the NSA's membership was consistently lied to, did not make a great deal of difference to them. Given the orientation of the American liberal community and the pervasive anticommunism of that period, the actions of NSA's leaders, anxious to preserve their organization and not in basic disagreement with the policies of their compeers in the CIA, are understandable.

NSA-CIA links were a closely guarded secret during the fifties and the number of individuals who were "witty" (in the parlance of the CIA, those who knew about the relationship) were limited to the president, the international affairs vice president of the NSA and, from time to time, a select few in the national office. That more people did not find out about the situation is surprising, particularly in view of the NSA's extremely incomprehensible financial picture. During the fifties, and for that matter into the early sixties, the NSA was considered by radical activists to be a somewhat over-careful, but still a solidly liberal, group which could be worked with. Indeed, radicals, pacifists, and others regularly attended annual NSA congresses to recruit adherents and lobby for a more liberal position within NSA. Several of the early leaders of the SDS were active in NSA, including at least one national affairs vice president.

It is difficult to assess the impact of NSA on the campus scene of the fifties or on the individuals who participated in it. NSA did involve a fairly large number of individuals in positions of regional or national leadership who learned a great deal about politics and organizational work as a result of their experience. Many went on to political careers or into government work. The involvement of NSA alumni as CIA functionaries was limited largely to ex-members of the International Commission. Quite a few NSA officers went into academic work and at least one has become a college president. Critics point out that NSA attracted "campus ward heelers" and that the kind of political education provided by the organization, particularly in the fifties, did not contribute to social change.[24] While this may be true, NSA did provide a valuable experience for many of its active members. Perhaps the greatest service of the organization was in opening up small denominational colleges which were members of NSA to the wider world of educational reform, campus politics, and international and national events.

The Students for Democratic Action

If the NSA was the broad umbrella movement of the liberals during the fifties, the SDA was the "cadre" organization which did the organizational work of the period. The SDA in a sense belongs to the tradition of the thirties, in that it maintained strong, although somewhat stormy links with an adult organization, the Americans for Democratic Action (ADA). The SDA was not a large organization, claiming only a few thousand members at its height, but by standards of the fifties it was one of the larger national student organizations. In addition, it exercised substantial influence on other groups, such as the NSA. The SDA also reflects the strong anticommunism of the Cold War period.

The Students for Democratic Action was founded in 1948 and functioned until its merger with its adult sponsor, the Americans for Democratic Action (ADA), in 1959. During those years, SDA was an affiliate of the adult ADA and had a degree of autonomy in its campus-based operations, although there were continuing conflicts between the student and adult organizations. Much of the budget of the SDA was provided by the ADA, and the SDA office was housed in ADA head-quarters in Washington, D.C. The SDA saw itself as the most important liberal political organization on campus. It worked with other organizations such as the NSA and occasionally with civil rights or civil liberties groups as well. The SDA was violently anticommunist in its orientation and many of the internal conflicts in which it was involved had to do with being "soft" on pro-Communist groups within the organization or sponsoring speakers who might be pro-Communist. In these cases, the ADA intervened and small organizational crises ensued.

The origins of SDA go back to the U.S. Student Assembly (USSA), which was organized in 1943 and represented groups on fifty-four colleges, mostly on the East coast, at that time. At its height in 1945-1946, the USSA had some 3,000 members and seventy campus chapters. In 1947, the USSA asked the ADA to accept it as an affilate and a founding convention was held in April of 1947.[25] The convention was attended by some 150 students from forty-four colleges. The convention excluded Communists from membership, strongly supported civil liberties and freedom of organization for students, condemned discrimination, and urged close cooperation between students and the labor movement.

The SDA was never very large. After an organizing drive in 1948, the SDA had about 5,000 members in 148 college chapters.[26] In 1951, SDA claimed 2,000 members in sixty-five active chapters, and the organization reported a large turnover of members in many chapters; by 1955, membership stood at 1,200 members in sixty-five chapters. And by 1960, a year after the SDA disbanded and merged into the adult ADA, there were thirteen campus chapters with some 300 members. Thus, the SDA declined continually after 1950. This decline occurred for a variety of reasons. For one thing, the SDA kept very accurate membership statistics and quickly dropped members who were not fully paid up. This is a rare situation for most American student organizations. The student movement in general was in a period of decline at this time and it is not surprising that an openly political organization like SDA experienced this decline as well.

Conflicts between the adult ADA and the SDA, and internal dissention within the SDA also added to the tension. On a number of occasions ADA made SDA groups cancel pro-Communist speakers and often intervened in SDA national conferences. Internal problems within the SDA were in part created by the involvement of a number of Socialist students who tried, unsuccessfully, to move the organization to a more radical position. These efforts involved a good deal of bitterness which no doubt alienated some SDA activists. In short, SDA functioned in a period which was difficult for student activism in America, and the leadership failed to take advantage of its position. As the end of the decade approached, the doctrinaire anticommunism of the SDA lost popularity, even with many moderate liberal students, in light of the Sino-Soviet dispute and thaws in the Cold War. The SDA did not change its views, and by 1958 had an ideological position which was not very satisfactory to most politically aware students. The adult ADA, of course, was a great hindrance both in organizational growth and in the evolution of an ideological position which would gain campus supporters.

Organizationally, the SDA was run by a small national staff which tried to travel regularly to campus chapters. At most, there were three full-time people in the national office, and the annual expenses for the organization ran to around $20,000 per year. The bulk of the expenses were met by the ADA and very little fund raising was done by the student group. The highest authority in SDA was its annual convention, which decided on policy and direction for the organization. These conventions were generally modest, with seldom more than 150 delegates from sixty or so colleges attending. They were, however, occasionally heated gatherings, particularly during the period in the mid-fifties when members of the Young Socialist League were active in the SDA and attempting to take it over. Occasional conflicts with the ADA also took place at the conventions, when students rebelled against the domination of the ADA officers. Throughout the history of the SDA, however, those loyal to the policies of the ADA and to moderate liberalism maintained control of the SDA, although as noted before, the cost of this control was high in terms of success as a student organization.

Why was there conflict within the SDA? Basically, the SDA leadership and its adult mentors wanted the organization to remain rigidly anti-Communist and to support official ADA policies. For example, representatives of the national office prevented the Swarthmore College chapter from sponsoring a speech by Alger Hiss in 1956. A number of the leaders of the chapter thereafter resigned in protest. At Brown

University, a large SDA chapter wanted to sponsor a talk by Mrs. Paul Robeson and was prevented from doing it. This act of censorship was also accompanied by internal struggles within that chapter. The Columbia University chapter was dechartered because of its refusal to support Adlai Stevenson for the presidency in 1956, because they felt he had abandoned his civil rights position. The undercurrent of adult interference and a consciousness of the appropriate ideological "line" seems to have permeated much of SDA thinking.

SDA chapters, located mainly at larger but geographically dispersed colleges and universities with some tradition of activism, engaged in a variety of activities. The most common emphases of SDA chapters were educational programs (mostly speakers) and participation in electoral politics, usually in support of a liberal Democratic candidate for office. During the early fifties, SDA was active in a number of other student organizations' actions, including NSA civil liberties and academic freedom work. SDA and CORE cosponsored civil rights workshops in Washington, D.C. and SDA collaborated with unions in giving students work and union experience. Meetings, speakers, programs, and other activities were held to focus attention on the importance of academic freedom. It might be noted in this regard that, while the SDA tried to oppose McCarthyism, it never took a stand against discrimination against Communists because of their political views. In 1953, the New York SDA region engaged in a campaign for revision of the McCarran immigration law, a drive for nondiscrimination in housing, a labor education project, and a civil liberties campaign. These are rather typical of SDA programming nationally. The Columbia University SDA launched a campaign against bias in fraternities and focused attention on campus discriminatory policies.[27] The SDA was successful in this effort. Other SDA chapters dealt with issues such as whether Communists should be allowed to speak on campus, universal military training, isolationism, while a few engaged in action projects such as collecting books for students in Uganda. At election time, SDA chapters were quite active in local, state, and national campaigns, and occasionally participated in campus election campaigns. At the University of Chicago, SDA was successful in capturing control of the Student Government in the mid-fifties.

SDA conventions and policies indicate a good deal about the organization. The 1948-1949 SDA chapter manual outlines organizational policies and programs. The SDA supported European recovery plans but opposed aid to China. It favored a strong United Nations and a strong American military presence around the world. It opposed universal military training, mentioned at the time as an alternative to the Selective Service System. In domestic policy, the SDA opposed discrimination in housing and education, but was for full academic freedom, for strengthening NSA and student cooperatives, and took liberal positions on issues like conservation. The SDA emphasized its support for and participation in campaigns of liberal candidates for public office. In the 1948 election, SDA supported William O. Douglas for the presidential nomination and had "great respect for General Eisenhower as a democratic leader" but refrained from supporting him for the Democratic nomination.[28] In general, the SDA's policies in 1948 were similar to those of the liberal wing of the Democratic party and, in general, remained that way throughout its history. The organization naturally emphasized campus issues, but even here it did not differ very much from most liberal Democrats. Subsequent SDA conventions, which generally had around 100 to 150 students from fifty to seventy-five campuses, took similar policy positions. The SDA can be characterized as "mainstream liberal" in its policy positions in the fifties, and the strong adult pressure and, at times, manipulation which prevented the organization from moving further to the left were resented by many active members and lay at the root of some discontent. The SDA maintained a strongly anti-Communist position on foreign policy, but was occasionally too liberal on domestic matters to suit the adult ADA leadership.

In 1955 and 1956, Socialists were active in the SDA, particularly at its conventions. Indeed, Socialists were able to win a majority at one convention and a split in the organization ensued. The issue on which the Socialists were able to rally substantial support was that of SDA's autonomy. Active members were sufficiently disgusted with adult manipulation that they sided with the radicals. Through additional manipulation and withholding of financial support, the ADA was able to regain control of SDA for "moderate" elements a year later but only after many factional disputes and disaffiliation of several "radical" chapters.[29] The factional disputes, however, made a bad impression on many SDA activists and contributed to the organization's demise.

SDA sponsored a number of special projects during its history which indicate the kinds of political action in which the organization was engaged. "Operation Free Thought" was aimed at securing civil liberties on campus and making students aware of general civil liberties issues.

Meetings were held on civil liberties and SDA members tried to stop "witchhunting" on campus. Another project, "Operation Brotherhood," publicized civil rights issues on the campus. SDA chapters tried to end local discriminatory practices on some campuses through petitions and related activities. Success was achieved at only a few schools. SDA had ties with a national scholarship organization for black students to raise the number of blacks attending major universities. SDA sponsored several summer labor projects in 1953 and 1954, with the financial and staff assistance of the United Auto Workers union. The aim of the project was to involve college students in work situations and to acquaint them with the problems and goals of the trade union movement. The 1953 project was successful, but in 1954 the number of participants was small and the project failed through lack of coordination by SDA and lack of cooperation from the participants.

Thus, the SDA engaged in quite traditional political activities for the period, and tried hard to build liberalism as an effective campus force. While it was not very successful, it was one of the major campus political groups of the fifties, a fast tenet says more about the weakness of other groups than the strength of the SDA. SDA was considered important enough by radical groups to be an "arena" for organizing. It was common for radicals to attempt to use other student organizations as a means of recruiting members as well as pressing their own positions. In the dozen or so universities where SDA had strong chapters, it was a fairly effective political force on campus, at least alerting politically aware students to the existence of a liberal student organization. Though the organization spent an inordinate amount of time in internal disputes and in efforts to keep its policies sufficiently moderate for the adult ADA, it participated in local elections and maintained the semblance of a national structure. Its decline in the late fifties was due to a number of factors, including the failure of the SDA to respond to changing and more radical currents on campus and the continuing interference, on the one hand, by adult ADA bureaucrats and by radicals, on the other. However, the SDA, and to a lesser extent the NSA, were the key national liberal organizations during the fifties and reflect, to a major degree, the nature and response of American liberalism to the decade.

The NSA and SDA were not the only liberal political campus groups of the fifties. There were a variety of local and unaffiliated campus organizations either devoted to discussions or to single-issue action, such as civil liberties or civil rights. Groups like International Relations Clubs were often politically liberal, but confined themselves almost exclusively to discussion and debate. The Collegiate Council for the United Nations (CCUN) was active during the fifties and had a respectable number of campus affiliated groups. The Young Democrats (YD) were also active and many local affiliates of this organization were quite liberal. There were perhaps 100 YD groups in 1949, and it is likely that this number remained constant throughout the decade. Typically, YD groups were most active around national election time. They were rarely militant, although they have usually been in the left wing of the Democratic party, often conflicting with the party on issues such as civil liberties. On some campuses, YD and SDA groups were closely allied, with an occasional YD organization controlled by SDA members.

The limitations of the liberal student movement can clearly be seen in the foregoing discussion. Ideological links with the Cold War politics of the period and an inability to shift positions when the national and international situation changed, marked the liberal organizations. The logic of the liberalism of the fifties led NSA to accept clandestine CIA funding. Liberals were unwilling to engage in militant tactics and had a profound fear of direct action. Given these factors and the general campus atmosphere, it is not surprising that the liberals failed to establish a viable student movement or to have much impact on the average American student. Yet, as far as political activism and consciousness on campus went during the period between 1945 and 1957, the liberals were the major force and attracted the largest amount of support.

NOTES

1. The best overall analysis of the peace movement, which has some discussion of the role of pacifists in the war years, is Lawrence Wittner, *Rebels Against War: The American Peace Movement (1941-1960)*, (New York: Columbia University Press, 1969).

2. While there is no fully satisfactory study of the fifties, see I. F. Stone, *The Haunted Fifties*, (New York: Random House, 1970) and Eric Goldman, *The Crucial Decade*, (New York: Vintage, 1960).

3. The best statement of the role and function of the American university in the late fifties and for that matter, at present, can be found in Clark Kerr, *The Uses of the University*, (New York: Harper Torchbooks, 1964). It was Dr. Kerr who coined the word "multiversity."

4. William McIntyre, "Student Movements," *Editorial Research Reports*, 2 (December 11, 1957), p. 926.
5. See "The Careful Young Men," *Nation*, 184 (March 9, 1957), pp. 199-206, "The Class of 1958 Speaks Up," *Nation*, 186 (May 17, 1958), pp. 432-439, Leslie Fiedler, "The UnAngry Young Men; America's Post-war Generation," *Encounter*, 10 (January, 1958), pp. 3-12, and "U.S. Campus Kids of 1953: Unkidable and Unflappable," *Newsweek*, (November 2, 1953), pp. 52-55.
6. David Riesman, "The Found Generation," *American Scholar*, 25 (Autumn, 1956), pp. 421-435.
7. "College Poll for Dewey," *New York Times*, (October 30, 1948), p. 9.
8. Charles Poore, "Class of '54: New Generation, New Hope," *New York Times Magazine*.
9. S. M. Lipset, *op. cit.*, p. 188. See also Edward Suchman, Rose Goldsen, and Robin Williams, Jr., "Attitudes Toward the Korean War," *Public Opinion Quarterly*, 17 (1953), pp. 173, 182.
10. "Newsweek Surveys Communism in the Colleges," *Newsweek*, 34 (July 18, 1949).
11. David McReynolds, *We Have Been Invaded by the 21st Century*, (New York: Praeger, 1970), p. 9.
12. C. M. Otten, *op. cit.*, p. 167.
13. See Shlomo Swirski, "Changes in the Structure of Relations Between Groups and the Emergence of Political Movements: The Student Movement at Harvard and Wisconsin, 1930-1969." (Unpublished Ph.D. Dissertation, Michigan State University, 1971).
14. Kalman Seigel, "Colleges Fighting Repressive Forces," *New York Times*, (May 11, 1953), p. 29.
15. Debbie Meier, "Careerism on Campus: Two Faces of Conformity," *Anvil*, 7 (Spring-Summer, 1956), pp. 9-12.
16. The statistics mentioned in this section come largely from the *Student Federalist* and other UWF publications.
17. There is no adequate analysis of the NSA, despite its importance to the American student movement. Much of the factual material described in this section is culled from the NSA's files, some of which are located in the State Historical Society of Wisconsin. Martin McLaughlin's thesis, *op. cit.*, is a useful research tool, as is Stephen C. Schodde, *Certain Foci of the U.S. National Student Association and Their Implications for Student Personnel Administrators.* (Unpublished Ph.D. Dissertation, Teachers College, Columbia University, 1965). Finally, see Philip G. Altbach and Norman Uphoff, *The Student Internationals*, (Metuchen, New Jersey: Scarecrow Press, 1973), offers some analysis of the NSA based on its international role.
18. Again, there is not as yet a full account of the relations between the NSA and the CIA and the implications of this relationship. The original exposé was published in *Ramparts*. See Sol Stern, "NSA-CIA," *Ramparts*, 5 (March, 1967), pp. 29-39. See also "The CIA and the Students," *Time*, 89 (February

24, 1967), pp. 13-17. See also Norman Uphoff, "The Viability of Student Internationals: Reflections on Their Organization, Relevance, and Financing," in P. G. Altbach and N. Uphoff, *op. cit.*, pp. 139-166.

19. Martin McLaughlin, *op. cit.*, p. 132.
20. "Birth of the NSA," *Newsweek*, (September 23, 1947), p. 86. See also Stephen Schodde, *op. cit.*, p. 23. For a radical commentary on the congress, see Marvin Shaw, "Toward Student Unity," *New Foundations*, 1 (Fall, 1947), pp. 71-74.
21. See Edward Garvey, *History and Development of the U.S.N.S.A.*, (Philadelphia, Pa.: U.S.N.S.A., 1963).
22. See Martin McLaughlin, *op. cit.*
23. For additional discussion of the IUS, the International Student Conference, and the NSA, see Philip G. Altbach and Norman Uphoff, *International Student Politics*, (Metuchen, New Jersey: Scarecrow Press, 1973).
24. Paul Weinberg, "Ward Heelers on the Campus," *Nation*, 190 (June 4, 1960), pp. 489-492.
25. Gerry Kramer, *SDA: A History*, (Washington, D.C.: Students for Democratic Action, 1955).
26. *SDA Chapter Manual, 1948-1949*, (Washington, D.C.: Students for Democratic Action, 1949).
27. These programs are culled from issues of the *Democratic Action Newsletter*, a publication of the ADA, as well as campus periodicals.
28. *SDA Chapter Manual, op. cit.*
29. Factual material on SDA conventions is taken from letters and reports in the files of the SDA, Wisconsin State Historical Society.

CHAPTER FIVE

Radicals and Others in the Fifties:
In and Out of the Wilderness

This chapter is concerned largely with the campus radical movement during the fifties. It also deals with the other major currents of socially concerned student organizations, the religious and conservative movements. None of the elements which are considered here has much relationship to the large majority of students attending college during the fifties. Yet, the radical groups provide a link between the thirties and the sixties. Indeed, the fifties can be seen as a kind of transitional period, with the early part of the decade resembling the thirties in terms of organizational forms and political concerns, and the latter marking a change in campus radicalism and a move toward both the styles and issues of the New Left. The late fifties saw a resurgence of campus social concern, which paved the way for the more active sixties.

If the liberal student organizations failed to establish a dramatic presence on most campuses, the radicals fared even worse. Indeed, many of the radical groups, particularly in the early fifties, functioned to a major extent within the liberal student movement and were unable even to capture control of them. Radical student groups of any ideological stripe were forces to be reckoned with on campus at perhaps a dozen colleges and universities in the United States until 1958. Schools like the University of California at Berkeley, the University of Wisconsin, Chicago, Harvard, Columbia, and some of the New York area schools maintained radical groups through much of the decade, although even at these schools the total local radical movement probably numbered fewer than fifty individuals on any given campus, and these were often divided into three or four warring factions of social democrats, Trotskyists, and Communists. By 1952 none of the radical national student organizations claimed a membership of more than a few thousand, and it is unlikely that more than 4,000 students belonged to radical groups in the United States.

The reasons for the decline of radicalism have been discussed earlier. Certainly the main cause was the general political atmosphere and the harassment of radicals, particularly Communists, during the fifties. At a time when students were literally afraid to sign petitions even on nonpolitical local issues, it is not surprising that Socialist or radical groups should find their memberships dwindling. While many academic administrators, particularly at the prestigious private universities, tried to protect the civil liberties and privacy of radical students, many schools demanded membership lists and other information of radical groups, and this caused several groups to disband or go underground to avoid giving it. The radical movement was forced to spend much of its time defending its right to exist, in fighting costly court cases, and trying to convince the American public that radicalism was not tantamount to treason. The Communists, particularly, were so harassed that legal expenses and campaigns to free their leaders from prison took the place of political organizing.

Many of the reasons for the eclipse of radicalism on the campus rest with the radical movement itself. Some of these factors seem, on the surface, to be without reason and merely self-destructive. Yet, there was reason for much of the ideological infighting of the period. While it is impossible to fully discuss the intricacies of left politics in this volume, it is important to mention some of the key elements. The entire radical movement had the problem of coming to terms with the Soviet Union and Communism. This was a particularly serious problem in view of the virulence of the Cold War and the strong anticommunism evidenced by most of the American people. For the Communists, of course, there was little choice. Traditionally subservient to the Soviet Union, the American Communist party continued to follow the dictates of the international Communist movement regardless of the domestic consequences. Non-Communist radicals also had to deal somehow with the question of the Soviet Union. Some groups were equivocal on the matter, such as the Socialist Workers Party, which maintained critical support. Others were extremely anti-Communist and anti-Soviet, in part for ideological reasons and in part because this stance permitted the Socialists to separate themselves from the Communists. The Socialist party and the Young Peoples' Socialist League were in this category.

Radicals had to deal with other ideological and tactical questions during the fifties which tended to limit their effectiveness. The question, for example, of whether the radical movement should be a "vanguard" movement or whether it should appeal to the largest number of people was an important one. Some groups felt that radicals must be highly committed to the cause and quite sophisticated ideologically, while others felt that it was most effective to organize large numbers of people around relatively popular issues such as civil rights or foreign policy. Splits within organizations occurred because of this and related questions.

Radical students often worked within other less radical groups, such as the NSA or the SDA, and seldom tried to organize direct political activism on campus. Their tactic was usually to function in small discussion groups which were close-knit socially and to aim at providing their members with a firm grounding in the particular ideological concerns of the organization. Much of the time of the radical movement was spent building up a high level of consciousness and ideological sophistication in very small groups rather than building a broad-based movement.

It can be said that, by the early fifties, the radical organizations, such as the Young Peoples' Socialist League, the Young Socialist League, the Labor Youth League (Communist), and a few other smaller groups were locked firmly into a "minority" mentality. They were, in essence, unable to perceive of themselves as anything but tiny sects isolated from the mainstream of American politics and from the mainstream of campus life. The radical student movement never seriously attempted to build a broader student movement; rather, it stressed a high level of political training for a few individuals. Thus, semiclandestine organizing within other student groups became a logical and much used tactic.

The student radicalism of the fifties can be divided into three somewhat distinct periods. The first was during the immediate postwar period before either the Cold War or the McCarthy period had started in earnest. During this period, there was some rebirth of radicalism on campus, spurred particularly by Henry Wallace's presidential bid in 1948 and the strong Communist support for that campaign. Following Wallace's defeat and the general collapse of the student movement, the period of the Korean War and McCarthyism marked the lowest ebb of American student activism since before the growth of the Intercollegiate Socialist Society in 1905. During this period, open radicalism all but ceased to exist on campus. Finally, the latter portion of the fifties, particularly after 1956, showed a rebirth of radical organizations and of activism in general and, by the end of the decade, some elements of the radical student movement had reestablished themselves as viable political organizations. During this time, the radical student movement moved increasingly into public view and involved itself in civil rights, civil liberties, and peace activities while preserving its organizational identity.

It was during the period of the rebirth of student activism in the late fifties that many of the roots of the New Left developed. A stress on single "issues," such as civil rights or nuclear testing, became an important aspect of the radical movement. Radicals tried, with some success, to link specific issues to broader political and ideological concerns. The weakening of ties between student groups and adult organizations also took place at this time and new groups, such as the Student Peace Union and the Student Nonviolent Coordinating Committee, developed which had no formal adult ties and were organizationally independent. The reestablishment of a sense of security about political expression and the end of the McCarthy era also helped to make campus activism "respectable" once again. A gradual liberalization in the nation as a whole, and such events as the Supreme Court's desegregation decision in 1954, paved the way for the civil rights movement.

The Communist Student Movement: The Popular Front Revisited

Student groups associated in some manner with the Communist party were very strong in the immediate postwar years and continued to function throughout the fifties, with a small break occurring after the demise of the Labor Youth League in 1957. The initial, although certainly limited success of Communist student groups was due in part to nostalgia over the student movement of the thirties, in which the Communists played an important role (with a relatively large Communist party membership of about 60,000 in 1946), as well as over the issues emphasized by Communists in the immediate postwar period. As in the thirties, the Communists tried to organize a broad-based student organization under its leadership which would focus largely on non-ideological issues and appeal to the broad liberal student community. In addition, Communist involvement in Henry Wallace's presidential campaign in 1948 attracted many unaffiliated radicals and liberals to Communist-dominated student groups for a short period. The failure of the Wallace bid and the growth of the Cold War spelled the end to effective Communist organizing in the student community. The Young Communist League had been abolished in 1943, and there was little direct Communist impact on the campus during this period.

One of the difficulties in analyzing the Communist student movement is the continual change in organizational titles that these groups went through in order to escape McCarthyism and conform to shifts in Communist party policy. The first of the Communist organizations of this period, and the successor of the American Student Union, was the American Youth for Democracy (AYD). Formed at a convention in October, 1943, the AYD was from the outset both strongly controlled by Communists and moderate in its political approach. According to one report, 242 of the 314 delegates to the founding convention were Communists.[1] At its founding, the AYD claimed 1,400 members in its Intercollegiate Division (the organization had off-campus members as well, mostly in the New York City area) and had sixty-five campus chapters. Although the House Un-American Activities Committee claimed that the AYD had 16,000 members,[2] it is highly unlikely that the organization had more than 2,000 dues-paying members in its history.[3]

AYD activities during the immediate postwar period were moderate. In the New York area, AYD groups at Columbia, New York University, and City College actively campaigned for Vito Marcantonio and the American Labor Party in the 1946 elections. AYD had vocal delegates at the various early NSA meetings, although its successes in NSA were limited. AYD either sponsored or cosponsored several periodicals. *Student Outlook* and *New Student* are two publications which reflected AYD policies and which were published for a year or two in the immediate postwar years. Neither journal had a large circulation, however, and both tried to appeal to the broad liberal student community. AYD supported campus labor unions, such as a strike of maintenance workers at Columbia University in 1946, and participated in veterans affairs actively. It tried to point out the negative aspects of the developing Cold War as well.

By 1947, AYD was attacked on many campuses as a "subversive" organization and a "Communist front" and its modest support began to decline rapidly. From this point on, AYD was forced to devote a good deal of its time defending itself from attacks and protecting its right to exist. In many cases, university authorities refused to grant recognition to AYD groups or disaffiliated local organizations. The attack on AYD by HUAC in 1947 led to its expulsion from a number of campuses, including Harvard and Queens College. AYD groups were also banned at UCLA, Syracuse University, and Michigan State. AYD, in response to these attacks, claimed that the organization never hid the fact that there were Communist members, but that these were only a small percentage of the total group.[4] After 1947, AYD tried to stress civil liberties, particularly its right to exist, but these efforts were not successful.

In 1948, when the Communist student movement shifted its emphasis from a general student organization to an effort to assist the election of Henry Wallace as President of the United States, several new organizational forms were developed, most notably the Young Progressives of America (YPA), which included both students and nonstudents but which had its major strength on campus. The YPA basically supplanted the AYD, and many of AYD's most active members simply joined the YPA. The YPA was founded in July of 1948 at a convention in Philadelphia attended by 1,930 delegates from forty-four states. Many of the delegates were not students. The meeting was free from major conflict until it became clear that the organizers were trying to elect their own slate of national officers without discussion. At this point, there was some heated debate and the slate was elected nevertheless.[5] A specifically student oriented group, Students for Wallace, was formed in April of 1948 at a meeting attended by representatives from 108 campuses and by the summer the organization claimed 300 campus Wallace for President Clubs. While many of the campus leaders may have been Communist, the rank and file were not.[6] The larger and politically sophisticated campuses had large pro-Wallace groups—at the University of Michigan there were 1,000 members and at Minnesota 200 had joined. Other universities had similar groups.[7] For a few months before the election, it is likely that the pro-Wallace students were the largest organized student political group in the United States.

The Wallace presidential bid got substantial campus support. The success of the Wallace campaign on campus reflected the desire of many students to "do something" about politics at a time when activism was at a relatively low ebb. Wallace was a popular figure among many intellectuals and his campaign was based on traditional values of Midwestern populism combined with an anti-Cold War stance. The Wallace campaign no doubt represented "the political energies of the Popular Front of the late thirties [which had] reached their final spasm."[8]

Wallace's defeat and indeed his very poor showing at the polls (some 1 million votes nationally) brought the Young Progressives and Students for Wallace organizations down like a house of cards. A Communist spokesman was disappointed at the size of Wallace's vote, but stated that a political party had been built in eight months and that the campaign was an important educational tool against the Cold War. He also noted that students played the key role in the Wallace campaign and provided much of his organizational strength nationally.[9]

The defeat of the Wallace campaign saw the end of Communist efforts to organize a mass student movement during the fifties. Demoralization set in among those who had been active in the Wallace effort, particularly when it became clear that the leadership for the campaign had mostly come from Communists. The end of the Young Progressives meant the end of any radical organization of any influence on the American campus until the rise of the Student Peace Union in 1959. In essence, the eclipse of radicalism in the fifties started with the defeat of Henry Wallace.

Communist organizing efforts did not stop, however. The organization which took over after the demise of the Wallace campaign was the Labor Youth League (LYL), which was founded in 1948 and officially dissolved in 1957. The LYL claimed a membership of 6,000 at its inception in 1948 and had declined to 400 when it dissolved. At the same period, the Communist party had a membership of 55,000 in 1950 and only 3,000 in 1958.[10] Although the LYL's membership was not limited to Communists, the organization made few efforts to conceal its Communist identification. *New Foundations*, a quarterly associated with the LYL, spoke of the "vanguard of the American working class—the Communist Party." The LYL's original program was aimed primarily at students, and it stressed its opposition to the Cold War, its support for peace, Negro rights, its opposition to anti-Communist hysteria, and its efforts to stimulate discussion of Marxism.[11]

In 1950, the LYL claimed 200 groups in nineteen states, forty of which were in factories. This is probably an overestimate. Even at this time, the organization admitted that it was under attack from "witch-hunters" and stressed its antiwar programming.[12]

While the LYL tried to attract nonstudents, it was not very successful in such efforts and remained largely rooted to the campuses. The 1949 LYL convention emphasized its program aims, which included support for the Soviet Union, unity of all youth movements, support for the labor movement, democratization of education, and opposition to "Wall Street" and its preparations for World War III. The LYL saw itself as primarily an educational organization dedicated to socialism in America, stressing the role of the working class and pressing a Marxist analysis. Its educational program was aided by two journals, *Challenge* and *New Foundations.* Neither of these periodicals was very influential, with *New Foundations* claiming a national circulation of around 5,000 in 1951. As early as 1951, the LYL's national leadership recognized that it was not effectively reaching American youth, or even the young on the campuses, and attributed this failure to ineffective educational programs and a low level of ideological sophistication among its new members.

By the early fifties, the repression of LYL local groups seriously threatened the survival of the organization. After the Supreme Court declared that Communists could be jailed under the Smith Act, many college administrators moved against the LYL and the organization was banned on many campuses. Among the schools which banned the LYL were CCNY and Brooklyn College, which had strong chapters. The University of Chicago narrowly allowed LYL to retain its recognition, but only after a long struggle, and the University of Wisconsin continued to permit an LYL group to remain on campus. Many universities demanded membership lists from LYL groups and, rather than provide such lists, they voluntarily disbanded.

Indeed, the organization had been weakened to such a serious extent by 1957 that it voted to dissolve itself. The final convention attracted only twenty-seven delegates, and the LYL claimed that it had lost contact with the mainstream of American youth (perhaps the understatement of the year), that it had been too subservient to the Communist party, and that repression had weakened its base of support. Of significance, although unstated at the convention, was the trauma for Communists of the Hungarian Revolution and Khruschev's denunciation of Stalin, both of which took place shortly before the convention. The final vote on dissolution was twenty in favor, four opposed, and three abstaining. Thus, one of the fifties student groups came to an end.

One other Communist effort to attract student support in the fifties should be discussed here. This was a series of ad hoc conferences and organizing campaigns aimed at attracting broad student support for radical or liberal issues not necessarily related to the ideological views of the Communist party. One such conference was held in Madison, Wisconsin in May of 1952. The meeting was entitled the "National Student Conference for Academic Freedom, Equality, and Peace." The conference attracted some 200 delegates and observers from thirty-three colleges. Many non-Communist liberals and radicals attended the meeting, and when it was clear that proceedings were dominated by Communists, a large number walked out in protest.[13] The conference passed resolutions on a range of issues: it supported student exchanges with the Soviet Union, called for an immediate cease fire in Korea, supported an end to racial discrimination, and called for academic freedom and expanded higher education facilities. One of the main aims of the conference was the creation of a new national student organization to be affiliated to the Communist-led International Union of Students. While a National Continuations Committee was set up and operated for a time, no organization emerged from the conference, and little seems to have been accomplished by it, although the organizers had hoped to form a counterweight to the NSA. Another Communist-led campaign in the early fifties which attracted some student support was an effort to obtain signatures on a peace petition drawn up at an international meeting in Stockholm in 1949. The petition was militantly anti-American in tone and did not attract major support among students. It was actively pushed by LYL and other Communist-related groups and provided a useful forum for them. None of the periodic efforts during the fifties, however, provided any lasting gains and none left a major impression on the student community.

The LYL was not the last of Communist efforts to organize among students. In 1960, a new group was formed by many of the (now rather old) student leaders formerly associated with the LYL. This new organization, called the Progressive Youth Organizing Committee (PYOC), attempted to be broad in its political tone and to recruit a range of students to its ranks. It was also somewhat freer of the jargon of the Communist party of the mid-fifties and therefore better able to speak to the concerns of the broader student community. PYOC tried hard to win broader student allegiance by gravitating to the student concerns most dramatic at the time—peace and civil rights. PYOC's periodical, *New Horizons for Youth*, issued first as a monthly newspaper and then as a magazine, featured articles on a range of student-oriented concerns, from culture to overtly political issues. PYOC continued for about three years, but failed to establish any major strength despite the general growth of the student movement. The cause for PYOC's failure was, in part, the organization's "old left" Popular Front style. Strong support for the Soviet Union was evident in PYOC publications and meetings, and its leadership was largely in the hands of old-line Communist functionaries. Most politically aware students were immediately alienated by both the style and substance of PYOC politics and by the manipulative nature of its organizational structure, which made sure that dissident elements did not take control.

When it became clear that PYOC had little potential for taking advantage of the upsurge in campus political awareness, it was dissolved and replaced with the W. E. B. DuBois Clubs, which were founded in 1963. While the DuBois Clubs represent a fraction of the broad New Left of the sixties, the organization was more successful than its predecessors, probably because of the fairly "open" political atmosphere of the 1960s and the fact that the DuBois Clubs remained fairly consistent (and fairly moderate) in their ideology and tactics during the period when most of the New Left was undergoing massive ideological upheaval. The DuBois Clubs had affiliated at a number of American universities and took part in many of the campus agitations of the 1960s. The Clubs have generally been on the "conservative" (nondirect action) wing of the campus movement, in keeping with the "legalist" views of the Communist party.[14] While the DuBois Clubs were not a major force during the sixties, several of their members, such as Bettina Aptheker at Berkeley and Steve Cagan at Indiana, were in local leadership positions. More recently, the Communists founded a new group, the Young Workers Liberation League, in order to reflect a trend away from the campus, and have dissolved the DuBois Clubs.

Just as the liberal student movement, in a sense, characterized American liberalism's paranoia about communism and its domination by adult organizations, the Communist student movement represented an ideological current which was beleaguered and intellectually stagnant during the fifties. The various Communist student organizations slavishly adhered to Communist party strategy which followed the not so consistent orientation of the Soviet Union. Even without the repression and fear that characterized the period, it is unlikely that groups like the LYL, YPA, or others would have had much success. For most of the period, the Communist student organizations were, in general, paper organizations with strength on only a few campuses and positions which attracted few students.

The Socialist Student Movement: Sectarian Survival

The Socialist student organizations of the fifties were essentially remnants from the thirties in their ideological orientation, organizational techniques, and in most cases, their self images. The Socialists never developed any broad-based student organization in the fifties. Even an organization analogous to the Wallace campaign was not forthcoming from the Socialists. The Socialist groups had more modest membership rolls than Communist student groups in the mid-fifties when less than 2,000 students belonged to any of the Socialist organizations. Socialist student activity was, like the radical student movement in general, concentrated in the larger, more cosmopolitan universities and some of the prestigious, liberal arts colleges. The vast majority of institutions of higher education had no Socialist student activity at all and few, if any students identified as Socialist.

The Socialist student movement is also more difficult to analyze than the Communist, if only because of its ideological diversity and the large number of small organizations, many of which spent most of their existence struggling with each other.

This section examines some of the more visible of the Socialist groups without attempting to be comprehensive in organizational coverage. The Socialist groups were active within broader student organizations; thus, a purely organizational description of their activities is somewhat misleading. Members of the Young Socialist League (YSL) attempted to work within the liberal SDA. Socialists were active in NSA on both regional and national levels, although they were never able to influence policy. Socialist students were particularly involved in civil rights activities and instrumental in early mass demonstrations such as the Youth March for Integrated Schools in 1957 and 1958 and the early Freedom Rides and sit-ins. Members of the Young Peoples' Socialist League (YPSL) worked in the Student Peace Union and provided some of its leadership. Socialist students were able to understand the direction of the student movement at the end of the fifties and to work constructively in some of the broader "single issue" organizations such as the SPU and in the civil rights movement. They successfully combined a radical perspective with a basically anti-Communist position. While the Socialist groups themselves had a modest rebirth in the late fifties, their major contribution was in helping other groups organize by providing them with energetic and politically sophisticated manpower. The Socialists, of course, continued the tradition of factionalism and in this sense did not serve the movement well.

Socialism is not a concept which has ever had a great deal of acceptability among Americans. This was especially true during the fifties, when socialism was linked to the Soviet Union and the Cold War. Thus, it is not surprising that Socialist students were organized into small educationally-oriented cadres and focused their energy on "mass" non-Socialist single-issue movements such as the peace movement. This orientation was both a strength and a weakness. On the one hand, it permitted Socialists to participate actively and effectively in movements which otherwise would probably have lacked sophisticated leadership. Socialists were able to recruit individuals from these broader movements into their own organizations. Often, their identification as Socialists was lost in the day-to-day organizational work of these "mass" movements.

The Socialist movement of the fifties had two basic streams: the social democrats represented by the Student League for Industrial Democracy (SLID) and the Young Peoples' Socialist League (YPSL); and the "revolutionary socialists" represented by the Young Socialist League (YSL), Socialist Youth League (SYL), and, at the end of the fifties, the Young Socialist Alliance (YSA). All of these groups were characterized by strong opposition to Communist (Stalinist) tactics and ideology and a commitment to the creation of a socialist society in America. Beyond this, there were substantial differences. The social democratic groups took a general "reformist" view of society and were committed to electoral politics as the key to achieving socialism. They identified with European social democratic parties such as the Labour Party in Great Britain and the Social Democratic parties in Scandinavia and West Germany. They did not claim, by and large, to be Marxist in their ideological or tactical orientation. The more revolutionary groups were Marxist and were committed to bringing socialism to America through a militant labor party or through revolutionary struggle based on the working class. The revolutionary Socialist groups differed substantially on tactical questions despite their common adherence to Marxist ideology. Their views toward the Soviet Union played an important role during the fifties, as they had in earlier periods. Indeed, internal struggles and interorganizational factional strife concerning the appropriate view of the Soviet Union bedeviled the Socialist movement.

The oldest consistently functioning student political organization was the Student League for Industrial Democracy (SLID), which dated back to 1905 and the founding of the Intercollegiate Socialist Society. At the end of the fifties, the SLID transformed itself into the Students for a Democratic Society and focused more on action-oriented programs. SLID, and its successor, the SDS, were affiliated to the League for Industrial Democracy (LID), an adult educational organization with moderate Socialist leanings which received much of its rather modest funding from the more radical elements in the labor movement. As the SDS grew more militant in the early sixties, it disaffiliated from the LID and became an independent organization. During the fifties, however, links between the LID and the SLID were strong and harmonious. The LID provided operating funds for the SLID, without which it could not have survived.

During the thirties, the SLID joined with the National Student League to form the American Student Union and from 1936 until 1945 there was virtually no separate SLID organization on the campus. As World War II ended, the LID moved to make funds available for student work and two student organizers were hired.[15] SLID never grew much in the postwar era. In 1947 it claimed 400 national members and fifteen affiliated chapters. Several regional SLID groups existed in Michigan (with three SLID chapters) and in New York City. Other active groups existed at Cornell, Pennsylvania State, Chicago, Wayne State, Wisconsin, and a few other schools. By 1950, SLID membership fell even lower and the annual convention that year drew only twenty delegates from New York University, City College of New York, Harvard, Brooklyn College, College of Wooster, Wayne State, and Columbia. During the fifties the organization focused on education, sponsoring campus meetings, speakers, summer conferences, and other national and regional meetings. The organization's 1951 convention was more successful than the 1950, with 150 students attending. In the 1950s organizational direction was a central concern of SLID conventions. A strong minority always pressed for a more activist orientation, while the majority, with LID support, favored an educational approach and moderate tactics. Since LID controlled the purse strings, the adult group's wishes were crucial and educational programming and ideological moderation were the dominant trend within the SLID of the fifties.

While SLID was strongly anti-Communist, it had no other positive ideological position. It was not even clear that a majority of SLID members considered themselves socialists.[16] The 1948 SLID convention voted that "all parties and/or factions based on Bolshevik principles will be excluded" and that no "advocates of dictatorship and totalitarianism" can become SLID members. During the fifties, the SLID worked more with liberal groups such as SDA than other radical organizations. It maintained ties with the labor movement, particularly the United Auto Workers Union, mainly through the LID.

Like other radical groups, SLID had its share of factional problems. Indeed, the lowest point in SLID membership and morale came in 1951-1952 when a group of radicals centered in the CCNY chapter tried to get the SLID to move further to the left and created a faction within the organization. The National Executive Committee postponed SLID's convention and spent much of its time fighting the radicals. As a partial result of this factionalism, SLID chapters fell to an all time low by the time of the convention in June, 1953. An energetic organizational campaign improved things in the following year. At no time in the fifties, however, did SLID's membership rise above 500 and its number of chapters above twenty-five.[17]

SLID remained ideologically and tactically open. Its official positions during the fifties did not emphasize socialism; in fact, they were rather liberal. SLID opposed universal military training, favored the Marshall Plan, opposed Soviet expansionism in Eastern Europe, placed great stress on academic freedom and civil liberties, opposed racial discrimination, and favored increased educational opportunities. SLID journals and pamphlets often stressed more radical ideas, such as nationalization of industry and workers' control and featured writers such as Norman Thomas and other leftist intellectuals. SLID engaged in an active publications program. Despite its small membership, it published a magazine and/or a newsletter regularly during the fifties. *SLID Voice* was its main publication. SLID also sponsored a series of pamphlets on a range of topics of economic and political interest from a moderate Socialist perspective. The organization maintained an active literature program and offered over a hundred publications for sale. SLID chapters stressed these publications in their local programming.

One of the features of SLID programs during the fifties, and perhaps one of the organization's most successful activities, was a series of summer conferences and conventions. The conferences, which usually attracted around forty students for a week of lectures and discussions, generally featured speakers from a range of radical perspectives, on such topics as civil liberties, the labor movement, leadership training, aspects of American foreign policy, and "The Silent Generation Speaks." SLID emphasized research by student members and published some of this research in pamphlet form. SLID's field secretaries, who during the fifties included a number of able individuals such as James Farmer (later National Director of CORE), were a key to the organization's modest strength. The secretaries travelled to most SLID groups once or twice a year to provide some educational input as well as to see that the groups were still functioning. They were also instrumental in setting up SLID chapters on campuses where none existed.

Around 1957, SLID members began to discuss the possibility of renaming the organization, mainly because many believed that the emphasis on industrial democracy that SLID had had in the past was no longer the most relevant issue for most American students, and that other questions, concerning the quality of life in America for example, were more important. This debate, which lasted several years, resulted in changing SLID's name to Students for a Democratic Society (SDS) in 1960. The SDS remained linked with the LID for a few more years, but increasing hostility between the adult organization and its student affiliate because of the latter's radicalism and direct action approach, led to an open break in January, 1966.

The development of SLID was somewhat typical of the decade. Organizational survival was assured only by subsidies and support from the adult LID, while, at the same time, relations between the SLID and the LID were occasionally strained. Pressure from the LID did prevent SLID from developing in ways which might well have moved the organization more into the mainstream of campus life. Efforts of more radical elements to move SLID leftward failed to some extent because of LID pressure and LID control of the organization's purse strings. SLID's emphasis on educational activities and its rigid anti-communism were typical of the social democratic student organizations of the fifties. SLID strength was concentrated largely in New York City and in the larger universities which traditionally had radical student groups. For some reason, the organization was especially weak on the West Coast. Indeed, the fact that SLID's emergence into the mainstream of student life necessitated a change in name, and eventually a total split from adult sponsorship, is highly significant.[18]

Another element of the socialist student movement has been described as "Third Camp" in the sense that it supported neither the Soviet Union nor the United States and kept to a more independent version of democratic socialism. All of the Third Camp organizations discussed here were quite small during the fifties and were important only because they had a dedicated membership willing to participate in other political movements, such as civil rights and civil liberties, as well as in the affairs of the Socialist movement. It is also difficult to clearly separate the various Third Camp groups because there was a good deal of interaction between them and much factionalism and conflict despite the fact that this entire section of the student movement probably had fewer than 1,500 members nationally for most of the fifties. Nevertheless, the Third Camp groups were instrumental in the revival of student activism at the end of the decade and helped keep alive the radical presence during the dark days of the early fifties.[19]

The Third Camp groups can be considered as a series of political and historical "streams." The mainstream social democratic group was the YPSL, which had a long organizational history and was closely tied to the adult Socialist party. A second stream was the Socialist Youth League (SYL), which represented a Trotskyist position and was more radical ideologically than the YPSL. At a point in the fifties, these groups merged, but later split over ideological and tactical differences. Later, another Trotskyist group, the Young Socialist Alliance (YSA), emerged and became one of the more important sectarian groups of the sixties. The YSA, unlike the YPSL and SYL, abandoned Third Camp ideology.

The ideological similarities and differences between the various Socialist organizations tell much about the concerns of student radicals during the fifties. The YPSL, as a social democratic organization, was basically gradualist in its approach, and saw socialism coming to the United States through the electoral process, while the SYL and other Trotskyist groups were more "radical" in the sense that they felt that some kind of revolutionary struggle based on the working class was necessary to establish socialism. None of the groups felt that such a "revolutionary" situation was in the offing and they concentrated on "arena" work—that is, working with other single-issue, often reformist groups such as the Student Peace Union or the civil rights movement in an effort to create a heightened sense of political awareness. Stress was also placed in some groups on developing highly committed "vanguard" cadres in the Leninist tradition. Foreign policy played an important role in the Socialist groups and it is possible that this emphasis on non-American concerns weakened its potential for growth. Arguments over the nature of the Soviet Union and over which revolutionary movements to support in the Third World were important to these Socialist activists.

The YPSL, probably the largest and certainly the most stable of the Third Camp groups of the fifties, managed to maintain its organizational identity throughout the fifties. It had very little organizational success and in the mid-fifties fell to an estimated national membership of 120.[20] In 1950, the YPSL claimed 500 dues-paying members, 500 "delinquent" members, and 300 individuals very active in local chapters but not actually members.[21]

YPSL membership and activity certainly decreased after 1950. A combination of political stagnation on campus, McCarthyism, and factional problems within the Socialist movement contributed to this decline. By 1952, SYL members were actively trying to push the YPSL to the left and, as a result, causing major rifts in the organization and friction between the YPSL and the Socialist party. The 1953 YPSL convention was attended by thirteen delegates and three alternates. The national secretary reported that fewer than ten chapters, several of these in New York City, were active nationally. YPSL's educational programming included an irregularly issued discussion bulletin aimed at YPSL members and occasional pamphlets.[22]

Between 1947 and 1954 the YPSL had almost no impact on the campus and only a modest role in the very small radical movement. YPSL tended to work more with the liberal SDA than with more radical groups such as the SYL during this period. Factional problems were endemic as early as 1947 and continued until the major split in 1954. In general, radical elements were attempting either to move the YPSL to the left and thus "take it over" or to recruit members out of the YPSL into their own organizations. Unsuccessful in the former effort, largely because of SP controls, the radicals were successful in recruiting many people out of the YPSL.

The YPSL's major leftist adversary during the pre-1954 period was the Socialist Youth League (SYL), the youth group affiliated to the Independent Socialist League (ISL), a small semi-Trotskyist party made up of Marxist but strongly anti-Stalinist Socialists.[23] Although a very small organization, the SYL managed to maintain an active internal education program, participate actively in broader politics, and function in other liberal and radical organizations. SYL's members were, in general, very committed to the organization and its political conceptions. As a cadre organization, the SYL screened its members and made sure that only the most committed and ideologically pure were admitted.

The SYL was founded in 1946 and by 1951 it had established itself as a national organization with chapters on twenty-five campuses. The 1951 convention of the SYL stressed the organization's commitment to a Third Camp foreign policy. At the same time, it also expressed willingness to work with non-Socialist groups on antiwar and other projects, and to oppose Stalinists in forming united fronts. The SYL recognized that its major role was as a student organization, and it adopted the *Anvil and Student Partisan*, a previously independent periodical, as its publication. *Anvil and Student Partisan*, one of the few radical student journals nationally circulated at this time,[24] appeared somewhat irregularly through the fifties. The SYL also published a discussion bulletin, aimed at internal education for SYL members. An active publications program was a key element of SYL work, and reflected its emphasis on education for its own membership.

SYL activities in the fifties combined "arena" work, with its stress on activism, with internal education and broader educational activities. The SYL was one of the few student organizations in that period which pressed for demonstrations and other public actions on various topics. Its demonstrations were rather small and infrequent, but it did attempt them. A series of national demonstrations against Franco and fascism in Spain in 1952 was typical of such efforts. But the bulk of SYL's activities were educational. Regular public meetings were held by many SYL chapters, including those in Berkeley, Chicago, and Brooklyn College. Regional conferences were also held on the West Coast and in other areas. Summer conferences on aspects of socialism were also sponsored. In general, SYL meetings and other activities were small—with a turn-out of fifty students to a meeting being an impressive number. Some, however, were larger, such as Max Schachtman's lecture to an audience of 500 at Berkeley in 1951. The reason for this large audience was that the university authorities refused to allow Schachtman to speak on campus and the matter became a civil liberties issue. A national tour by Hal Draper for the SYL attracted students to meetings at the University of Wisconsin, Michigan, Oberlin, the University of Washington, and other schools. Internal education programs for SYL members included reviews of articles in discussion bulletins, serious study of Marxist classics, and discussions of current political affairs and organizational matters.

SYL's activities did not greatly differ from those of other radical student groups at the time. Its policies were broadly Third Camp Socialist and frequently contained denunciations of other radical and liberal groups for their inconsistency, or "Stalinist" views. SYL was, of course, particularly critical of Communist groups, but it also attacked social democratic and liberal organizations. If nothing else, the SYL was consistent in its views. For example, the organization opposed the draft and military conscription, and criticized other radical groups for supporting student deferments (a popular measure on campus) because this support involved compromise with the conscription issue. On foreign policy questions, the SYL took a very consistent Third Camp position, regardless of the tactical consequences. The SYL was successful at least in the limited aim of preserving its organizational identity and functioning effectively in a difficult period largely because of the dedication and political sophistication of its members.

The SYL was active in other student organizations. At times, this was helpful to the organizations invaded, since SYL activists were willing workers. On other occasions, however, SYL members seriously damaged the organizations by creating factional disputes. The SDA, for one, suffered factionalism as a result of SYL attempts to take an active role. In this case, many of SDA's problems were caused by its unwillingness to allow internal democracy.

The most important of SYL's excursions into other organizations was into the YPSL. This resulted in the merger of the YPSL and the SYL into the Young Socialist League in 1954. SYL members had worked in YPSL on the local and national levels for several years and had convinced a majority of YPSL members that a new, independent, and more radical organization was needed if the student Socialist movement was to grow. The unity convention took place in February, 1954. It began as a separate convention of each group, followed by a joint meeting that officially proclaimed the new organization. The bases of unity were that the new organization be 1) internally democratic, 2) open to all antiwar Socialists and not officially Marxist, and 3) independent of all adult organizations. The new organization agreed to support *Labor Action* in return for a page in it to be edited by the YSL. A joint slate of former YPSL and SYL members was proposed to form the new group's National Executive Committee.[25] While formally independent of any adult organization, the ISL had a good deal of influence on the YSL, and the link between *Labor Action* and the YSL's newspaper further solidified ISL-YSL ties. The ISL exercised its influence on the YSL by intellectual and ideological skill rather than organizational manipulation. The YSL functioned effectively until 1957, when most of it merged with the YPSL, at the same time that the ISL was moving into the adult Socialist party. A small group, the left-wing Opposition, refused to join the YPSL and later became the nucleus for the Young Socialist Alliance (YSA).

The YPSL had existed throughout the years of YSL activity. A small right-wing faction, based mainly in Los Angeles in 1954, had refused to merge with the YSL and had retained the YPSL name. It was this group that fused with the YSL in 1957.

Relations between the SP and the YPSL throughout the fifties were strained, mainly because the YPSL, even its right wing, was to the left of the party on almost all issues ranging from internal party democracy to the nature of socialism. The events leading to the formation of the YSL were beliefs on the part of the YPSLs that the SP had worked to isolate left-wing leadership in the YPSL and had imposed its own political position. Further, the SP was hostile to the YPSL's antiwar politics and refused to publish any YPSL antiwar material in its journals. Finally, the SP refused to allow organizational democracy; it investigated the YPSL and expelled its New York District organization. When the YPSL and the YSL merged, only fifteen YPSLs supported the SP.[26]

The new YSL committed itself to concentrating on campus, although it recognized that the primary revolutionary force in America was the working class and not students. One of the new organization's immediate problems was to recruit new members and revitalize the student Socialist movement. While orienting itself primarily toward education, the YSL recognized the importance of working with the antiwar movement, supporting anti-ROTC campaigns, civil liberties struggles, and similar enterprises. The organization continued to stress its strong commitment to a Third Camp position on foreign policy.[27]

The YSL emphasized publications and speaking tours by national officers. A discussion bulletin, the *Young Socialist Review*, was published in mimeographed form ten times a year and *Anvil* was the YSL's magazine. Regional educational conferences, summer meetings, and other activities were also stressed. In 1954, fifty persons attended a YSL summer camp, and regional meetings were held in Chicago and New York covering a range of Socialist issues. Debates between the YSL and other groups were reasonably popular on campus and a number of these occurred in Chicago, Berkeley, Detroit, New York, and other areas of YSL strength. In addition to the major metropolitan areas, where small radical groups had traditionally functioned, YSL chapters existed at Wisconsin, Oberlin, Antioch, the University of Washington, and other schools. In all, the YSL had about twenty active chapters in the mid-fifties.

Like almost all of the radical student organizations in the fifties, the YSL was centered in New York City and the strong radical traditions (and factionalism) of New York shaped its reality to a great extent. Since New York radical politics were atypical—it was more factionalized, more sectarian and had more participants—the radical movement became far removed from campus currents.

By 1957, the YSL began to move toward merger with the reformed YPSL. This was very much in line with the adult Independent Socialist

League leadership, which was negotiating with the Socialist party. The YSL's proposed merger with the YPSL caused a split within the organization. A "Left-Wing Caucus" was formed which strongly opposed the merger and called for a continued YSL. The Left-Wing Caucus contended that the merger represented a right-wing antiworking-class ideological tendency. The majority of the YSL, however, felt that the time had come, in 1957, to form a new Debsian Socialist movement which could move from a small radical sect into the mainstream of American politics. By late 1957, the YSL had officially merged with the YPSL, creating a larger and more radical YPSL. The minority of the former YSL joined with youth affiliated with the Socialist Workers Party (SWP), a Trotskyist political party, to form the American Youth for Socialism (AYS). This group had only a small membership in the late 1950s. In 1959, it became the Young Socialist Alliance (YSA), the unofficial youth group of the SWP.

The newly merged YPSL was far from a mass organization. Indeed, as of 1960, it had at most twenty-five chapters and under 500 members, although a larger number were active in YPSL-sponsored activities. Most YPSL members were college students, although some of the most active chapters were located in large cities and had nonstudents as well as students in them. The YPSL, which was under the leadership of former YSL activists, was consistently to the left of the Socialist party, and major disputes with the SP were common. Indeed, the SP expelled a segment of the YPSL with left-wing views in 1963 and this group went on to found another small organization. Factionalism within the YPSL was also endemic.

The YPSL was heavily involved in what activism there was in the late 1950s. It was particularly active in organizing the Youth Marches for Integrated Schools. YPSL members were also active in the campaign against compulsory civil defense drills in New York City. The campaign was one of the first civil disobedience efforts and attracted national attention despite the modest numbers of individuals participating in them. YPSL members worked in the peace movement. They supported the founding of Student SANE as well as the Student Peace Union (SPU). While the merged YPSL remained a fairly small organization, it became for a while part of the mainstream of the student movement and in 1958-1960 had a substantial impact on the direction of the reviving student movement.

The final Socialist student organization, which merged in the late fifties, was the Young Socialist Alliance (YSA). The YSA was formed by various groups dissatisfied with Socialist groups like the YPSL. From the beginning, it was under the tutelege of the SWP. The SWP claimed to be the orthodox Trotskyist organization in the United States, with its own ideological view of both foreign policy and the role of Socialists in the United States. The SWP's view of the Soviet Union as a Socialist country that had "degenerated" but was still worthy of critical support, placed it in direct conflict with other Socialists. Further, its emphasis on building a vanguard of committed cadres and functioning as a revolutionary political party organizationally set it apart from the social democrat. Thus, the YSA, while subject to major factional disputes (which resulted in small groups, like the Sparticists, leaving the organization and forming splinter groups), did not allow much of the factionalism to dominate the public image of the organization. They did this through democratic centralism and party discipline.

The Socialist student movement of the fifties had a consistent pattern of development. Most of its concerns were internal, and the movement tried hard, but without much success, to develop a consistent attitude toward the Soviet Union and American capitalism, and build an American Socialist movement. It split into camps that wanted to form a vanguard Leninist organization like part of the YPSL. But the delineation between mass and vanguard parties was never purely organizational, and splits occurred from time to time within groups such as the YPSL or the YSL as perspectives changed. These internal questions preoccupied the student groups which, until the late fifties, emphasized only Socialist educational efforts. The Socialists moved out of their ideological torpor only after a student movement began to revive.

OTHER CURRENTS IN THE STUDENT MOVEMENT: CONSERVATIVE AND RELIGIOUS ACTIVISM

In this volume, major attention has been given to organizations and movements involved directly in student activism and politics, generally from a liberal-radical point of view, since this has been where the mainstream of the student movement lies. However, as pointed out previously, the liberals and radicals were by no means the whole of the student movement, nor during some periods were they numerically the most influential. This section is devoted to several nonliberal elements of the student political scene, particularly to the conservative and religious student movements which were significant in the fifties. It should be pointed out that the religious groups particularly cannot be totally separated from student liberalism or radicalism. At various times there were strong ties between some of the Protestant student organizatio. s and the liberals and radicals. If there was any political current on mo t American campuses, it was some sort of mild liberalism. The campu s press, organizations like the National Student Association, and group like the International Relations Clubs and most student governments were mildly liberal in their views. Anti-Communist views were taken for granted, and liberalism was largely directed at domestic issues. The religious and conservative student groups, therefore, were somewhat out of the mainstream of overt political concern and activism in the fifties. At the same time, they both represented, in a sense, only the tip of an iceberg. There were (and are) many students who were conservative in their politics and who took religion seriously. Public opinion polls consistently showed large minorities of politically conservative students. While religion clearly declined as a force among educated young people and as an organized movement on campus, a large proportion of the student population numbered themselves as believers in organized religion and were nominally members of religious organizations. In analyzing both conservative and religious organizations, one must keep in mind that these groups were not the most important centers of activism and concern on university and college campuses during the fifties. At the same time, the conservatives were more representative of the thinking of students in general than liberal organizations and movements. Since this volume is not concerned primarily with currents of student opinion but with organized groups and movements, conservative and religious groups do not merit the same amount of attention which has been given to other elements of the student movement.[28]

The Conservative Student Movement

The decade of the fifties was a period of apathy rather than reaction on the campuses. The general weakness of the right-wing student movement demonstrates this fact. The immediate postwar period was almost overwhelmingly liberal, and right-wing opinions had been tainted by association with fascism and Naziism. Even the onset of the Cold War, the Korean conflict, and McCarthyism did not produce a groundswell of reactionary organizations on campus, although several such groups did develop in the early fifties. Student opinion during the fifties seems to have been fairly similar to opinions of the general public—that is, highly conservative with only limited support for civil rights and liberties and strongly anti-Communist. Nevertheless, no strong conservative student movement emerged.

At the end of the decade, a reasonably large and well-organized national conservative student organization, the Young Americans for Freedom (YAF), emerged on the scene. Even the YAF, despite lavish financial support from adult conservatives and an active and articulate leadership, was unable to make a major impact on campus. The reasons for the lack of a powerful conservative student movement in America are complicated. When the society itself is reasonably conservative and those in positions of authority share many of the views of conservatives, there is little reason for activism. Indeed, it has been pointed out that campus conservativism has tended to be reactive, that is, it reacts to liberalism on campus and seeks to counteract it. One of the main themes of the campus conservative movement in the fifties was to counteract the effects of liberalism.[29] During the fifties, however, liberal activism was not dominant on the campus and conservatives felt little need to counteract it. In addition, conservative students tended to respect authority and generally did not wish to engage in "confrontation" tactics. This left them with few practical targets at which to aim campus activism. Indeed, as Lawrence Schiff has pointed out, conservative students tended to be "young fogies" in many of their attitudes toward society and education.[30] Psychological and sociological studies of conservative students indicate that they are, by and large, career-oriented and respectful of authority. These two elements strongly mitigate against activism.

There has never been a strong tradition of conservative activism on campus in America. When one thinks of student movements, one generally thinks of movements associated with radical politics, social reform, and humanistic values, and not with status quo politics. Further, conservative organizations on the adult level have traditionally distrusted intellectuals and universities and have not tried, with a few exceptions, to influence the academic world. The professoriate, even during the fifties, was liberal in its orientation, and was certainly one of the few groups in America which provided some opposition to McCarthyism.

Thus, historical traditions, the sociological and psychological make-up of conservative students, and the attitudes of the faculty all militated against the emergence of a strong conservative student movement in America.

Despite this, conservative student groups functioned during the fifties. The first national conservative student group of the fifties was the National Collegiate MacArthur Clubs, which was founded in Los Angeles in 1951. After a brief and unsuccessful effort to get Douglas MacArthur nominated by the Republicans for the presidency, the group changed its name to Students for America (SFA) in 1952 and began publishing a monthly newspaper, the *American Student.* The SFA was formed in part to oppose leftist domination of the American campus. SFA felt that most American student groups were led by Communists and other leftists, and one of its first publications was entitled, "Students Answer to the Marxist Challenge."[31] The organization claimed a membership of 2,500 on 120 campuses in 1954. Its focus was educational, and it claimed to have published 100,000 pieces of literature in a single month in 1954. SFA had few financial problems as it was funded by adult conservatives. To combat left-wing activities on campus, the SFA hired a National Security Director to keep tabs on radical campus activities and to spy on radical professors. SFA leaders urged their members to infiltrate leftist groups and report to the authorities on their activities.

According to M. Stanton Evans, a conservative commentator, the "SFA was intensely nationalistic, and proffered a broad, unsophisticated appeal for renascent 'Americanism'. But, for the times, SFA's approaches were apparently not right. The movement did not survive, although a number of the students continued to work in behalf of conservative principles, and have played influential roles in the current revival."[32] Due largely to lack of interest, SFA virtually disappeared from the campus after 1955.

The SFA seems to have had relatively few strong local groups. An SFA chapter of twenty members existed at the University of Wisconsin, and affiliates were active in the Midwest and in California. There is little indication, however, that the organization had much of a national or local impact. The SFA strongly attacked the National Student Association in 1952, calling it a Communist front, and the NSA felt that the threat was important enough to spend a good deal of energy responding to it.

Another national conservative student organization was the Intercollegiate Society of Individualists (ISI). It was started mainly to disseminate libertarian conservative literature to college students. The ISI began with the aid of the right-wing journal, *Human Events*, and functioned out of the *Human Events* offices for some time until it moved to its own headquarters in Philadelphia.[33] The ISI organized a number of discussion groups, mostly at Midwestern colleges, and was instrumental in the founding of two conservative student journals, the *New Individualist Review*, founded in 1961 and published from the University of Chicago, and *Insight and Outlook*, issued by students at the University of Wisconsin. The ISI's own journal, the *Individualist*, featured reprints from other conservative publications and had a circulation of at least 13,000 in 1960. ISI officials reported that more than 40,000 students had requested ISI literature. Although the ISI did not conceive of itself as a membership organization and had no clear ideological position, it did support a number of field workers, organized campus discussion groups, and assisted in distributing ISI literature. In the sixties, the ISI sponsored a series of summer schools which featured prominent conservative thinkers as resource persons. In all, the ISI saw itself as an educational undertaking and engaged in little or no direct action on campus. Although the organization reached a fairly substantial number of students, it made little overt impact on the campus.

The most active and action-oriented national conservative student organization to emerge in the postwar period was the Young Americans for Freedom (YAF) which, since it was started in 1960, is dealt with in more detail in the following chapter. YAF's roots are, however, very much in the same tradition as the ISI and the other conservative organization of the fifties. Conservative student groups also existed locally. By the late fifties, independent conservative organizations had sprung up at such campuses as Harvard, Princeton, Pennsylvania, Purdue, Minnesota, Washington, Southern California, Indiana, Miami, Maryland, and Holy Cross. Some of these organizations were affiliated with national conservative groups, but most were independent and were started with local initiative. In a few cases, conservative journals arose, among which were the Cornell Conservative Club's *Gentlemen of the Right*, the *Flat Hat* from the College of William and Mary, and *Analysis* from the University of Pennsylvania. Wisconsin's *Insight and Outlook*, founded in 1958, was one of the first and most successful of these journals. Most of these publications were fairly short-lived and circulated for the most part locally. But they did indicate the existence of active organizations. Conservative students also tried, with some success, to take over existing student organizations which they felt were dominated by "liberals." The Harvard-Radcliffe Committee to Study Disarmament found itself taken over by conservatives and its name was changed to the "Council Against Appeasement." Student governments were taken over by conservatives at a number of schools, usually for short periods of time, including Harvard, Northwestern, and Chicago.

The conservative "resurgence" at the end of the 1950s was related to the general rise in student awareness and political activism at the end of the decade.[34] The major impact of the campus conservative movement came at the end of the decade and was linked both to the revival in activism and the growth of Barry Goldwater's drive for power in the Republican party in the 1960s. Conservative groups, like liberals, were subject to the apathy of the fifties, and a highly conservative national posture during this period did not significantly contribute to a resurgence of conservatism on the campus. Some students actively supported McCarthyism, and there are many stories of students reporting "subversive" statements of faculty members to the authorities. But by and large, the conservative student "revival" occurred simultaneously with the growth of liberal and radical activism.

Religious Student Organizations

Religious student groups have been most influential at times when the overt political movement has been weakest. This was true during the fifties, when religious organizations were often the most radical and politically concerned groups on many campuses. As in other periods, socially concerned religious groups were often the only remotely "political" groups on campuses, particularly in smaller church-related colleges and schools in the Southern and Midwestern states. The religious student groups, when socially concerned at all, were predominantly liberal in their orientation. The very large majority of religious groups, however, were apolitical. In the fifties, the socially concerned religious organizations which were national in scale were limited to the YMCA-YWCA; several denominations such as the Methodists, Unitarians, Quakers, and some Jewish groups; and small segments of more traditional religious organizations. Of the total religious student movement, only a very small proportion were socially active to any significant degree. And where social activism existed, it was often only a small part of a much broader program of activities.

Nevertheless, the impact of the student religious movement on political activism in the fifties cannot be ignored. Many groups spoke out against McCarthyism, particularly against right-wing attacks on the National Council of Churches. Religious groups sponsored conferences on topics of political concern and some were sympathetic to pacifism. Toward the end of the decade, some of the religious groups began to participate in the civil rights and peace movements, and were responsible for sending some of the early activists into the field. Several nationally circulated student religious magazines, such as *Motive* and the *Inter-collegian*, dealt often with political themes, and reported on the development of the activist movement in the late fifties and early sixties.

The campus was not dominated by religion in the fifties; in fact, the impact of religious groups had declined from its previous period of influence in the twenties. Greater numbers of students declared themselves religiously unaffiliated, and the proportions of the student population directly affiliated to religious groups declined. At the same time, a large majority of American students claimed that they believed in organized religion, and on some campuses the religious groups retained a great deal of prestige.

The YM-YWCAs have always been among the most active social concern organizations in the Christian community. In the fifties they continued this tradition, maintaining, as always, a "low profile" in terms of participation in controversial activities. The Y movement was not involved in social action projects with liberal or radical groups, but rather it undertook its own projects. National Y conferences continued to take strong social action stands. In 1953, for example, it called for the desegregation of colleges and formed a committee to promote integration in Y activities.[35] The 1954 annual conference of the National Student Council of the YMCAs adopted a number of liberal policies: it supported academic freedom and called for curbing the investigative powers of Congress. On national issues, the council called for racial integration, an equitable tax system, and social welfare programs. The Y strongly supported the United Nations, favored disarmament, and advocated the free flow of international communications (at a time when many sought to prevent Communist propaganda from entering the United States). Thus, the Y movement maintained a liberal stance through the fifties, and devoted a reasonable amount of time at its conferences and regional meetings to political and social affairs.

The Y, and other liberal Protestant student groups, were closely associated with the World Student Christian Federation (WSCF), which was headquartered in Geneva, Switzerland and represented many of the Protestant student organizations around the world. The WSCF has been a radical voice in world Christian circles, strongly supporting anticolonial movements in developing areas and focusing attention on racism, imperialism, and other controversial questions. The Y movement and the broader Student Christian Movement (SCM) in the United States publicized WSCF positions and distributed its literature. This was another means of stressing social concern. A number of active SCM and Y leaders participated in WSCF conferences and work camps, increasing their political and social awareness in the process.

The YM-YWCA sponsored a variety of activities, generally of a noncontroversial nature, which focused on social problems and issues. Many regional meetings; Washington, D.C. conferences on world and national affairs; work camps in urban slums, and Southern tenant farms; and other programs brought middle-class students in contact with pressing social problems. Students-in-Industry programs in a number of locations focused attention on the problems of workers and the trade union movement. National Y officials circulated program planning documents which focused on social action questions and publicized successful local Y programming on such questions. The professional staff recruited by the Y was often involved in social action efforts. The Y participated early in interracial activities and was particularly strong in its opposition to racial discrimination. The Y movement in the fifties was not the force on campus that it was in the twenties. The proportion of students belonging to Y groups declined throughout the period.

Several of the denominational Protestant groups were also involved in social action. The Methodists were particularly active, in part through *Motive* magazine founded in 1941, and in part through organizations like the National Council of Methodist Youth (NCMY) and later the Methodist Student Movement (MSM). The NCMY, organized in 1941, was an attempt to unite all Methodist youth work. Students constituted only a portion of its membership of some 1 million. Like the YM-YWCAs, the NCMY was generally liberal and in 1955 declared its opposition to universal military training, favored rights for conscientious objectors, opposed ROTC, and opposed the use of nuclear weapons. These were fairly strong stands for that time. NCMY sponsored regional meetings, work camps, and similar activities, and its program emphasized both religious and social action. An outgrowth of the NCMY was the Methodist Student Movement (MSM), which focused solely on the campus and provided professional staff for campus organizing. MSM's policies were, if anything, more radical than those of the NCMY.

Most of the mainstream Protestant denominational student federations were, to some extent, involved in social action programming and took stands on many semipolitical issues. Few were as "radical" as the Methodists, but all were to some extent concerned. Denominations, such as the Baptists with a strong Southern contingent and a relatively fundamentalist theological position, were the most conservative of the major denominational groups.

Efforts at unity among Protestant student organizations were quite intense during the fifties, although none of these "federations" ever managed to achieve substantial legitimacy among the rank and file of members of religious student groups. Among the first of these efforts was the United Student Christian Council, which was founded in 1944 as a federation of many of the Protestant denominational student groups as well as the YM and YWCA. In 1951, the USCC changed its name to National Student Christian Federation (NSCF), perhaps the largest of the umbrella organizations. The NSCF included the SCM (USCC), the Student Volunteer Movement, and the Inter-Seminary Movement, an organization of socially conscious seminary students from many of the nation's better-known Protestant theological schools. The NSCF itself in 1966 merged into the University Christian Movement (UCM), the closest thing to a genuine ecumenical Protestant student movement in the postwar period. The UCM, in turn, dissolved itself in 1969 in the turmoil of the New Left, leaving the Protestant student community with no unifying body. Various journals were sponsored by these federations, including *Motive, Campus Resource, Wind and Chaff,* and *The Source.* With the exception of *Motive,* none of these journals was influential on campus. The federations generally took a very strong interest in social action questions and were actively involved in international Christian student activities, particularly with the World Student Christian Federation. The federations also maintained contact with, and occasionally cosponsored activities with nonreligious student organizations. As the sixties approached, the various Christian student groups became active in the civil rights movement, and such activities were often coordinated by organizations such as the NSCF. Conferences sponsored by the federations, particularly during the early and middle fifties, were among the main arenas for discussions of civil liberties and other "controversial" issues of the period.

The Roman Catholic student movement was, overall, less radical and less political than its Protestant counterparts during the fifties, but there were some Catholic social action student groups. The most radical of the Catholic organizations was the Young Christian Students (YCS), a Chicago-based group with affiliates on many campuses. YCS emphasized social action and, in the fifties, stressed activism. YCS was particularly interested in racial integration. In its own words, the YCS was "a movement of the specialized lay apostolate in the colleges and universities. Through its social action nature, it seeks to answer the needs of people by answering the needs of students and civic communities of which the student is a member. YCS aspires to make it more possible for all people to lead a fully human and fully Christian life." These were strong words during the fifties and particularly in the Roman Catholic community, which was generally conservative. It is perhaps significant that the YCS dissolved in the late sixties after internal dissension and protracted the conflict with the Church hierarchy.

The National Federation of Catholic College Students (NFCCS) was founded in 1937 with thirty-five campus affiliates. The NFCCS was from the beginning concerned with creating unity among Catholic students and in expressing views on social and political questions.[36] By 1946, the organization claimed ninety-seven campus affiliates. At its 1946 conference, the NFCCS agreed to sponsor a National Commission on Interracial Justice and agreed to sponsor Interracial Justice Week. In 1948, the organization came out against universal military training, supported student relief efforts, agreed to help combat magazines featuring sex and crime, and called for a strong civil rights program. While probably not as liberal as its Protestant counterparts, the NFCCS was among the more outspoken Roman Catholic organizations during the fifties.

Probably the largest of the Catholic student groups was the National Newman Club Federation, founded in 1915, which had some 90,000 members in the early sixties, most of whom were college students. The Newman Clubs were only occasionally concerned with social action questions and probably were the most conservative of the national Catholic groups.

All three Catholic groups—YCS, NFCCS, and Newman Clubs—sponsored their own magazines, and all were primarily educational in social concerns during the fifties. As noted, the YCS was the most action-oriented and, by the early sixties, was involved with many New Left organizations. There was fairly little contact, in a direct organizational manner, between Catholic and Protestant student organizations.

All active religiously-oriented groups have not been dealt with here in detail. Several others should be mentioned as particularly concerned with political questions. The Unitarian youth movement, Liberal Religious Youth (LRY), which included the campus-based Channing Murray groups, was throughout the fifties strongly liberal in its orientation and willing to collaborate with political orientation of the adult Unitarian movement. The American Friends Service Committee (AFSC) was also active among students although it was not a national membership organization. AFSC's activities were limited to campus conferences, regional meetings, and work camps concerning social action and political questions. AFSC, often in cooperation with local campus Y groups, sponsored some of the most "radical" meetings on the campus scene in the fifties, and was not afraid to bring Communists and others to the campus to discuss questions related to civil liberties. As a fairly respected Quaker organization, AFSC had sufficient respectability to successfully sponsor these activities. Jewish organizations, particularly the widespread Hillel Foundations, were not involved in activist politics, but were generally fairly liberal in their orientations and often sponsored social action meetings of various kinds.

Thus, while the religious student organizations were by no means in the forefront of the activism of the fifties, and the majority of their energies were not directed at social action issues not to mention activist politics, the religious groups did play some role during the decade.

Again, as with the other organizations, the religious students grew more socially concerned as the decade drew to a close. During the depths of apathy, they kept some social concern alive on many campuses. And their national statements provided some counterbalance to the otherwise conservative trends.

To call the fifties a "silent decade" characterized entirely by apathy, is not quite the case. Without doubt, activism was at a low ebb, and the political consciousness of the student community seems to have been quite limited. Yet, organizations continued to function, and groups not normally directly involved with political concerns, such as religious organizations, took a fairly active role. The most influential elements of the activist movement during the early fifties were the liberal student groups, and these set the tone for the political culture on campus—although this culture was more limited and ineffective than it had been in the previous two decades. In this chapter, radical, religious, and conservative groups have been considered. These groups also played a key role in the small activist movement of the period. They maintained a political "presence" on campus in the case of the Socialist groups. Religious organizations played an active social action role and filled an important gap left by the demise of the large political groups of the thirties. And the conservatives, although limited in size and scope, presented a differing political ideology which had limited appeal among students.

In the next chapter, we turn to a consideration of the rebirth of activism. This rebirth, however impressive, could not have occurred without the existence during the "dark days" of the early 1950s of the political elements discussed in this chapter.

NOTES

1. "Memorandum on AYD" (document in the files of the Students for Democratic Action, November, 1944).
2. "House Unit Scores AYD as Subversive," *New York Times*, (April 16, 1947).
3. "Join Now! 600 AYD's Goal," *Student Outlook*, (October, 1946).
4. Stuart Cleveland, "Attack on the Campus," *New Masses*, 63 (April 29, 1947), pp. 18-20.
5. P. Des Marais, "The Young Progressives of America," *New Leader*, (August 14, 1948), p. 5.
6. Marvin Shaw, "Student Life," *New Foundations*, 1 (Summer, 1948), pp. 212-216.

7. *Ibid*

8. George Rawick, *op. cit.*, p. 395.

9. Marvin Shaw, "November 2nd and After," *New Foundations*, 2 (Winter, 1949), pp. 104-105.

10. Arthur Liebman, "The Active and the Silent Generations: Student Politics in the 1950's and 1960's," (Unpublished paper, Harvard University, 1971), p. 18.

11. *New Foundations*, (February, 1949), p. 19.

12. Leon Wofsy, "Report to the 2nd National Council of LYL, 1950," (New York: LYL, 1950).

13. George Rawlings and Dora Miller, "Stalinist Plans Thwarted at Madison Student Meet," *Labor Action*, (May 19, 1952), p. 7.

14. For a view of the Communist position on the student movement, see Gil Green, *The New Radicalism: Anarchist or Marxist?* (New York: International Publishers, 1961).

15. Much of the factual data in this section is taken from Bernard Cornfeld, "Leadership Training in an Oriented Agency," M.A. Thesis, New York School of Social Work, Columbia University, 1954, and from *SLID Voice*, the organization's newsletter.

16. Andre Schiffrin, "The Student Movement in the 1950's: A Reminiscence," *Radical America*, 2 (May-June, 1968), p. 28. See also Harold Lewack, *Campus Rebels: A Brief History of the Student League for Industrial Democracy*, (New York: SLID, 1953).

17. Harold Lewack, *op. cit.*, p. 23.

18. It is not possible here to develop a complete analysis of the growth of the New Left, of which the SDS was an integral part. For such an analysis, see James O'Brien, "The Development of the New Left," in P. G. Altbach and R. S. Laufer, eds., *The New Pilgrims*, (New York: David McKay, 1972), pp. 32-45.

19. There is no effort here to present a complete history of the Third Camp Socialist student movement, since there were during the fifties a number of other tiny fragments of organizations and journals from time to time. Nor is it possible to present a complete ideological picture of this element of the student movement. Curiously, there is no such analysis available. Examples of such tiny factions are the Libertarian Socialist League and the Industrial Workers of the World.

20. Arthur Liebman, *op. cit.*, p. 18, notes this may be a low figure since many student Socialists participated in activities without paying membership dues, particularly in the fifties, when organizational membership often required a strong moral and political commitment.

21. *Proceedings of the 17th National Convention of the YPSL, New York City, September, 1950*, (New York: YPSL, 1950).

22. *Proceedings of the 19th National Convention of the YPSL, New York, 1953*, (New York: YPSL, 1953).

23. A full discussion of the politics and history of the ISL is beyond the scope of this analysis. The ISL emerged from the Workers Party in the late forties under

the leadership of Max Schachtman and continued to function as a left-wing sect until 1958, when it merged into the Socialist party. The ISL's journal, *Labor Action*, which was edited by Hal Draper, was one of the few continuously publishing Socialist papers of the period which took an active and consistent Third Camp position. *Labor Action* featured many articles on students at this time. For a fictional account of the Workers Party and its participants during the forties, see Harvey Swados, *Standing Fast*, (New York: Doubleday, 1970).

24. Most of the data on this section is taken from *Labor Action* and *Anvil and Student Partisan.*

25. "Youth Unity Moved Up to February 12," *Labor Action*, (January 18, 1954), p. 4.

26. Bogdan Denitch, "YPSL Breaks Ties with Socialist Party," *Labor Action,* 17 (September 7, 1953), pp. 3-4.

27. *Young Socialist Review*, (May 15, 1954).

28. Neither conservative or religious organizations have received much serious analysis from scholars or journalists. In the rapidly expanding literature on student activism, only a tiny proportion of the material concerns these organizations while most deals with leftist groups.

29. See especially, Lawrence Schiff, "The Conservative Movement on American College Campuses," (Unpublished Ph.D. Dissertation, Harvard University, 1964).

30. Lawrence F. Schiff, "Dynamic Young Fogies—Rebels on the Right," *Transaction*, 4 (November, 1966), pp. 30-36. See also Lawrence F. Schiff, "The Obedient Rebels: A Study of College Conversions to Conservatism," *Journal of Social Issues*, 20 (October, 1964), pp. 74-96.

31. Douglas Cater, "Undergraduate Underground," *Reporter*, 10 (March 2, 1954), p. 31. For other commentary on conservative student groups from a generally friendly perspective, see M. Stanton Evans, *Revolt on the Campus*, (Chicago: Henry Regenery, 1961) and Edward Cain, *They'd Rather Be Right*, (New York: Macmillan, 1963).

32. M. Stanton Evans, *op. cit.*, p. 34.

33. M. Stanton Evans, *op. cit.*, p. 67.

34. Russell Kirk, "From the Academy: Campus Bugaboos," *National Review*, 2 (June 13, 1956), p. 19.

35. Factual materials have been culled from the *Intercollegian*, the organ of the National Student Council of YM-YWCAs.

36. *New York Times*, (February 16, 1946), p. 11.

CHAPTER SIX

The Revival
of Student Activism:
The Late Fifties

The late fifties saw a substantial revival in student activism in the United States and paved the way for the New Left, and the most substantial student movement in American history. This chapter is concerned with some of the trends and events which marked this resurgence of activism.[1]

Three issues were crucial in the revival of student activism at the end of the 1950s: civil liberties, peace, and civil rights, in that order. Established liberal and radical student organizations became increasingly involved with these questions, especially civil rights. Peace (including nuclear testing and the arms race), civil liberties, and civil rights were logical issues to spark student activism. The concern for civil liberties, evident throughout the 1950s among small numbers of students, was necessary in order to restore simple freedom of speech on campus and to assure students that speaking out on public issues was no longer dangerous.

Civil rights later became the focus of the student movement because of its dramatic nature and the nonviolent black movement in the South which developed in the years following the 1954 Supreme Court decision on desegregation. The emergence of a militant, nonviolent, direct action movement among Southern black students was a powerful impetus to Northern white college students. It provided white activists with important lessons in both tactics and depth of commitment necessary for student activism. It was also a major source of student disillusionment with the government and thus paved the way for the more militant New Left.

An interplay of many elements helped to stimulate the revival of activism. On the international scene, the Cold War had abated. The threat of a "monolithic Communism" was less imminent to many because of the fissures in the Soviet bloc evident in the Sino-Soviet dispute and the Hungarian uprising. Senator Joseph McCarthy was thoroughly discredited and the kind of repression which he represented had come to an end. Under President Eisenhower the country was at peace and (except for a short period) in the midst of general economic prosperity. A political relaxation affected the campus community, where in loco parentis began to weaken and administrators allowed increasing amounts of free speech. Faculty liberals, who had been silent for the most part, began to speak out and eased the way for similar student behavior.

One should not get the idea, however, that the end of the decade marked an immediate upsurge in activism. While growth did occur, the campus still was apathetic as a whole and only a tiny minority participated in any activist or liberal organizations. Yet, the atmosphere on campus did change, organizations started, and articulate and politically aware students formulated policies and perspectives for a growing nexus of groups and individuals active in a range of causes. It was a time of rebirth rather than of dramatic successes for the activist movement.

CIVIL LIBERTIES ACTIVISM

It is not at all surprising that civil liberties should have been an important issue to politically minded students during the fifties. Indeed, civil liberties was of direct interest and concern. As has been pointed out elsewhere, the fifties was a period when elemental rights of free speech, political association, and other liberties were abridged. In the universities, questions of civil liberties and academic freedom were actively discussed. A number of states, California, Illinois, and Massachusetts, among others, instituted loyalty oaths for teachers and professors and this became a controversial issue in academe. The most dramatic struggle over the loyalty oaths took place in California in 1949. A number of

University of California professors refused to sign the Regents-imposed oaths and were dismissed from their positions.[2] While the brunt of the struggle was carried by the faculty, students were involved in it as well. A number of other states also imposed loyalty oaths for teachers, including Illinois and New York, and similar campaigns to have them repealed occurred. Other abridgements of civil liberties were common on campus, and many of the key elements of civil liberties, common on campus in the sixties, were causes for dispute even in the late 1950s. University administrators, in keeping with the current of the times, often denied controversial speakers the use of campus facilities; some demanded membership lists from radical student organizations. These infringements often provoked sharp student reactions, especially among many liberal and radical groups who spent most of the fifties defending their right to exist as organizations. These groups were forced to focus on civil liberties questions rather than on their own political programs.

Before a broadly based student movement could arise on campus, the right to free speech and free assembly had to be reestablished, for few students were willing to put their futures on the line for political involvement as minimal as signing a petition. Thus, the student civil liberties movement was a prelude to the student activism of the late 1950s.

Activities related to civil liberties were evident throughout the decade. In 1951, students at the University of Washington organized the American Association of University Students for Academic Freedom, which quickly became a national organization, complete with newsletter. The organization never grew very large, but it collaborated with the American Association of University Professors and with other student groups. Its orientation was liberal. The group's publication, *Academic Freedom Newsletter*, contained news of threats to academic freedom. For instance, it discussed the new Oklahoma loyalty oath, the expulsion of a student at Wayne State University for refusing to testify before the House Committee on Un-American Activities, the firing of a professor at the University of Minnesota because of his politics, and attempts to censor the *Daily Californian* at Berkeley.[3] National liberal groups, such as the SDA and NSA, were actively concerned with civil liberties and academic freedom as well, and by the mid-fifties, the NSA sponsored a number of conferences on civil liberties and created an "academic freedom" project which issued publications and provided resources to campus groups. Religious student groups were also involved in civil liberties activities.

Communist student organizations were especially active in academic freedom and civil liberties cases. Communists were the group most seriously threatened by the repression of the fifties, and they saw the issue as attractive to liberal and uncommitted students. Most Communist-dominated efforts were in the form of ad hoc committees, such as the "National Youth Committee to Defeat the Mundt-Nixon Bill." Major amounts of time and energy were spent on defending Communists accused of violations of the various state and federal subversive laws. Few of these committees resulted in any ongoing organization. Liberal and other radical groups were more involved in broader questions related to civil liberties, or in campus-related issues such as the right of a speaker to be heard at a particular university. Issues such as the effort to repeal the loyalty oath attached to the National Defense Education Act in the late 1950s, were typical of those which aroused a good deal of interest on campus and which actively involved liberal students.

Much of the civil liberties activism of the early fifties was local or regional. For example, an attempt to remove Robin Hood from libraries in Indiana stimulated the formation of "Robin Hood Clubs" in Indiana and in other Midwestern areas for the purpose of defending civil liberties and engaging in anti-McCarthy activities.[4] Within a short time after its founding, Robin Hood Clubs existed at Wisconsin, Michigan, Michigan State, Roosevelt, and Wayne State Universities. Most of the activities were educational, focusing on raising consciousness about civil liberties causes. At Berkeley, a Student Civil Liberties Union (SCLU), loosely associated with the American Civil Liberties Union, was active in the continuing struggles concerning the loyalty oaths and other infringements on civil liberties. The SCLU expanded to other California campuses and sponsored several statewide conferences. The SCLU was supported by most of the political groups on the Berkeley campus and became a center of factional disagreement between them. Nevertheless, the SCLU was effective in arousing concern over civil liberties.

Specific infringements of academic freedom or civil liberties often stimulated student campaigns. At the University of Washington, students organized a large protest movement when three professors were fired in 1949. When the Ohio State University Board of Trustees refused to let a representative from the American Friends Service Committee speak on campus in 1952, most of the religious and political groups on campus protested and attempted to get the rule changed. An all-campus Civil Liberties Committee was formed at the University of Chicago to fight the proposed Broyles Loyalty Bill in the Illinois legislature. The campuses which were especially active in protesting the right of free speech, were those that had the highest political consciousness and had experienced the most political activity in the past, namely the larger, prestigious Northern and Western universities and some of the best private colleges. Smaller colleges, denominational institutions, and Southern schools generally were not the scenes of student protests.

The student civil liberties movement reached its height during a series of protests against the House Un-American Activities Committee (HUAC), the national symbol of the repression of the fifties, in May of 1960 in San Francisco. At that time, a session of HUAC was disrupted by protesting students. Some sixty-three students were arrested and many others injured in a large and violent demonstration. The affair received national publicity and brought the Berkeley student movement into national prominence.[5] The House Un-American Activities Committee produced a film concerning these demonstrations entitled "Operation Abolition" which was so biased that it actually helped to recruit supporters for the civil liberties movement and further discredited the Committee on campuses throughout the country. Local Committees to Abolish HUAC were organized in many areas.

In addition to local and regional activities, a degree of national organization around the civil liberties issue emerged. A federation of local civil liberties and anti-HUAC student groups was organized which provided speakers and literature to local groups, and coordinated the showing of films on campuses throughout the country. This federation was under the leadership of radical students, most of whom had previously been involved in campus politics, but it had no specific ideological viewpoint and was devoted to purely civil libertarian and anti-HUAC activities. While the civil liberties campaigns did not build a continuing student movement in America, and the coordinating activities ceased when the HUAC issue was no longer a key campus issue, the civil liberties movement laid the groundwork for more widespread and politically focused activity. First and foremost, they proved that political expression was possible as growing numbers of students participated in politics without repression. The civil liberties movement used a range of tactics, from educational campaigns to direct action projects which included the disruption of meetings of official agencies. This was an important step for the American student movement since, before the 1960 San Francisco riots, few students were willing to risk arrest or academic discipline for political aims. The movement also reached a broad segment of the student community. It involved a range of other organizations, from many campus religious groups to the small Communist and Socialist student groups. Further, the civil liberties groups by and large had no adult sponsorship and few financial resources, although many liberals supported the movement. In this sense, it was a beginning of the New Left tradition of independent student organizations.

THE STUDENT PEACE MOVEMENT

The student peace movement was one of the major movements of the late fifties and early sixties. It involved larger numbers of students than the civil liberties efforts and was effectively coordinated on a national basis. By the early 1960s, the peace movement was able to attract national publicity with demonstrations in Washington, D.C., with 5,000 participants being the largest such turnouts since the 1940s.

While the peace movement had been dormant in the late forties and early fifties, several of the organizations which later led the resurgence of peace activism existed throughout the period and influenced the types of projects later groups took up. Two of the mainstream peace organizations of the period were the Fellowship of Reconciliation (FOR) and the American Friends Service Committee (AFSC), both of which were pacifist. The FOR and the AFSC, often in cooperation with campus religious organizations or with Socialist student groups, sponsored summer programs, peace caravans which involved small numbers of college students in travelling to various campuses speaking on antiwar subjects, and occasional demonstrations. Both groups suffered a decline in the early fifties. The FOR, which was the largest pacifist organization in the country lost 3,000 members in the 1950s, bringing its total membership, only a small proportion of which was students, to around 9,000.[6] The American Friends Service Committee, with the

FOR, kept concern for peace alive through its regional programming and occasional conferences related to international affairs and pacifism. But, by and large, until the late 1950s, the peace movement lay dormant, devoting itself to educational programs. Only the Peacemakers, a tiny radical pacifist group, engaged in direct action.

During the early fifties, there was almost no antiwar activism on the campus despite the fact that, as noted previously, there was a good deal of student discontent with the Korean War. Prior to 1956, the little antiwar activism that there was came from three sources: Communist, Socialist, and pacifist students. One of the major focuses of Communist students was antiwar projects. They operated through ad hoc campaigns, such as the one to collect signatures on the 1949 Stockholm Peace Petition. Socialist students were active after 1955 in periodic demonstrations protesting armed aggression like the Suez Invasion in 1956 and the Soviet intervention in Hungary in the same year. Socialist students picketed the French consulates in protest against French colonial policies in Algeria in 1955. They also participated in established peace groups.

The pacifists were few in numbers but were well organized and represented on a number of campuses around the nation, particularly at the more liberal theological seminaries, such as Union Theological Seminary in New York and Chicago Theological Seminary. Affiliated with national groups like the Fellowship of Reconciliation (for religious pacifists) or the War Resisters' League (for nonreligious pacifists), pacifists were involved mainly in educational activities. They had relatively little impact on the campus as a whole. In the late fifties, they helped form more radical direct-action oriented groups like the Committee for Non-Violent Action (CNVA), which was instrumental in developing the tactics of nonviolent civil disobedience which were used so effectively by Dr. Martin Luther King and the civil rights movement.

While the peace movement, both on and off campus, was fairly small and certainly without influence during the period from 1949 to 1957, the major adult peace groups kept the movement alive and, from time to time, involved students in various activities. The legacy of Henry Wallace's presidential campaign, which was focused on war-peace and foreign policy questions as much as anything else, was used without much success by the Communists. Thus, despite the lack of notable success, antiwar groups and sentiment did not disappear from the American scene during the fifties, and the revival of the peace movement depended, at least for organizational support, on these remnants.

The student peace movement was not mainly a phenomenon of the fifties, indeed its main strength, particularly that of the Student Peace Union (SPU), its main organizational manifestation, was between 1960 and 1962. Devoted to a single issue, the peace movement was able to attract many students who had no previous experience in ideological politics. Despite this, some broader ideology underlay most peace groups' activities and programs. In some cases, the ideology was pacifism; in others, socialism, communism, liberalism, or strong Christian concern. Like the civil liberties or civil rights movements, the peace movement trained many in political activism, and many alumni of groups like the SPU later became active in SDS or other New Left groups.

The student peace movement developed during the Cold War, at a time when the large majority of Americans were convinced that there was a danger of Soviet expansionism and that the United States was the main bulwark against international communism. Most antiwar activists shared this anti-Communist perspective, and almost all agreed that it was tactically impossible to confront some of the basic ideological tenets of American public opinion. Thus, the ideological atmosphere in the middle and late 1950s was far different than during the sixties, and the character of student activism was also different. In this sense, there is a wide gulf between the perspectives of student activism in the fifties and that of the New Left. By and large, the antiwar movement dealt with issues which were somewhat peripheral to the mainstream of the Cold War—questions such as nuclear testing in the atmosphere and biological weapons, or issues surrounding a nuclear test ban treaty. By the end of the decade, the political equation changed somewhat. The Sino-Soviet dispute proved that "monolithic" communism was not so monolithic. Dulles' notions of "massive retaliation" began to seem ludicrous in the eyes of Americans increasingly sophisticated about foreign policy. Scientific evidence concerning the dangers of atmospheric testing of weapons, the dangers of nuclear fallout in case of attack, and other matters received attention in the mass media. In 1957 the National Committee for a Sane Nuclear Policy (SANE) was organized by a number of prominent liberals and radicals in New York and spread rapidly throughout the country. SANE's emphasis was educational and it strove to influence national policy about disarmament. Although some tried to taint SANE with the "red" label, the more liberalized atmosphere of the late fifties permitted SANE to function effectively. Many have credited SANE with helping to prepare American public opinion for the Nuclear Test Ban Treaty signed in 1962.

The major national student peace organization was the Student Peace Union (SPU), which flourished as a national force on campus from 1959 to 1963, although it continued to survive as a smaller, mostly regional organization centered in New York, for several years longer. There were, however, several other national or regional groups which existed at the same time. The student affiliate of the National Committee for a Sane Nuclear Policy was formed in 1957, two years before the SPU, largely by Socialist students in New York City. Student SANE became a national organization, with chapters in many of the larger campuses; its main strength was in New York City and in the middle-Atlantic states. Student SANE's official policies were controlled by adult SANE and its offices were in SANE's national headquarters in New York City. Much of its budget also came from the adult organization. Despite these links, the student group moved to the left of adult SANE. The adult organization's lack of a clear ideological position and its rather ill-defined liberalism were translated on the student level into a willingness to accept any and all ideological viewpoints within the organization. As a result, students who were pro-Soviet joined the organization in large numbers and assumed major leadership roles, particularly in New York. Despite this, Student SANE's programming and orientation remained tied to the adult group's policies, and this "conservative" current was largely supported by pro-Soviet elements and Communists.[7] But the McCarthy period was not quite at an end, and SANE was attacked by Senator Thomas Dodd and the Senate Internal Security Subcommittee for having Communists in its organization, particularly in the New York area. National SANE, after much debate, moved to "purge" Communists and other pro-Soviet elements, and demanded that members adhere to a strict pro-West position. Student SANE, in response to this interference with the ideological freedom of its members, was vociferous in its opposition to the national organization's policies, and as a result lost much of its strength as well as support from adult SANE. The students were very much concerned about civil liberties within the peace movement, and were joined in this debate by many more radical elements in the peace movement.[8] Due in part to the internal crisis in SANE and in part to the emergence of the SPU, Student SANE was virtually dead by 1960. Pro-Soviet students continued to participate in the peace movement, although there was no national organization which expressed their position. The journal, *Sanity*, published for several years by an independent group at the University of Wisconsin, in part represented Student SANE in the movement.

An organization exemplifying the pacifist trend in the student peace movement was the College Peace Union (CPU), founded in 1959 by New England students aided by the regional Fellowship of Reconciliation and American Friends Service Committee. The CPU's staff was paid by either the FOR or the AFSC, although the CPU had a great deal of autonomy. The CPU coordinated student peace activities in New England, and was instrumental in establishing CPU groups on campuses without peace groups. The organization combined local groups which were strongly pacifist, some which were oriented toward radical action, and affiliates like Harvard's Tocsin, which was concerned with effective research on disarmament and foreign policy issues. A fairly broad policy statement united these groups effectively, and regional conferences and the activities of the full-time staff provided some sense of unity. The CPU merged with the Student Peace Union in 1960, becoming the New England Region of the SPU.

The analysis here of the post-1958 student peace movement focuses largely on a single organization, the Student Peace Union (SPU), which was founded in 1959 and functioned actively until 1963.[9] The SPU was not the only element in the student peace movement, but it was the largest and most geographically diverse organization of its time. Between 1960 and 1962, it was probably the largest radical student organization, with a paid membership of over 4,000 and a monthly *Bulletin* with a circulation of more than 10,000. Moreover, the SPU's membership contained most of the political elements in the student peace movement except for the Communists. Independent of adult organizations, the SPU was strongly supported by the FOR, the American Friends Service Committee, the Socialist party, and several other groups. Thus, the SPU was the mainstream of the peace movement at the time, and a good example of the scope and orientation of the political student movement in general.

The origins of the SPU lie in the pacifist stream of the antiwar movement and in the Middle West. In this sense, it was similar to the College Peace Union. The impetus for the organization came from a small nucleus of pacifist students active in the regional programs of the American Friends Service Committee. The AFSC had, through an active program of speakers and conferences, helped establish peace groups at a number of local campuses in the Chicago area. Most of these groups were small and pacifist in their orientation. The Students for Non-Violence, a group at the University of Chicago which contained both pacifists and Socialists, was in contact with interested students in the area. With the assistance of a staff member of the Chicago office of the AFSC, a regional newsletter was established and a national conference called. Some fifteen schools were represented at this meeting, which took place in 1959, and the SPU was officially founded. Due in part to the organizing work of several of the regional staff members of the AFSC in various parts of the United States and in part to the fact that there was no national student peace organization to which local groups could turn, the SPU grew rapidly into a national organization. The SPU's *Bulletin*, a monthly printed publication featuring reports on chapter activities, national peace actions, and some discussion of relevant foreign policy related issues, provided further cement to the growing peace movement.

Organizationally, the SPU was controlled by its annual national conventions. These meetings, which attracted up to 400 students during SPU's most successful period, made basic policy and elected a National Council, which in turn elected a Chicago-based National Steering Committee. The National Council met twice a year and the Steering Committee, composed of national office workers and some of the most active Chicago-area leaders, met weekly to make policy decisions. A good deal of power, naturally, devolved on the Steering Committee. There was a good deal of diversity in SPU local groups, with the national organization encouraging local autonomy. The only requirement for SPU membership was agreement with a fairly broad statement of purpose, a statement which emphasized the futility of war, the responsibility of all of the great powers for the arms race, and a commitment to social justice. This statement, with its emphasis on a "Third Camp" position—placing responsibility on both the United States and the Soviet Union for the arms race and the Cold War—effectively eliminated

Communists from membership, but left the organization open to almost anyone with a concern for peace, save the most progovernment conservatives.

The organizational strength of the SPU rested with its local chapters, of which there were about sixty in 1962, and on its regional groupings, which existed on the West Coast, New England, Northern Ohio, Southern Ohio, the Chicago area, New York, Washington, D.C., the South and Middle Atlantic. These regions held conferences and, in several cases, supported regional field staffs. The national office in Chicago supported several field secretaries, whose responsibility was travelling to various campuses, maintaining contact with existing SPU groups, helping with educational programming, and organizing new chapters. Through these field secretaries it was possible for the national office to maintain its communication with local groups and also keep some political and tactical control over quite a diverse organization. The national office also published the *Bulletin* and a *Discussion Bulletin*, which was mimeographed and sent to all SPU members and which featured longer articles on a range of matters relating to tactics, organizational philosophy, and politics. The national office also took responsibility for fund raising, a very difficult undertaking for an organization which had no specific commitments from adult organizations. SPU relied heavily on support from several adult groups, including the AFSC and the War Resisters' League, local chapters and individual membership dues, and from individual adult contributors. While a substantial share of the budget was paid by SPU members, the largest single source of revenue was from individual adult contributors.

The political orientation of the SPU was an important aspect of its development and a source of both strength and weakness. As noted, the early orientation of the SPU was strongly pacifist, but pacifist with a strong radical bent. The organization's first national secretary and the individual primarily responsible for its founding was both a pacifist and a Socialist. Another strong element in the SPU's leadership was socialist. Soon after the SPU's founding, members of the Young Peoples Socialist League, especially the left Labor party faction, became active in the organization and exerted an important influence on the national office and the Steering Committee. These YPSL members strongly adhered to a Third Camp position and steered the SPU consistently toward a position which criticized both the United States and the Soviet

Union and committed the organization to a radical stance on both domestic and foreign issues.[10] A final element in the SPU, which was perhaps strongest among the majority of rank-and-file members, was a brand of liberalism. Most SPU members had little previous experience in politics and had no coherent ideological position. They were simply concerned about the dangers of nuclear war, willing to participate in a movement which opposed the arms race, and fairly pragmatic in their politics. The ideological subtleties of the SPU's Third Camp position probably had little impact on most of these individuals. These ideological currents—pacifism, socialism, and liberalism—coexisted in the SPU, although not without periodic factional struggles.

The SPU, like most other student political movements, had its share of factional problems and disputes, but power was consistently retained by the pacifist-socialist alliance which was responsible for the group's early organization. Strongly Third Camp policies kept out most Communists and pro-Soviet elements although, since the SPU did not conduct careful investigations of its members, a number of such individuals were members and a few were influential in local chapters or regional federations. The national staff tried, with reasonable success, to maintain the ideological "purity" of the organization through intense political work among affiliated groups and at times by trying to manipulate the selection of delegates to conventions. The national office was particularly interested in preventing members of the Young Socialist Alliance (YSA), a Trotskyist organization, from achieving leadership positions in the SPU. It is unlikely that the majority of the SPU's members were very concerned about the nuances of Socialist politics. While the SPU was not driven apart by these factional problems, as the SDS was a decade later, factional politics played a somewhat disruptive role in the organization.

The SPU, as an independent student organization not affiliated with any adult group, was in a sense a precursor of the New Left in this regard. In fact, the SPU had important relations with adult liberal, radical and peace organizations, but the important difference between the SPU and, for example, Student SANE or the SDA, was that no adult organization could dictate policy or shape the direction of the SPU. Indeed, there were important differences between the SPU and those adult groups which most actively supported it—the War Resisters' League, FOR, and AFSC. In 1963, for example, the SPU leadership took a rather critical stance on the Cuban revolution that conflicted with the views of a number of the prominent radical pacifists who were instrumental in providing money. SPU strongly opposed SANE's "purges" of its pro-Soviet elements on the basis that this action was an infringement of democratic process. But because of its independence and the basic direction of SPU policy, none of the adult groups cut off the organization's resources completely. Prominent pacifists and radicals, such as Norman Thomas, A. J. Muste, Bayard Rustin, David Dellinger, and David McReynolds, were important in helping the SPU maintain its financial stability. It is nevertheless true that the SPU was never lavishly supported and its annual budget of some $20,000 in its most active years was always in jeopardy.

SPU local groups differed substantially in size, political orientation, style, and activities. And while SPU had active chapters at most large and traditionally political campuses, such as Chicago, Harvard, Illinois, Berkeley, and Columbia, it was particularly strong at smaller colleges and universities. The largest SPU chapters existed at Antioch and Oberlin Colleges in Ohio. At Antioch, at one time, close to half the student body belonged to the SPU. Strong chapters also existed at Shimer, Knox, North Central, and Lake Forest Colleges in Illinois, at Carroll and Lawrence in Wisconsin, at Drake and Grinnell in Iowa, and at Dartmouth, Brown, New Hampshire, and other schools in New England. The organization was especially strong in the smaller Midwestern schools which had some tradition of radicalism or pacifist sentiment. The orientation of a particular SPU chapter depended often on the individuals who were most active in it. Some were strongly pacifist in orientation (this was true of some of the smaller schools and of theological seminaries such as Union Theological Seminary in New York). Others were dominanted by Third Camp Socialists, as were the chapters at the University of Chicago, Columbia and Berkeley. Probably the majority of SPU groups were rather unclear of their precise political direction and not overly concerned with it.

The style and activities of local SPU groups differed as well. The major emphasis of the SPU nationally and locally was on educational programming. Direct action was also a strong element in the organization. Active local SPU chapters sponsored speakers on topics related to foreign affairs and the arms race. National SPU field secretaries were occasionally speakers as were local faculty members who agreed with

SPU views. Debates between faculty members for and against a specific topic were also sponsored. Occasionally, nationally prominent radicals would speak for SPU groups. Such individuals as Bayard Rustin, Linus Pauling, David McReynolds, and Norman Thomas spoke for the organization. The more active chapters sponsored study groups in which members read books in common and discussed them. Sessions oriented around discussions of national SPU policy also occurred. Regional groups held periodic conferences, which provided opportunities for activists from various schools to meet. Some SPU groups were more active than others. Some stressed educational campaigns, local petitions, and "traditional" activities, while others were more radical in their approach, engaging in direct action projects, picketing missile bases, and the like. Most SPU groups participated in direct action projects, and this was something of a transition from the almost purely educational orientations of the early fifties to the much more action approach of the New Left. Anti-ROTC campaigns were common, as were "anti-military balls." In the early sixties, SPU groups and SPU individual members were actively involved in the civil rights movement and the national SPU strongly encouraged students to participate in civil rights work.

The SPU sponsored a number of national peace actions and regional demonstrations and was successful in mobilizing for the period large numbers of students. Beginning in 1959, SPU organized "Students Speak for Peace" demonstrations on November 11. These campus-oriented activities provided a national focus for a series of local events which differed substantially from campus to campus. A nationally coordinated leaflet was distributed, but local groups planned their own activities. SPU was also a sponsor, along with other national peace organizations, of the annual Easter peace marches, which were held in major metropolitan areas. Students were usually among the most numerous participants in these marches.

In February, 1961 the SPU sponsored its first major national Washington, D.C. demonstration. Masterminded by the Harvard SPU affiliate, Tocsin, the demonstration aimed at underlining student opposition to a resumption of atmospheric nuclear testing, and speaking directly with government officials of the Kennedy administration in an effort to "communicate" with them. The SPU somewhat reluctantly agreed to this approach, although it was clear to most of the National Council that the "power elite" were not about to listen to a group of students. The Washington Action Project was quite successful and attracted some 10,000 participants, the large majority of them students. Observers noted that it was the largest such demonstration since the thirties. It received national publicity and, despite the fact that student leaders were invited into the White House to speak to some of President Kennedy's aides, nuclear testing in the atmosphere was resumed a few weeks later.

After the Washington Project, the SPU became the largest radical student organization in the United States. Established in most parts of the country, reasonably well coordinated nationally, and with 4,000 national members (and at least that many who considered themselves SPU members but did not pay dues), the organization was at the height of its influence. The SPU's *Bulletin* achieved a circulation of 10,000 or more, and was one of the first radical publications to focus substantial attention on the Vietnam war. The focus of the peace movement remained on nuclear testing, disengagement in Europe and various disarmament plans, but the political situation in America and the world was gradually changing. The Cuban missile crisis of 1962 was a severe shock to the peace movement, which was totally unable to influence the course of events which brought the world to the very edge of nuclear war. The signing of the Nuclear Test Ban Treaty in 1963 had a similar effect for a different reason. Many in the peace movement thought that they had won a major victory and that further activism was unnecessary. Finally, the focus of the student movement was shifting from foreign policy to civil rights with the explosion of the sit-ins and freedom rides and the tremendous moral appeal of civil rights activism. The SPU, which supported the civil rights movement, was still a "single issue" movement concerned with foreign policy and could not take leadership in the civil rights struggle.

Thus, in late 1963 and 1964, it became clear that the Student Peace Union had reached its high point and was on the decline. The 1964 convention attracted many fewer delegates, and the leadership of the organization pressed the SPU to disband and participate in other radical groups. The convention agreed to disband the organization, but a group of delegates, mainly from the New York area, decided to continue with the SPU name and function as a national organization. While the "reformed" SPU was largely centered in the Middle-Atlantic states, it continued with the help of the War Resisters' League to function until 1966.

The decline of the SPU was due not only to the changing domestic and international political situation but to internal factors as well, factors which have direct relevance to the later development, strengths, and final decline of the New Left. The SPU was dominated by pacifists and Socialists who adhered to a Third Camp position. This political tendency was able to maintain its hegemony over the organization for its entire existence (even after it moved to New York), but the cost proved to be stultifying ideological appeal and to some extent tactics. The SPU refrained from cooperating fully with student groups which did not share its viewpoint. For example, cooperation between the SPU and the journal *New University Thought*, which was also headquartered at the University of Chicago, was very limited for ideological reasons. Such cooperation might have aided both enterprises and strengthened the student movement as a whole. The factional disputes between the SPU leadership and Trotskyist students is another example, although in this case it is clear that the Trotskyists would have simply used the SPU for their own aims. The SPU's national leadership was unable to develop younger leaders who could have taken over the organization and by 1964 found that there were few experienced activists who were ideologically "trustworthy" to assume key leadership positions. This failure to look to the future, either in terms of ideological changes or new leadership, was a defect of the organization. While the political perspective of the SPU brought it a good deal of strength in its early years, it was a source of rigidity later. At the beginning, the SPU remained somewhat in the mainstream of American politics by its Third Camp policy and its strong criticism of the Soviet Union. Later, with the clear development of the Sino-Soviet dispute and other international changes, the SPU retained a rigid response to international questions based on its unchanging ideological position.

Despite its ultimate, and perhaps inevitable decline, the SPU played an important role in the growth of the New Left. It proved that it was possible to build an independent radical student movement and to effectively function without adult ties. It demonstrated that a combination of traditional educational approaches and militant direct action was a viable program for a student organization, and it indicated that a radical leadership could direct a mass a good deal less sophisticated and activist than itself.

THE CIVIL RIGHTS MOVEMENT

Two elements took over the leadership of the student movement from the student peace movement generally and the SPU in particular. These were the civil rights movement, particularly the Student Nonviolent Coordinating Committee (SNCC), and the Students for a Democratic Society (SDS). Clearly, the most important element in the 1962-1965 period was the civil rights movement. The student civil rights movement was, along with the antiwar movement, the most important contribution that students have made to American society. They focused substantial attention on the plight of black people in America. The experiences of white college students in the various summer civil rights campaigns provided some tangible results in terms of voter registrations; it also provided those students with tactical and ideological training which was very important in later stages of the New Left. It is not possible here to survey the entire student contribution to the civil rights movement, but some attention is given to its early period and the contribution which the civil rights movement made to the broader student activist movement in America.[11]

Race relations were, of course, a concern both on campus and in society before the growth of the militant civil rights movement in the early sixties. While no major national civil rights movement emerged prior to 1960, and there was no effective nationally coordinated effort in the area, there was nevertheless substantial concern with civil rights and some activity on campuses in various parts of the country. Despite the growing public concern with the rights of minorities and particularly of blacks, there was no major breakthrough in civil rights until the Supreme Court decision of 1954, which outlawed racial discrimination in public education. Further court decisions concerning interstate transportation, the courts, and other aspects of American life followed. Organizations like the National Association for the Advancement of Colored People (NAACP) pressed in the courts for a further lowering of the barriers of discrimination, and the NAACP and other groups such as the Congress of Racial Equality (CORE) engaged in various public campaigns to press for racial equality. The Montgomery Bus Boycott of 1956, organized by Martin Luther King, Jr., brought the tactic of non-violent resistance and civil disobedience to national attention and made King a prominent figure. The organization of the Southern Christian Leadership Conference (SCLC) under King's leadership opened a new chapter in the civil rights struggle since the SCLC was a Southern-based organization with a commitment to direct action. By the end of the decade, both blacks and whites felt an active civil rights campaign was possible, and the stage was set both for the militancy of SNCC and other civil rights groups and for the move toward "black power" on the part of the activist black community.

Civil rights activity occurred on campus at a rather modest level between the end of the war and 1958. There was a growing awareness, at least in the more liberal Northern and Western universities and colleges, that the plight of the black, both on and off campus, was unjust. A number of universities gradually dropped overt discriminatory practices, integrated dormitories and other facilities, and modestly increased the numbers of blacks studying at the institutions. But the proportion of blacks in the student population remained extremely low and many of the black students were in black colleges in the South. Campus-related facilities also received some attention during the fifties, and fraternities were under pressure to end discriminatory practices. Liberal white students were often in the forefront of these activities and political student organizations were very much involved with race relations. Yet, while small beginnings were made, race relations was hardly an issue which shook many campuses.

The largest and most important civil rights organization of the fifties, the NAACP, had an active youth division which was founded in 1936 and which during the fifties had a membership of 20,000 nationally. While only a small minority of these were on campuses, there were eighty-five college NAACP chapters in the late 1950s, many of which were located in predominantly white schools. The NAACP was concerned with educational programming and legal action to end segregation, and their college affiliates were never particularly activist oriented. Typical college NAACP activities were pressure to remove racist textbooks at Queens College in New York and a campaign to establish scholarships for black students at Oberlin College in Ohio.[12] In the mid-fifties, the NAACP was active in legislative work, and attempted to enlist student support in pressuring Congress to enact meaningful legislation to end discrimination. From time to time, liberal and radical white students were active in NAACP youth work, but the organization never achieved major campus significance in the fifties.

The first major civil rights organization which had its roots on the campus was the Congress of Racial Equality (CORE), which was founded by a group of pacifist students at Chicago Theological Seminary in 1942. Among the founders was James Farmer, long-time director of CORE and a key figure in the civil rights movement of the fifties and sixties. Farmer, like many of the other early CORE activists, was both a pacifist and a Socialist. In its early days CORE had strong ties to the Fellowship of Reconciliation. CORE pioneered nonviolent direct action by picketing a downtown Chicago restaurant which would not serve blacks. At the time, this kind of activity was quite novel. Later, CORE affiliates in many Northern cities (CORE remained largely a Northern urban-based organization) applied direct action tactics to many projects.

One of the first campus sit-ins took place in 1948, when CORE members at the University of Kansas had to be carried from a football field after protesting racial discrimination in Kansas athletic programs. CORE also engaged in sit-ins at a local campus restaurant which would not serve blacks. CORE's focus moved away from the campuses in the early fifties as it established itself as a national civil rights organization. Direct action projects against discrimination in theaters, efforts to integrate eating facilities and other public facilities, and similar concerns were the mainstay of CORE activities in the fifties. CORE also sponsored annual interracial institutes in the summer which many students attended. These institutes were both educational and action-oriented, and participants often researched a particular racial problem and then tried to solve it, first through negotiations with those involved and later with direct action demonstrations if negotiations failed. CORE, more than any other organization, pioneered the adaptation of Gandhian nonviolent direct action techniques to the solution of American social problems. The unique blend of pacifists and those concerned mainly with civil rights made this possible. The leadership of several articulate black pacifists, such as James Farmer and Bayard Rustin, was crucial in this effort.

The most important campus civil rights activities of the fifties were local. For example, when Autherine Lucy was denied admission to the

University of Alabama in 1956, students there circulated a petition in her behalf. A few other schools engaged in support action, including the University of California at Berkeley, where 3,000 students signed a petition for Lucy's admission to Alabama. Student efforts had some effect in ending segregation in women's residence halls at Indiana University in 1953; in the mid-fifties, students at the University of California tried to obtain pledges of nondiscrimination from Berkeley landlords (with moderate success); and a number of Northern universities began exchange programs with Southern black colleges. These, and many other similar actions, were undertaken by a variety of groups, ranging from student religious groups (as at North Carolina, where students tried to persuade merchants to pledge nondiscrimination in 1960) to student governments, local CORE or NAACP chapters, or occasionally liberal or radical political groups. These local actions were sometimes successful and often for the first time raised the issue of race relations on campus. While it is difficult to estimate how many campus-based action projects occurred in the fifties, their number must be in the hundreds, involving colleges and universities in all parts of the nation. In some cases, as at the University of Chicago in 1948, student pressure on the university to move toward racial equality brought favorable response from academic officials. In others, such as Alabama and many other Southern schools, student pressure had few results.

Fraternities were one of the foci of civil rights activists in the fifties. One of the last bastions of the "traditional" values of the college campus, most fraternities engaged in blatant discriminatory practices. These were often due to the policies of their national organizations. The fraternity movement, while still strong, was losing its position of dominance on many campuses.[13] By 1956, there were as many University of California students living in private housing as in fraternity houses, a marked change from previous periods.[14] Due to the influence of the veterans who invaded the campuses in the late forties and to a growing liberalism among young people, neither the fraternity sorority subculture nor the various discriminatory practices of these organizations had the attraction they once had. Many local campuses, including Michigan, Berkeley, Chicago, Wisconsin, and Amherst, were the scenes of campaigns to end fraternity discrimination.

Two large civil rights demonstrations took place in the fifties, which indicated something of the potential for mass civil rights activity. These two demonstrations, called the Youth Marches for Integrated Schools, took place in 1957 and 1958 in Washington, D.C. They were organized by the more radical wing of the civil rights movement and were coordinated by Bayard Rustin. Among the largest demonstrations in Washington, D.C. since the thirties, the marches attracted some 10,000 to 15,000 young people, many from college campuses in the East and the Midwest. The marches were strongly supported by CORE, YPSL, and other radical groups, and by some labor unions. The students who participated in them had a feeling, rare in the late fifties, that a mass civil rights movement was a possibility in America.

All of these activities—the marches, local campus campaigns, and educational activities—were a prelude to the main thrust of the civil rights movement which began in 1960 in Greensboro, North Carolina and continued for several years, the sit-in movement. The sit-ins were, of course, the first major mobilization of Southern black students and, in this sense, were a breakthrough in American student activism. The civil rights movement also greatly affected Northern white students and stimulated major organizing efforts.

The Student Nonviolent Coordinating Committee (SNCC), the main group in the student civil rights movement, was organized in 1960 by black and white militant students in the South, and within a short time supported more than 100 full-time organizers in its various projects in the South. SNCC was an organization of organizers, and not a mass membership group, but its influence on the student community was very great. Not only did it succeed in mobilizing unprecedented numbers of previously uninvolved black college students in the South, but "Friends of SNCC" groups were started on many Northern campuses and contributed to the struggle by collecting money for the Southern movement, engaging in direct support activities in the North, and from time to time sending Northern volunteers to the South to participate in projects. One of the most widespread support activities was a national picketing campaign against the Woolworth company for its refusal to serve blacks in its Southern stores. (CORE was also actively involved in the boycotts of Woolworth.) Woolworth stores in many college towns in the North were picketed for varying periods of time in a campaign which eventually was victorious. Out of the "Friends of SNCC" came the Northern Student Movement (NSM) in 1961, a predominantly white middle-class student organization centered in Eastern, prestigious colleges. NSM was primarily a support organization for the Southern civil rights struggle, and it collected funds for the Southern groups, sent volunteers, and engaged in political work in the North.

As is well known, the sit-ins and the later Freedom Rides attracted both national attention and sympathy. The liberal American middle class admired the black (and some white) students who engaged in nonviolent tactics for the elemental rights of public service and transportation. It became clear only later that the struggle for racial equality was very complex, and extended not only to the "racist" South but to the "liberal" North, where de facto housing and school segregation was endemic. Civil rights activists also felt in the late 1950s that it was increasingly important to shift the focus of the civil rights movement from the campus and to involve more ghetto and rural blacks in the struggle. The emergence of the ideology of Black Power in the civil rights movement and the subsequent departure of whites from the movement was caused in part by a realization by blacks that the achievement of racial equality was a very difficult task and that masses of black people had to be mobilized in order to attain the desired goals.[15] The emergence of Black Power essentially forced white students out of the civil rights movement, substantially disorienting politically active whites, and served to force a reassessment of the white radical movement.

When the civil rights movement began, many thought that moderate pressure from socially concerned young people would end segregation and racism. The enthusiasm for the civil rights movement in 1960 was substantial. At least 3,600 were arrested in the South in the year following the Greensboro sit-ins and 50,000 participated in demonstrations.[16] The reasons for Southern black students embracing the sit-in struggle are not difficult to understand. Martin Luther King's nonviolent movement showed that it was possible for blacks to struggle for equality without unacceptable physical risks. The mood of the nation was perceived to have changed, even if the South remained implacably racist. Thus, the typically politically quiet and solidly middle-class black Southern colleges were producing a new generation of students who were willing to take risks for racial equality and were able to organize a movement. Indeed, although the SNCC was no paragon of organizational efficiency or political sophistication in its early days, it was still able to pull together an effective national movement.

SNCC quickly became the key black student organization in the

South. In the early sixties, its leadership, while militant in terms of nonviolent action, was not revolutionary in the ideological sense of the term. SNCC closely cooperated with SCLC, CORE, and other civil rights groups to organize the various summer projects which brought many white students to the South to work on voter registration and other projects. Many of the experiences of the civil rights movement of the early sixties proved quite sobering to militant black activists. While marginal gains were made in opening up public accommodations to blacks, in voter registration, in school desegregation, racism remained the order of the day in the South, and de facto segregation in education, housing, and the economy remained intact in the North. In addition, blacks who came up against the power structure found that Southern officials were serious in their effort to crush the civil rights movement and that substantial risks were often involved for activism. The federal government, while maintaining outward commitment to desegregation, moved slowly if at all much of the time. Thus, events had a "radicalizing" effect on militant black student leadership. It was at this time that Black Power developed as an ideological current in the black student movement and by 1966 had become a dominant force. The ideological underpinnings of SNCC, and many other black student groups, became self-consciously revolutionary, the commitment to nonviolence as a means of social change weakened and then totally disappeared, and links with white radicals were gradually severed. In the mid- and late sixties, SNCC under the leadership of Stokely Carmichael, who himself shifted from nonviolent activist to Black Power revolutionary in a matter of a year or so, was a far different organization than it had been during the period of the early sit-ins. Indeed, its impact on the student movement as a whole lessened. Other groups, such as the Black Panther Party, developed and became important among black students with a good deal of support, although with very little *direct* participation, from white student activists. It is perhaps significant that two of the key founders of the Panthers, Huey Newton and Bobby Seale, were students at the time.

The white student movement was also greatly affected by the civil rights movement, particularly by the sit-ins and the aftermath. The current of interest in civil rights activity was maintained through the fifties, as has been noted, especially after the Youth Marches for Integrated Schools. The radical organizations such as YPSL, the SPU, and others took a strong interest in civil rights activities. Other student organizations from the National Student Association to most of the liberally oriented Christian student movement did also. Thus, while the sit-ins were hardly expected, Northern white students were already interested in race relations and quite sympathetic to civil rights activity. Indeed, the sit-in movement had a profound moral impact among Northern students. The issues were so morally clear and the tactics seemed so correct that few in the student community opposed the sit-ins.

The National Student Association, the National Y, and other groups moved quickly to supply assistance to the Southern movement and by 1963, recruited hundreds of volunteers to participate in summer civil rights activities. Various projects, such as Freedom Summer and the COFO voter registration campaigns of the early sixties attracted substantial Northern support. Many of those who came South to participate found themselves in an environment quite different from their campuses or from the middle-class surroundings in which they had grown up. The experience, in addition to being quite dangerous, was shattering emotionally and intellectually for many. Many of the alumni of the Southern movement came home committed radicals. It is not surprising that many of the alumni of the civil rights movement became campus activists at home and effectively changed the orientation of the Northern student movement. Mario Savio, of Berkeley fame, got his first experience in the South, as did many other radical leaders like Tom Hayden of SDS. Almost immediately upon returning home, many of the veterans of civil rights activity applied tactics learned in the South to civil rights activities in the North, often with quite dramatic results. In San Francisco, students conducted sit-ins against a number of automobile dealers in order to insure the hiring of more blacks. These demonstrations resulted in many arrests and contributed to the atmosphere of the Berkeley student revolt of 1964.

In a sense, the complexity of the civil rights question and the unwillingness of the nation to make more than token changes both destroyed the civil rights movement itself and contributed to a major radicalization of the American student movement. As students began to search for the reasons why it was impossible to achieve racial equality in the North and why repression of civil rights workers was commonplace in the South, they began to look to the "system" itself as the source of evil. And, with the exception of a very small minority of Socialists in previous periods, the realization that revolutionary change by over-throwing capitalism was necessary to assure social justice was something quite new to the vast majority of even those involved in activist movements.

THE CONSERVATIVE REVIVAL

While the thrust of this volume—and of student activism in the fifties—was in a liberal or radical direction, the conservative student movement saw something of a revival in this period too. The most important conservative student organization in the United States is the Young Americans for Freedom (YAF), founded in 1960. Unlike the education-ally oriented Intercollegiate Society of Individualists, the YAF saw it-self as an "activist" organization and had engaged in a series of direct action projects, including sometimes violent confrontations with radical groups. The YAF was founded at the initiative of William F. Buckley, Jr., and its first conference, held in September of 1960, occurred on his estate in Connecticut and attracted a hundred students from forty-four colleges. The original YAF program stressed anticommunism and a commitment to individual freedom and a free-market economy. In 1960, YAF played a key role in defending the House Un-American Activities Committee, which was then under attack from liberal and radical students. In 1961, the organization established its journal, *Young Guard*, which was published monthly. By 1961, YAF claimed a membership of 21,000 on 115 campuses, but it is quite clear that this is an exaggerated figure.[17] By 1970, YAF claimed a membership of 50,000, which was said to have doubled from the previous year's fig-ures. About 60 percent of this was made up of college students.[18] Its 1970 convention was attended by 500 delegates, who vowed to actively attack campus radicals, to infiltrate student newspapers and govern-ments, which it claimed were dominated by liberals. Much of the stress of the YAF has been on combatting the overwhelming liberalism on campus.

YAF undoubtably had more influence on campus and on the na-tional scene than any of the conservative groups of the fifties. For example, a national rally it sponsored in New York City in 1962 at-tracted 18,000 people and featured many nationally prominent conservative speakers. YAF sponsored a campaign to take over the National Student Association in the early sixties and generated some support, although it was unable to achieve its goal. The YAF then urged colleges to disaffiliate from the NSA and had some success in this regard, particularly among smaller schools and Southern colleges.

The YAF had a good deal of influence within conservative circles, even if it did not shift the American student community away from its overwhelming political liberalism or stem the rise of the New Left and the antiwar movement. YAF activists were key elements in the presidential campaign of Senator Barry Goldwater in 1964, for example, and were a powerful influence in Young Republican circles in the sixties. Indeed, a number of YAF alumni found themselves on the staffs of conservative senators and now hold staff positions in the Nixon Administration. YAF activities include the publication of the *Young Guard* and the holding of annual conventions, which generally attract up to 1,000 students. While YAF has on several occasions claimed financial difficulties, the organization has continued to provide salaries to a number of staff members and to publish an expensive journal. In comparison to liberal and radical groups, the YAF is wealthy indeed.

CONCLUSION

It is clear from this chapter that the New Left was not merely a product of the 1960s but had important roots in the previous decade and began in the late 1950s. The "silent fifties" produced, in fact, the vociferous and militant student movement of the sixties. Indeed, it can be argued that the campus provided a degree of leadership in terms of reviving political activism in the society as a whole. A large constituency, although by no means the entirety, for civil liberties, peace, and civil rights activity came from the campus, particularly from students.[19] But prior to the New Left of the sixties, it was seldom true that the student activist community provided the major leadership for broad social movements. Up to the development of the independent student organizations of the late fifties, student activists took their leadership from adults. As is indicated in this chapter, the end of the fifties marked a critical turning point in American student activism as students struck off on their own.[20]

The period covered in this chapter marks both an end and a beginning. Some of the characteristics evident among students in the early part of the decade—careerism, fear of political expression or action, overwhelming anticommunism, and a feeling that liberals or radicals were a beleaguered minority—marked the activism of the middle and late fifties as well. The leaders of the SPU and early SNCC were very careful not to stray too far from the mainstream of American society, which was militantly anti-Communist, somewhat anti-intellectual, and strongly nationalistic. The memory of McCarthyism was strong, particularly for the sons and daughters of the liberal middle class—and these provided much of the support for student activism. Activists weighed the implications of their programs carefully, not only in terms of the possible success or failure of a particular demonstration but in terms of government investigations and expulsions from the university. Such considerations were very far from the minds of the activists of the sixties.

The campus culture of the fifties also had something to do with the nature of student activism, although it is very difficult to provide quantitative evidence on this matter. Most commentators indicate that the basic life styles and mores on campus were not very different from those of the rest of the society. Generational conflict, as measured by public opinion polls as well as overt signs, was nonexistent. Styles in clothes, music, and dance were, of course, distinctive to some degree, but they were not in basic conflict with the society. Indeed, during the early and mid-fifties, folk music, which later became an important part of the political revival, was limited to a very tiny proportion of the student population, particularly those involved in politics. The "radical subculture," which existed on many of the more active campuses, was small and generally fairly self-contained. In the late fifties, this subculture expanded somewhat and, perhaps most significantly, received widespread attention in the mass media. The Beat Generation, while not centered on the campus, had an impact on campus and provided a "model" for an alternative life style that was, to some degree, influential among increasingly large numbers of students.[21] There is no doubt that the hippies and the more generally widespread counterculture of the sixties were stimulated by the experiences of the late fifties. In the late fifties, there was probably less contact between the political subculture on campus and the small counterculture.

The late fifties marks the rebirth of a student movement of significant proportions in the United States. This rebirth was centered around important political issues rather than ideologies, and the "old left" ideological groups, while active, did not grow dramatically or become a key political force. They did, as has been pointed out, provide much of the leadership for the "single issue" movements which led the revival. The student movement of the late fifties reflects rather accurately the political concerns of the middle classes at the time—civil liberties and the reestablishment of free speech, peace and particularly a slowing of the arms race, and civil rights, with an emphasis on fulfilling the promise of the 1954 Supreme Court decision on desegregation. As students began to see the ideological implications of their actions and understand the limited success of the movement, it was possible to pull together the specific concerns of the late fifties into a student organization which linked many issues and began to provide the beginnings of an ideological framework—the Students for a Democratic Society.

The late fifties developed some of the tactics used in the sixties. Direct action leading to and including civil disobedience were used with much effect in this period. The combination of educational efforts on and off campus and increasingly militant action became a hallmark of student activism. While by no means original to the late 1950s, the use of nonviolent direct action of the kind pioneered by Dr. Martin Luther King and the civil rights movement was perfected at this time and became a hallmark of American social protest activities.

And the revival of the late fifties was not limited to the left. Conservative student groups experienced unprecedented growth, and although the campus remained dominated by liberal sentiment, the conservative revival of the period was probably the highest point for such student activism in recent American history. The religious social action emphases continued, but were by and large taken over in organizational terms by politically oriented groups. Organizations like the YM-YWCA were not generally in the forefront of social concern as they were in previous years, in large part because many of their members simply participated in existing political groups. Thus, the late fifties was a period of key importance to American student activism, and marked the real origin of many of the currents felt so dramatically in the New Left of the sixties.

NOTES

1. Several recent volumes have attempted, with only limited success, to deal with the history of the sixties, and to some extent these studies are useful for understanding the context of student activism in this period as well. See William O'Neill, *Coming Apart: An Informal History of the Sixties*, (Chicago: Quadrangle, 1971), and Ronald Berman, *America in the Sixties: An Intellectual History*, (New York: Harper, 1968). For a more radical perspective, see Carl Oglesby, "Notes on a Decade Ready for the Dustbin," *Liberation*, 14 (August-September, 1969), pp. 5-19.

2. The story of the California oath controversy is described in D. Gardiner, *The Great Oath Controversy*, (Berkeley: University of California Press, 1967).

3. *Academic Freedom Newsletter*, 1 (March, 1952).

4. George Rawlings, *Young Socialist Challenge*, (May 17, 1954).

5. The rise of the Berkeley student movement, and particularly the events surrounding the 1960 riots, are covered in David Horowitz, *Student*, (New York: Ballantine Books, 1962).

6. For an overall analysis of the American peace movement, see Lawrence Wittner, *Rebels Against War: The American Peace Movement 1941-1960*, (New York: Columbia University Press, 1969). See also Patti Peterson, *op. cit.*

7. Interview with Richard Sack, former president of the University of Pennsylvania Student SANE chapter, May 20, 1972.

8. For a detailed discussion of the "purge" in SANE, see A. J. Muste, "The Crisis in SANE," *Liberation*, 5 (July-August, 1960), pp. 10-13.

9. Much of the material on the Student Peace Union comes from the author's own experience as National Chairman from 1959 to 1963, and from the archives of the SPU, located in the University of Chicago library. For post-1964 development of the SPU, see Francis Carling, *Move Over: Students, Politics, Religion*, (New York: Sheed and Ward, 1969). See also Alan Brick, "Peace Moves on the Campus," *Fellowship*, 19 (September 1, 1959), pp. 8-12, Kenneth Calkins, "The Student Peace Union," *Fellowship*, 26 (March 1, 1960), pp. 6-8, and Philip G. Altbach, "A History of the American Peace Movement," *Fellowship*, 31 (January, March, July, and September, 1965), pp. 22-27, 28-32, 25-29, and 28-32.

10. An interesting political analysis of the SPU is provided by Donald McKelvey in his unpublished paper "SPU and SDS: Continuity and Change," (1967). In his paper, McKelvey argues that the SPU was totally dominated by the YPSL, and the organization was manipulated to remain faithful to the YPSL position.

11. Much has been written about the student role in the civil rights struggle. Perhaps the best account remains Howard Zinn's *SNCC: The New Abolitionists*, (Boston: Beacon Press, 1964). See also Southern Regional Council, *The Student Protest Movement: A Recapitulation*, (Atlanta: Southern Regional Council, 1961), and Staughton Lynd and Roberta Yancy, "Southern Negro Students: The College and the Movement," *Dissent*, 11 (Winter, 1964), pp.

39-45. For the participation of white Northern students, the best discussion is N. J. Demerath, III, Gerald Marwell, and Michael Aiken, *Dynamics of Idealism*, (San Francisco: Jossey Bass, 1971).

12. NAACP, "Crusade for Freedom: The Story of the NAACP's Youth Program," (New York: NAACP, n.d.).

13. For a detailed discussion of the role of fraternities in discrimination, see Albert McClurg Lee, *Fraternities Without Brotherhood*, (Boston, Beacon Press, 1955).

14. Verne A. Stadtman, *The University of California, 1868-1968*, (Berkeley: University of California Press, 1970), p. 431.

15. See Gene Roberts, "From 'Freedom High' to 'Black Power:' The Story of SNCC," *New York Times Magazine*, (September 25, 1966), pp. 21-29, 119-125.

16. Calvin Lee, *op. cit.*, p. 111 (quoted from Howard Zinn).

17. Calvin B. T. Lee, *op. cit.*, p. 114.

18. *New York Times*, (September 14, 1970), p. 1.

19. The role of faculty, particularly in the middle and late fifties, should not be overlooked. This role is particularly dramatic when contrasted with the overwhelming attention given to the student role in activism in the sixties. This topic is dealt with briefly in S. M. Lipset, *op. cit.*, pp. 197-235.

20. There are, of course, important exceptions to this generalization. The Trotskyist Young Socialist Alliance, for example, was always closely controlled by the adult Socialist Workers Party, as was the Progressive Labor Movement in the sixties. Adults continued to provide guidance to the YPSL, although not without conflict.

21. The best account of the "Beats" is found in Bruce Cook, *The Beat Generation*, (New York: Scribners, 1971).

CHAPTER SEVEN

Continuity and Change:
The New Left
in the Context
of American Student Activism

This chapter delineates some of the major themes in American student activism and links the movement of the past to the New Left of the sixties. There is a good deal of historical continuity in student activism, as there is in other areas of American politics, and therefore it is important to consider events on campus in social and in historical terms. It is very difficult to make firm predictions about future trends on campus on the basis of the material presented in this volume. Some claim that the emergence of such a potent student movement during the sixties will have a long-term effect on the nature of student activism in America. On the basis of this historical analysis, however, it would seem that such a development is not at all assured. There is no question but that American students can again take an important place in the political equation on campus and in the nation—but their assuming such a role is by no means assured.

THE IMPACT OF STUDENT ACTIVISM

When placed in comparative perspective, American student activism appears to have a minimal impact on either society or the university. American students have never overthrown a government, nor have they been a cause of major political instability. The campus has not been the locus of any moderately successful revolutionary movement. The nation has been politically stable and most of the major political currents of the twentieth century have not begun among students. Yet, students have had some effect, even if it has fallen short of fomenting revolution. The campus community was the primary source of counterculture in both the 1920s and the 1960s. Politically, students in the 1930s kept an awareness of foreign policy issues, particularly the issue of peace, alive. In the 1960s, the student movement was partly responsible for making anti-Vietnam war sentiment a majority opinion. This antiwar movement was in large part responsible for the withdrawal of Lyndon Johnson from the 1968 presidential race and the success of George McGovern's bid for the Democratic nomination in 1972. Students were instrumental in the early days of the civil rights movement in dramatizing the plight of blacks and assisting in the passage of the landmark civil rights legislation in the early sixties. In short, the political impact of student activism, while not as dramatic in the United States as in some other countries, has been felt from time to time.

The cultural impact of activism has also been substantial, and is perhaps more difficult to quantify. The Beat Generation of the fifties, while not originating on campus, had a good deal of support among students. Both the folk song revival of the fifties and the growth of rock in the sixties had strong campus support. The various counterculture movements of the sixties had strong campus support. The spreading use of various kinds of drugs has been particularly marked on campus, and has spread from the universities to other segments of society. Changing attitudes toward marriage and the family have been reflected on campus and only thereafter spread more widely. Again, whether these developments are a permanent part of the American culture remains to be seen, but it is certainly true that university students and the campus community have been the seedbed for many of the cultural innovations of recent years.

On campus, the effects of student activism have been mixed. By and large, the direction of the American university has not been determined by students, but by forces in society combined with the academic community itself. Students have, of course, been the consumers of higher education, and have had some influence in this capacity.[1] But they have seldom been involved at the policy-making level and have only recently been taken into account by academic decision makers. There is in America no tradition of student co-government, as there is in Latin America, and the concept of in loco parentis has further removed students from policy making because of its assumption that students are wards of the university and that the university has responsibility for their moral well-being as well as their intellectual training. It is in the case of in loco parentis that students have been most successful in modifying policy and eventually eliminating parentalism in the university.

American students have seldom been interested in participating in academic governance, nor in formulating plans for university reform. Student activists have been from time to time quite critical of the universities, but they did little more than complain. During the 1960s, a significant portion of the student community was highly critical of the nature of higher education and of the direction of the university, but few proposals for change were forthcoming. It is perhaps significant that, in general, those students who have taken an interest in academic reform have been the more moderate elements of the activist movement. The level of discontent during the sixties was unprecedented and perhaps, as a result, academic policy makers began to include students at various levels of the governing process, while some curriculum changes were made to meet student demands. It has been common at many universities for many formerly required courses to be dropped, for a relaxation of the foreign language requirement, and for more "relevant" courses to be included in the curriculum. At a few institutions, students have been included in policy-making positions, and students are now commonly part of the evaluation process for faculty promotion. For the most part, however, these measures have not changed the basic nature or direction of American higher education, and are limited to a small proportion of the universities.

American student activism has been focused almost entirely on broad political and social questions and not on academic or university matters. The few instances of concern for campus-based issues have been linked to political questions in society, such as the campus free speech issues of the 1950s or the links between the universities and the Vietnam war in the 1960s. The size and scope of student activism has depended on political currents in society. During the twenties and fifties, when political repression was in evidence and the general mood was fairly conservative, student activism was limited and had little impact on or off campus. However, in the thirties, a period of social crisis when the society was looking for economic and political alternatives and dissenting political views were more accepted, student activism reached a high level. The early fifties, which was the lowest ebb of student political organization and concern, were notable for their generally apolitical atmosphere and repressive tendencies toward dissenting groups. The sixties was the height of student activism and forces in the society at large contributed to it. An increasingly unpopular war (especially among educated young people), elements of a counterculture spreading to larger segments of the population (particularly the young), the perceived failure of accepted liberal alternatives to solve pressing social problems, and a sense of security in political expression, all led to the growth of a potent social protest movement on campus, a movement which had repercussions in society as well.[2]

American student activism is, of course, not isolated and is related to currents around the world. Indeed, some comparative perspective is quite useful when examining activism in the United States. In the recent past student movements in advanced industrialized countries have had less of an impact on their societies than student movements in developing countries. The political, social, and economic infrastructure of advanced societies is much more dense than in developing societies, and students must compete with many other elements for influence. In the United States, a well developed press and mass media, fraternal organizations, a complex network of local, state, and federal government agencies, all limit the power of the student community on national, or even statewide events. There is, in America, no clear tradition of student activism, and such activism is not considered a legitimate part of the political culture. In many other countries, students are considered political actors by the public and often by the government. This gives a student movement an entree to the political system which it does not have in the United States.

American higher education is a very large and complex enterprise and cannot claim to educate an elite in American society. There is little elite consciousness among American students, as there is in many other countries, and no expectation that the student leaders of today will be the government leaders of tomorrow. Furthermore, the universities are geographically spread out, and significantly there is no large and prestigious university in the vicinity of the national capital. For students at the militant University of California at Berkeley to physically confront the national government is a difficult task. The social class origins of the American student population are also diverse, as are their political backgrounds. These factors make the organization of an effective mass student movement in America very difficult, if not impossible. There are some exceptions to this general situation. The mass media, combined with the clear social crisis of the 1960s, gave an unprecedented section of the American student population—primarily those in the prestigious universities and in metropolitan areas—a sense of community for perhaps the first time, a consciousness which made the coordination of the national protests following the Cambodia-Kent State events possible.

The American university also mitigates against continuing political activism. The American system of courses and credits, with frequent examinations, makes sustained activism more difficult. The pressure for students to keep up with their academic work is great, and there is little of the tradition of the "professional student leader" as there is in some other countries. In many nations, examinations at the end of a year of work or even after several years is common, and this permits activists to ignore academic responsibilities for fairly long periods of time. The growth of nonstudent youth communities in major centers of activism in the United States (Berkeley, Madison, Ann Arbor, for example) is changing this situation somewhat by creating a semipermanent community of individuals inclined to participate in activist movements.

Finally, the American political system has proved fairly impermeable to pressure from students. The political structure has been stable over the years, and there is a tradition of distrust of both the involvement of intellectuals (and, by implication, students) in politics and against the creation of nonmainstream political parties and pressure groups. Indeed, one of the few times that student activism had an impact on national politics, the antiwar movement of 1968, was a time when the government suffered from a great deal of distrust among significant proportions of the population because of the Vietnam war. It remains to be seen whether the "McGovern Phenomenon," which has included many non-Establishment elements, will remain a force in American politics.

Only a minority of American students have been active in student movements. Indeed, politically involved students have been less than 15 percent of the student population at any period between 1900 and the present. At times, like the 1920s, the proportion of activists fell to 1 percent or 2 percent. Larger numbers have participated in demonstrations at one time or another during periods of high activism, such as the "peace strikes" of the thirties and the Kent State-Cambodia crisis of 1970. This does not alter the fact that the minority of activist students have shaped the political culture of the campus and by and large made it liberal in orientation. At times, such as in the fifties, the predominant overall campus trend was apathy, but still whatever political current existed on campus was liberal. During periods of activism, this political minority has had quite an impressive impact on the campus. Thus, data from campus opinion polls which emphasize the conformist and conservative nature of the student community do not negate either the impact or the importance of the activist minority.[3]

THE ORIENTATION AND IDEOLOGY
OF AMERICAN STUDENT ACTIVISM

One of the themes of this volume is that student activism in the United States has exhibited a strong degree of continuity over time. While organizations and movements have been short-lived and ephemeral, there are issues and ideological concerns which are common throughout its history. There are three "streams" evident in American student activism; the liberal-radical, the conservative, and the religious. These streams have persisted, in various guises, over the period under discussion.

The concerns of American student activism have exhibited amazing constancy. Foreign policy has been the key thrust of student activism, particularly of left-of-center activism, although many other topics have attracted the interest of students. Foreign policy was the issue around which the National Student Federation of America was organized in 1919, and it was the moving force behind the American Student Union in the 1930s. It was also responsible for the short revival of activism at the end of World War II, and was one of the major elements in the rebirth of activism in the late 1950s. Cultural concerns have also been a continuing theme, particularly in the twenties and sixties, when there was widespread discontent with American culture. Students, when they have been concerned with culture, have been critical of the established norms; certainly, the recent counterculture reflects this historical current. This emphasis on foreign policy and on culture reflects the middle-class nature of American student activists. The liberal American middle class, from which most students emerge, has not been very much concerned with labor unions, working conditions, or similar matters. They have been interested traditionally in foreign policy questions, cultural issues, and such matters. The recent student concern about the environment, for example, fits well into the framework of middle-class concerns in America. Concern with labor organizing and other more working-class oriented questions has been, in general, limited in the development of student activism, although radical groups have from time to time made strenuous efforts to move in this direction.

Other issues that have preoccupied student activists have been more varied and specific to particular periods. The interest in civil rights in the late 1950s and early 1960s was in response to a growing concern in society. The movement was initiated by black students, and provided an opportunity for white Northern college students to express the moral concern and the feelings of many middle-class Americans, and to use newly developed tactics (nonviolence). A desire to change education has cropped up from time to time in response to conditions both within the universities and in society. In the twenties, the development of the American university into a larger, more impersonal institution triggered criticism of the process of education and of the universities, and initiated several educational reforms, such as experimental colleges like the new educational program at the University of Chicago under President Hutchins. Similarly, in the sixties, students, who were dissatisfied with the continued growth of higher education and with university involvement in the government and its foreign policy, turned their attention of questions of "student power." Students were successful in achieving some curricular reforms and stimulating the establishment of several experimental colleges.

While many issues have remained central since 1900, the nature of student activism and student organizations has changed. The traditional links between student organization and adult parties and groups have been weakened, if not eliminated. One of the great strengths of the student movement of the sixties was its independence, in both an organizational and an ideological sense, from adult political movements of the "old left." Many of the more socially concerned Christian student groups have split from their adult sponsors and, as a partial result, have lost organizational purpose and stability. The factionalization of the SDS and the dissolution of the University Christian Movement in the late 1960s exhibit some of the dangers of total independence.

The cultural content and impact of the student movement have changed. While the sixties resemble the twenties in the sense that segments of the student population disagreed with the current of the culture, the nature and impact of the cultural "revolt" of the sixties has been more far reaching.[4] The growth of the Beat Generation in the fifties and the hippies in the sixties was important to student activism, despite the fact that neither of these were specifically student phenomena. Both the beats and the hippies represented a dissatisfaction among a portion of the youth population with the overall direction of American life and culture. This dissatisfaction was translated into overt rejection of standard norms and the adoption of new ones which were at odds with much of the establishment culture. Neither the beats nor the hippies played a directly political role—indeed, the Beat Generation made its disdain for political activity quite clear. However, both had an impact on political activism on campus and helped to infuse the student community with a certain style of activism[5] through their attacks against the achievement orientation of the broader society and a concomitant emphasis on noncompetitive values and experiments with new life styles. Self-awareness, and the use of drugs to achieve it, and rock music are other characteristics of counterculture. Many committed devotees of the counterculture are no longer enrolled in the universities, although they often remain in university communities and provide manpower for the student movement. In and around such academic centers as Berkeley, Ann Arbor, Madison, as well as in the larger cities, nonstudent members of the "youth community" can be found in significant numbers. This is a new phenomenon.

While American student activism shows a good deal of historical continuity in terms of key issues and concerns, it also displays it in its ideological orientation. Ideologically committed radicals have been active in liberal and radical student groups since 1900. In addition, ideologically oriented groups of various kinds have existed through most of the century, with varying degrees of cohesiveness and impact. Yet none of these ideological organizations was able to recruit large campus memberships. American students have never been willing to join organizations like the Young Communist League or the Young Peoples' Socialist

League in large numbers because of their primary orientation toward ideological politics and their commitment to a special *weltanschauung*. They have actively involved themselves, however, in organizations and movements like the American Student Union or the SDS which have been led by ideologically committed radicals but which focus on broader social issues and do not require their members to become committed to an ideological position. It is perhaps significant that both the SDS and the ASU began to decline precisely when their ideological component became more pronounced. Socialism, Marxism, and other ideological perspectives have attracted small numbers of students but never have been able to make mass converts among students. Thus, American students have been attracted to issues rather than ideologies, and the best efforts of committed Socialists and others to infuse large student movements with a conscious brand of ideological politics have been unsuccessful in every case. Mass student movements have taken radical positions; for example, the American Student Union in the 1930s was explicitly anticapitalist and the SDS anti-imperialist, but a full-scale ideological critique of American society has never been very attractive to participants in activist movements, not to mention the broad masses of American students.

The ideological orientation of much left-of-center student activism, if it has existed at all, has been left-liberal in its direction rather than radical or basically anticapitalist. Specific demonstrations or campaigns may have strong anticapitalist implications, but most of the participants and, for that matter, most of the organizations have not shared this view. This impression is backed up by both the policy positions of student organizations and opinion surveys of American students at various periods of time.

The size and scope of American student activism have changed at various periods. The American Student Union of the thirties had a larger membership than the SDS of the sixties, but it is clear that the SDS and its supporters had a greater impact on both campus and society than did the ASU. According to S. M. Lipset and E. C. Ladd, Jr., American students have become more liberal over a period of time, and thus the constituency for liberal and radical activism has probably grown.[6] Due to a dramatic increase in the student population itself, there is no question that the absolute numbers of students involved in activist movements have increased, although it is not clear that the proportion of students involved is greater than it was during the militant thirties.

The involvement of student organizations such as the Student Christian Movement or the YMCA in social concern activities has changed over time. The most socially active of the religious groups have remained predominantly liberal in their orientation and have committed themselves to social activism during much of the twentieth century. They have, however, been most visible during periods of general quiet on campus. When nonreligious organizations have been active and involved, the religious groups have generally supported their work rather than undertaking their own. Indeed, when activist groups are strong, the whole spectrum of campus politics moves in a more active direction. This is as true for religious and conservative groups as it is for liberal and radical organizations.

THE SIXTIES IN THE CONTEXT OF STUDENT ACTIVISM

The 1960s was the period of the greatest national impact of student activism, and while this volume cannot deal in detail with this decade, it is appropriate that it be discussed in the broader context of American student activism. The movement of the 1960s represents a continuity with the themes and, to a lesser extent, the organizational and ideological patterns of previous periods of student activism. Despite this continuity, some of the innovations made by the movement in the sixties, such as the dissolution of major links with adult organizations and parties and the lack of reliance on traditional "old left" politics and ideologies, were the very elements that made it possible to build a student movement of substantial proportions.[7]

The major thrust of activism in the sixties was the antiwar movement, and this focus clearly reflects the historical traditions of American student activism. Despite this similarity, the anti-Vietnam war movement diverges from the movements of the 1930s: earlier movements were more "ideological" in the sense that, at their height, the United States was not at war and students were not directly threatened with the draft. This was the case with the Oxford Pledge movement. The protest against the Vietnam war differs with previous antiwar movements precisely because it is one of the very few antiwar movements which flourished while the country was at war. Previously, student antiwar movements collapsed when the fighting began. During the Korean War, while there was much student opposition, there were few overt protests against the war itself and little draft resistance. In the seventies, when students are no longer directly threatened by the draft due to draft reforms and the lessening of the American combat role in Vietnam, there is a lower level of student activism and antiwar organizing. Despite the divergencies with the past, the broad antiwar theme is still one of the constants of American student activism.

Many of the ideological orientations of radical student activism can be traced to previous periods, although the dominance of adult groups has substantially diminished. The varieties of Marxism, social democracy, and other ideologies still affect political activists, although in the sixties and seventies new ideological strains have developed which are represented by Marxists like Herbert Marcuse and Mao Tse-tung and less ideologically oriented thinkers like Wilhelm Reich and Paul Goodman. The movement of the sixties managed to synthesize various ideological and cultural positions more successfully than its predecessors—the SDS certainly exemplifies such synthesizing at some stages of its development. Yet, the ideological positions taken by the leadership of groups like the SDS—and these positions changed rapidly owing to changes in both leadership and circumstances—had relatively little effect on the rank and file membership of most New Left groups. The overriding concerns of most activist students in the sixties, as at other periods of American student activism, remained issue-oriented.

In addition to the more traditional kinds of ideological orientations, a number of other developments characterized the sixties which are both very important and somewhat different than currents observable in the past. Of perhaps most importance is the counterculture—the hippie movement, the widespread use of drugs on campus and off, the dramatic (although perhaps not permanent) shifts in life styles among young people, rock music and its impact among the young, and other elements. While the counterculture has been largely apolitical in the direct sense, there is no question but that it has contributed to anti-establishment views on campus and has been by and large sympathetic to the political New Left. While it is almost impossible to define an "ideology" for the counterculture in its many aspects, there is no question but that the mixture of culture and politics in the sixties was a key element in the popularity and strength of the New Left.

Ideologically, there were a number of currents which characterized the sixties which were somewhat unique as well. The splits in the SDS in the late sixties exhibited some of these elements.[8] The emergence of the Weatherman faction of SDS is the most dramatic of these new developments.[9] This group, devoted to urban guerilla warfare and violent confrontation with the "system" attracted a fairly small but very committed following and for a short time had substantial sympathy among campus radicals. Both the theory and, more importantly, the practice of terrorism by student groups was an unprecedented event. Another current in student activism in the late 1960s was a substantial anti-intellectualism among some elements of the New Left. Again, this was a major change from the past, since student radicals have, if anything, been overly concerned with ideological disputation and the attempt to create a viable ideological position. Many in the late 1960s, however, including the Weathermen, were openly scornful of the ideologies of the "old left" and uninterested in creating a new synthesis. They were, rather, concerned largely with "action" and a dramatic effort to end the Vietnam war and bring about major social change.

One final element of the student movement of the sixties which was unprecedented was the growth of the women's liberation movement. While by no means limited to the campus, a substantial impetus for the women's movement came from women who had been involved in the radical student movement and who were dissatisfied with the role of women in these organizations.[10] Without doubt, the women's movement has had a major impact both on student radicalism and some impact on society at large. The existence of independent campus women's organizations and the injection of women's issues into campus politics for the first time is certainly an important development, and one which will without question have a continuing impact on the nature of student activism and perhaps on university life generally if current discussions about eliminating sex discrimination in hiring, opening day care centers, and other aspects are followed through. Thus, it can be seen that many changes occurred in the sixties which are both linked to past elements in student activism and at the same time are differentiated from them.

Ideology has been an important factor in the student movement. It often has been preoccupied with searching for a "correct" and sophisticated ideological position and an accompanying analysis of the nature of American society and the tactics for social change. Such was the character of the YSL, the YPSL, and at times the SDS of the 1960s. At times this ideological concern has hindered effective action.[11] The example of the American Student Union, by hewing to the line of the Communist party, succeeded in destroying itself in 1939-1940; the Student Peace Union, in part because of its adherence to a "pure" ideological position, was unable to link up with other forces in the student community which might have strengthened the peace movement in the late fifties. The Port Huron Statement of the SDS, drafted in 1962, tried to free the movement from the focus on ideology and was the impetus for developing a new analysis of American society which would have more appeal to the campus.[12] The SDS in the early 1960s, if anything, stressed activism and derided ideology. Only in the late sixties, when the situation on campus had become difficult, did the organization and the movement become bogged down in factional ideological struggle.

An examination of Students for a Democratic Society (SDS), the major student organization of the 1960s, illustrates the degree of continuity between the sixties and earlier periods. During its early period, the SDS brought an original political approach emphasizing activism and cooperation among all students. The SDS stressed a campus orientation and accepted students as legitimate participants in social change in America. This was a significant different from many previous student groups, which tended in the past to consider students a secondary element, in part because orthodox Marxist theory did not see students or intellectuals as important elements in radical change. SDS theorists posited the idea that educated people constituted a kind of "new working class" in a technological society and thus, in part, students had a role in furthering social change.[13] This SDS emphasis gave student activists a greater feeling of self-confidence and the idea that they were part of a historical movement.

The SDS emerged at a time when the Vietnam war was escalating and campus protest against the war was emerging as a major concern. It was also a time when the civil rights movement was undergoing a change as the result of the failure of nonviolent tactics to bring the required changes and blacks shifted to Black Power as an ideology and organizing tool. Because the SDS was a multi-issue movement, it was able to shift from issue to issue in order to appeal to campus activists.

Of course, the SDS miscalculated on several occasions as to what issue would capture students' imaginations. For example, it stressed economic action programs among white working-class elements in 1966 instead of participating fully in the antiwar movement.[14] But, by and large, its lack of ideological dogma permitted SDS to join in and lead various activist movements. SDS did have a fairly consistent, "loose" ideology stressing the need to overthrow American capitalism. Within this anticapitalist stance, SDS was able to concentrate on a range of issues, from welfare problems of poor people to imperialism in Latin America or Vietnam.

SDS experimented with new organizational forms. The most famous of these was the notion of "participatory democracy."[15] Previous radical student groups were either based on "democratic centralism" (which permitted the group to impose discipline on its members in their public statements and action) or on parliamentary democratic processes. SDS instituted a new means of operation based on the equal voice of all participants, somewhat in the traditional Quaker manner. Participatory democracy was also partly a result of the influence of the counterculture's emphasis on encounter groups and person-to-person interaction. In the end, however, participatory democracy did not work since ideological differences could not readily be solved by methods of consensus. But regardless of its success or failure, participatory democracy was an innovation for student political organizations. SDS's decentralization was also a part of its approach, at least until bitter factional disputes developed at the end of the sixties, and participatory democracy fit well into a decentralized organizational structure. For most of its early history, the national SDS leadership did not try to maintain ideological hegemony over its affiliated chapters, as was common with most student organizations in earlier periods. Indeed, the diversity of SDS campus affiliates in the mid-sixties was quite large. One of the reasons that large numbers of students identified with SDS was precisely because of its laissez-faire attitude toward ideological currents. If a student considered himself a radical, then the SDS was the natural group with which to affiliate.

The SDS was not controlled by any adult organization, nor even informally influenced by them. After 1963, when the SDS and the League for Industrial Democracy formally parted company, the SDS functioned completely independently. Noninvolvement with adult movements had both advantages and disadvantages for the SDS. Independence enabled SDS to engage in projects without sanction from any outside organization and permitted it to develop new analyses without the constraints of the ideological doctrines of adult groups. Freedom from adult control or influence also brought the SDS more into the mainstream of campus life, at least during its early and middle periods. The SDS was able to sense the direction of student concern and respond to this concern with new programs without the limitation of adult authorities. Thus, the independent student movements of the sixties were perhaps more "indigenous" than their predecessors, at least in the sense of maintaining strong links with the continuing situation on campus.

Independence also brought problems for the SDS, and for similar student groups. Financial problems were particularly serious, since affiliation with an adult group in the past had meant basic financial support. Traditionally, it has been very difficult for student organizations to finance even modest programs on their own. For one thing, students do not have access to large sums of money despite the fact that most come from relatively affluent families. Student leaders have seldom been willing to devote themselves to the often difficult and sometimes demeaning tasks of fund raising. And the changing personnel of any student organization prevents the sense of continuity which permits ready access to funds. Indeed, one of the major worries of leaders of groups like the SDS and the SPU were financial and much time was spent on finding adequate resources. Even the National Student Association found it impossible to finance its operations with membership dues from affiliated student governments and eventually turned to the Central Intelligence Agency. The lack of adult affiliation also makes organizational continuity difficult since student groups are inevitably transitory phenomena and the presence of a permanent national office often helps to maintain organizational cohesion. It can be argued, of course, that student groups which are unable to maintain themselves without adult financial and administrative support should not survive in any case. It is clear, for example, that many of the student groups of the fifties, if left to themselves, would not have endured with the handful of members they attracted. The SPU, for example, went out of existence quickly when it failed to attract a substantial membership. On the one hand, the survival of groups like the YPSL, the SLID, and the

SDA in the fifties may have helped to facilitate the growth of a student movement at the end of the decade. On the other hand, the "artificial" survival of such groups may have hindered the effective and ideologically unfettered growth of a new movement. But for better or worse, the period of effectiveness for the SDS was marked by independence from adult organizations and a substantial degree of organizational and ideological freedom.

The historical development of the SDS in the sixties reflects, rather accurately, the story of the New Left—both its successes and failures. The SDS began as a moderate and generally reformist organization led by highly intellectual, social democratic students from major universities. Its focus was on social reform, and the Port Huron Statement, the organization's first manifesto, was concerned with beginning a new analysis of American society at mid-century and at articulating the vision—and the frustration—of politically minded students at the time. The early moderation of the SDS is reflected in the organization's slogan in the 1964 presidential contest: "Half the way with LBJ." Early SDS leaders were very much interested in the Peace Corps, worked closely with NSA, and were engaged in white working-class areas in organizing projects funded by the United Automobile Workers union, among other groups. The focus of the SDS changed quickly. The political situation in America deteriorated rapidly from 1964 on, from the point of view of many liberals and radicals. The growth of Black Power among black activists effectively excluded the white student movement from participation in the civil rights movement, a substantial blow to white activists. The escalation of the Vietnam war by Lyndon Johnson provided a stimulus to the further leftward movement of the SDS. The tactics of the antiwar movement, from teach-ins to campus activism, to massive national demonstrations, and finally to disruptive activism on both local and national levels, dramatically shows the drift of the SDS and student activism in general in the mid-sixties.

The final period of the SDS, from 1969 onward, was marked by major factional disputes, an increasing radicalism, and a turn toward violent tactics, as well as the development of a Marxist-Leninist analysis of both American society and of the means of bringing about social change. The SDS, in its own words, moved from protest to resistance to revolutionary action. And the final period brought internal strife based largely on differing conceptions of the means to revolution. The final split of the organization, at its 1969 convention in Chicago, into two separate organizations marked the culmination of this internal struggle. The two currents of the SDS, the Weathermen and the Worker-Student Alliance, dramatically show the changing nature of the SDS. The analysis of the Weathermen was based on the need for revolutionary violence aimed at triggering mass struggle. The logical outcome of this policy were the sporadic bombings and accompanying repression which eventually forced the movement underground. The Worker-Student Alliance, dominated by the Maoist Progressive Labor Party, had a more complicated analysis of the road to revolution, but in general it was characterized by a doctrinaire view of American society and an emphasis on working-class organizing. Significantly, neither of these factions had much success in organizing on campus, and by the end of 1970 it was clear that both had failed as student movements and as revolutionary forces in society.

The development of the SDS during the sixties says a great deal about the nature of American politics at that period and the tremendous frustration which many students felt at that period. Unprecedented numbers of students were radicalized, and a large and sometimes effective movement was created. Universities were disrupted and, in a few cases, damaged in an unprecedented manner. But, in the long run, the SDS failed as an organization and provided neither an analysis of American society which proved a useful guide to organizing, nor a tactical means of achieving change or even of organizing a student movement.

The SDS was not the only student organization functioning during the sixties. And although it is the most important symbol of the national student movement at the time, the SDS as an organization did not play the key role during the decade. Rather, much of American student activism, and most of the dramatic acts of disruption and dissent were locally organized and carried out by various ad hoc committees and movements. The Berkeley student revolt, the agitation at Chicago, Wisconsin, and even Columbia (which was nominally under SDS leadership) were locally organized and spurred no national movement. The wave of Dow protests in 1968, and the unprecedented series of demonstrations after the events at Kent State University and the invasion of Cambodia were almost entirely spontaneous and clearly not under the leadership of any existing student organization. It is perhaps significant that these ad hoc groups were not able to maintain their momentum on campus (the Berkeley Free Speech Movement failed when it tranformed itself into the Free Student Union in an effort to maintain its organizational strength) or to build a national student movement. It is probably fair to say that most of the militant activism of the sixties relied on committed local organizers and not on nationally dictated policies or ideologies. Nevertheless, for much of its history, the SDS national office was able to maintain a reasonably effective coordination of activities, and its efforts at nationally focused demonstrations and programs achieved, with some exceptions, notable success. It is true, however, that no firmly coordinated, ideologically cohesive national organization dominated the campus scene during the sixties. Single issues, and particularly questions related to the war in Vietnam, attracted the support of large numbers of students. In many, although by no means all, of these cases, effective national coordination was provided by SDS or by some ad hoc group with close ties to SDS.

A number of somewhat more specialized student groups also were active during the sixties and had some impact on campus. The various black student organizations were unique to the sixties, and although they descended from SNCC and the other civil rights groups of the early sixties, they were different in their orientation and programs. Such organizations were very active in the struggle for black studies programs and were instrumental in local campus disruptions. The "traditional" student political groups were also active in the sixties, although their impact was overshadowed by the locally oriented agitation mentioned previously and by the broader appeal of the SDS.

The "old left" was far from dead during the sixties, and the existing student groups tied to traditional radical organizations and parties show a closer continuity with the traditions of student activism than the SDS. The most important of the "old left" organizations of the sixties was the Young Socialist Alliance (YSA), which maintained organizational continuity and a coherent ideological position throughout the period, something of a feat in this turbulent decade. The YSA, which has received very little analysis from commentators, was closely tied to the Trotskyist Socialist Workers Party. It maintained a hostile position on most elements of the counterculture, and was somewhat unique in this "puritanical" position. The YSA has also been sharply opposed to "adventuristic" tactics in the student movement, and has urged a more moderate tactical position. Perhaps the main strength of the YSA was the fact that it did maintain consistent politics and organizational direction throughout the decade; and as a result, when the SDS was splitting in the late sixties, the YSA attracted many disillusioned former SDS activists. Furthermore, the YSA's tactical moderation, which was at first a disadvantage in terms of attracting large numbers of students, became an asset as the "revolutionary" tactics of the Weathermen and other groups proved a failure. The YSA was also an important element in many of the massive Washington antiwar demonstrations of the mid-sixties, further adding to its strength. As the decade ended, the YSA was probably the largest single radical student organization, although its membership and active participation was but a shadow of the SDS at its height.

Other "old left" groups continued to function during the sixties, although they were clearly on the periphery of the student movement. The W.E.B. DuBois Clubs, which were linked to the pro-Moscow Communist party, maintained a high level of activity during much of the decade, but due to their links with the "conservative" Communists and their extreme tactical moderation, they were unable to attract massive support. The moderate and social democratic Young Peoples' Socialist League also continued to function, but was at the extreme right of the activist movement and, as a result, quite small nationally. The Progressive Labor Party, a Maoist offshoot from the Communist party, was active on the student scene, first as a sponsor of the May Second Movement, an antiwar group, and later as one of the elements in the SDS which eventually caused the organization to split in 1969.

What, then, is the "balance sheet" of the student movement of the sixties and how does this movement fit into the broader perspective of American student activism? The sixties marked the height of student activism in the United States. While the student movement did not come close to threatening the stability of the national government, it did severely shake the foundations of several of America's most prestigious universities and brought higher education into the limelight as an issue of major national concern. Furthermore, students came to be considered important factors in the national political scene. True, the antiwar movement did not succeed in bringing the Vietnam conflict to an end, and the civil rights movement a few years earlier did not end racial inequality. But these movements did shape, to some extent,

American public opinion and prepared the way for legislation in the case of civil rights and a more vocal criticism of the Vietnam war by more moderate elements. Students had a role in providing the backbone for Eugene McCarthy's presidential bid and Lyndon Johnson's decision not to run in 1968 and were instrumental in providing the early manpower for George McGovern's candidacy in 1972.

One sees the seeming paradox that at precisely the time that American student activism was considered by most Americans to be the number one issue in the nation, according to the Gallup Poll, most American students were both uninvolved in activist politics and prowar in their attitudes. Thus, one can see the phenomenon of the activist minority—albeit a rapidly growing and unprecedentedly large one— shaping the orientation of the campus and providing the "image" of the American student community. In historical context, this is not especially surprising, as has been pointed out, since the activists have generally shaped the political culture of the campus.

Other issues were also important during the sixties, and these issues had effects both on campus and in society. The civil rights question and the student response to it is one of these issues. For it is unlikely that the civil rights movement of the sixties would have developed in the way that it did without student participation. The sit-ins, after all, were sparked by black college students and many of the early volunteers in civil rights campaigns in both North and South were students. Even when white college students were eliminated from the movement, much of the leadership of the militant wing of the civil rights movement remained with black students. SNCC and the Black Panthers were both substantially under the leadership of students or ex-students.

Thus, the student movement of the sixties had some impact on the broader American society during the decade, but its impact was mixed. The social movements of the day were very much in the mainstream of student activism and were influenced by this student participation, but the society at large remained stable and basically unchanged by the participation of the student community. This lack of immediate and direct success in moving the society toward change was a matter of great frustration for many student activists and helped steer the movement toward an increasingly violent approach. In broad historical terms, however, the movement of the sixties was unprecedented in that American students became a force to be reckoned with in the social equation.

The reasons for this unprecedented level of participation are manifold. Of course, the level of activism and the numbers of students involved in it were key factors. So too was the militancy of the student movement—petitions signed by thousands of students could be ignored; but disruptions of campus life and bomb scares in major business districts had to be dealt with in some manner. The role of the mass media in catapulting the student movement to the center of national attention was also a key variable, and deserves a full analysis. Unlike the thirties, when the labor movement, political groups, and other elements in society were actively involved in movements for social change, in the sixties the students were almost alone in their involvement. This no doubt placed them in a more important position nationally than if they had been but one of a number of elements involved in such movements.

Perhaps the most important aspect of the student movement of the sixties was its effect on the student community itself and on the university. The political style, attitudes, and cultural forms of the student movement had a profound effect on a large number of students not directly involved in activism. The student movement combined in a somewhat unique manner both the political dissent and the cultural criticism which characterized many students during the sixties. Thus, to some extent, culture and politics were linked. Even the generally apolitical hippies were influenced by the oppositional politics of the SDS, while politically minded students were in turn influenced by the drug culture and rock music. And this combination of politics and cultural dissent had a powerful impact on the student community at large. The use of drugs, for example, often took on political significance. In the popular vision, drugs and politics were closely linked and while this was something of an exaggeration on the part of the mass media, there is a good deal of truth to it. And, of course, the student movement was greatly strengthened by the development on many campuses, and particularly in the prestigious schools, of an "opposition" culture which fit in very well with an increasingly militant atmosphere.

While the student movement of the sixties had the greatest impact on the university of any period in student activism in American history, the nature of this impact is not entirely clear. For a variety of reasons, student activism in the sixties focused on the university—an entirely new phenomenon in American history. In previous periods, most activists have either looked on the university as a kind of sanctuary from a rather less tolerant society and excused any failings of American higher education, or simply felt that the university was not the key to social change and therefore left it pretty much alone. In the sixties, students saw the universities as exemplars of much that was wrong in society and turned on it because it was a relatively defenseless institution in a society which was increasingly repressive. The increasing involvement of the university with the government, most dramatically in the area of defense-related research, made it a target of student criticism.

Student activism acutely disrupted many American universities and caused substantial damage to several of them. Some institutions reexamined their military-related research programs. Many institutions tried in various ways to repress student activism. Both the dissenters and the subjects of their dissent became topics of importance for the academic community and for the public. The sixties showed that universities were indeed fragile institutions and that they were much more prone to disruption and damage than other segments of the society.

At least part of the attack on the university was based on matters of curriculum and the nature of modern American higher education. Few doubt that undergraduate education has suffered as a result of the research and graduate orientation of American higher education since World War II. And few question the notion that the administrative structure of the university was and still is in need of overhaul. Students were critical of what they perceived as the "alienation" of modern mass higher education, of a curriculum which they felt was not "relevant" to current social problems, of teaching methods which prevented contact between professor and student, and of the traditional conception of in loco parentis, which seems to be particularly ill-suited to the sixties. The thrust of the student movement was not in the direction of curriculum reform and similar matters, and little in the way of coherent analysis was provided by activists. This lack of constructive criticism was combined with the natural conservatism of the academic community. But some things were changed as a result of the experience of the sixties. The last vestiges of the doctrine of in loco parentis were eliminated on most campuses, for example. Many universities were stimulated to think carefully about their curricula and about their goals, and numerous reports and other documents on university reform were issued. While the basic direction of higher education has not changed, some reforms have been made, and there is little doubt that without the pressure of student activism of the sixties, few institutions would have changed by themselves. Thus, the impact of student activism on the student community and on the university as an institution was mixed, although probably greater than at any other time in the history of America.

The movement of the sixties seems to have been, in the last analysis, unsuccessful in developing a long-term student movement in the United States, although a resurgence of campus activism is by no means out of the question. The thrust of the New Left of the sixties ended essentially by 1970. Whatever activist currents emerge after 1970 may look back on the sixties for lessons and a historical tradition, but they will be entirely new organizations. The New Left did not provide any coherent ideological analysis of either American society or of the university which might provide guidelines to future generations of students, nor did it develop new organizational forms which might be useful. The major organizations of the sixties have disappeared, and their histories do not provide much cause for emulation. The SDS, in particular, shows many of the pitfalls of the radical student movement in its later period, although the organization lasted longer than most student groups as an effective campus force. None of the journals which flourished in the late fifties and early sixties remain to provide guidelines. And this generalization is not only true for the radical student movement, but by and large for religious and conservative groups as well. The major liberal Protestant student organization, the University Christian Movement, dissolved itself in 1969, and by 1970 even the lavishly financed conservative Young Americans for Freedom was in some difficulty. Thus, no model for student activism emerged from the sixties despite the unprecedented nature of the student movement.

The radical student movement made some efforts at a new analysis of modern American society, and while no full-scale analysis has as yet emerged, there is no question but that some of the younger intellectuals involved in student activism in the sixties made an original contribution. The student journals of the late fifties and early sixties, such as *New University Thought* and *Root and Branch*, used historical, sociological, and economic analyses to understand American society from a radical perspective. Later, *Studies on the Left, Radical America,* and to a more modest extent *Leviathan,* and other journals continued this effort. The thinking represented in rather broad terms in the Port Huron Statement and based on the writings of such individuals as

C. Wright Mills, Herbert Marcuse, William Appleman Williams, and a few others has permeated much of radical analysis in the United States and has contributed to new developments in sociology, among the revisionist historians and among some younger radical economists. Much of the tactical and ideological thinking of the emerging women's movement came from radical women involved in student activism.

Yet, despite these efforts, "movement" thinkers were unable to develop either an analysis of American society which was convincing or a tactical approach for the activist movement to follow. In short, the beginnings of a radical critique of America and its role in the world were developed during the sixties, but no full-scale analysis emerged from these beginnings. Perhaps such a synthesis of a very difficult period of American history was too much to ask of a rather small number of young radical thinkers very much involved in the day-to-day problems of a political movement. But in contrast to some of the European radical student movements, the American activist thinkers were perhaps not as productive as their European counterparts. At least the New Left broke free for a time from the traditional canons of radical orthodoxy and perhaps came closer than at any other time in the history of American student activism to providing an effective and original analysis.

CONCLUDING COMMENT

American student activism deserves to be carefully studied by those interested in the future and direction of higher education and by those who wish to have a convenient tool to understanding some of the major currents in American history. If this volume has any contribution to make, it is to point out that the history of American student activism contains many useful lessons. It has not been argued that student activism has been of revolutionary importance in the United States, nor that it is in any sense the "wave of the future." Indeed, a careful reading of this volume will perhaps be a useful antidote to the mass media in periods of campus turmoil, since it is important to keep the student movement in perspective, in periods of both intense activism and apathy.

The major theme of this volume is that American student activism does have a historical tradition and that this tradition can provide useful clues to the current development of the student movement. Such an analysis of this history can also provide some insights into trends in American political history and into the directions of American higher education. While it is unlikely that the American student movement has the same revolutionary potential which can be found in many developing countries, a significant role for student activism cannot be ignored, particularly in the light of the events in France in 1968, when a seemingly weak student movement came close to bringing down the government. The potential for the student movement to have an impact on higher education greater than heretofore evident is quite real.

NOTES

1. It is perhaps significant that few of the many books which deal with the history of American higher education and with its governance have dealt extensively with students as an element of the current history of the university.
2. See Robert S. Laufer, "Sources of Generational Consciousness and Conflict," in P. G. Altbach and R. S. Laufer, eds., *op. cit.*, pp. 218-237 for an elaboration of these points.
3. For a good summary of opinion surveys concerning American students, see S. M. Lipset, *op. cit.*, chapter 2. See also S. M. Lipset and E. C. Ladd, Jr., "The Political Future of Activist Generations," in P. G. Altbach and R. S. Laufer, *op. cit.*, pp. 63-84.
4. See Philip Slater, *The Pursuit of Loneliness*, (Boston: Beacon Press, 1970), and Philip Pettitt, *Prisoners of Culture*, (New York: Scribners, 1970) for insightful analyses of both generational conflict and cultural developments among American youth.
5. Theodore Roszak's book, *The Making of a Counter Culture*, (Garden City, N. Y.: Anchor Books, 1970), is probably the best discussion of this development at the end of the sixties.
6. S. M. Lipset and E. C. Ladd, Jr., *op. cit.*
7. The best overall analysis of the development of the New Left in the United States is James P. O'Brien, "The Development of a New Left in the United States, 1960-65," (Unpublished Ph.D. Dissertation, Department of History, University of Wisconsin, 1971). See also James O'Brien, "The Development of the New Left," in P. G. Altbach and R. S. Laufer, eds., *op. cit.*, pp. 32-45.
8. This late period of SDS is covered in more detail in Alan Adelson, *SDS: A Profile*, (New York: Scribners, 1972). The earlier periods are covered adequately in James P. O'Brien, "The Development of a New Left in America, 1960-1965," *op. cit.*

9. For a discussion of the "Weatherman" and its ideology, see Harold Jacobs, ed., *Weatherman*, (Berkeley, Calif.: Ramparts Press, 1970).

10. For a discussion of the women in the radical movement, see Marge Piercy, "The Grand Coolie Damn," in R. Morgan, ed., *Sisterhood is Powerful* (New York: Vintage Books, 1970), pp. 421-437. Other essays in Robin Morgan's anthology are useful in gaining an understanding of the women's movement, as are those in Edith H. Altbach, ed., *From Feminism to Liberation*, (Cambridge, Mass.: Schenkman, 1971).

11. Among the elements most concerned with the creation of an ideological perspective for the New Left has been the journal *Studies on the Left* and its successor, *Socialist Revolution*.

12. For a partial text of the Port Huron Statement and representative commentary on aspects of New Left ideology, as well as an excellent historical discussion of the growth of the New Left, see Massimo Teodori, *The New Left: A Documentary History* (Indianapolis, Indiana: Bobbs-Merrill, 1969), particularly pp. 163-196.

13. The writings of Richard Flacks have been particularly lucid on the concept of the "new working class." See particularly Richard Flacks, *Youth and Social Change*, (Chicago: Markham, 1972).

14. For a sympathetic yet critical discussion of SDS and its development, see Norman Fruchter, "SDS: In and Out of Context," *Liberation*, 16 (February, 1972), pp. 19-23.

15. For a discussion of SDS internal functioning from a sympathetic viewpoint, see Rich Rothstein, "Representative Democracy in SDS," *Liberation*, 16 (February, 1972), pp. 10-18.

APPENDIX

American Student Organizations Concerned with Social and Political Action

Radical

a) *Socialist groups*

Young Peoples' Socialist League (YPSL), 1907-

Young Socialist League (YSL), 1950s

Socialist Youth League (SYL), 1946-1954

Young Socialist Alliance (YSA), 1958-

Intercollegiate Socialist Society (ISS)—Student League for Industrial Democracy (SLID)—Students for a Democratic Society (SDS), 1905-1965

Youth Against War and Fascism, 1960s

Students for a Democratic Society (SDS), 1965-1970—Worker-Student Alliance, 1970—Weatherman, 1970-

b) *Communist groups*

Young Communist League (YCL), 1921-1941

American Student Union (ASU), 1935-1940

National Student League (NSL), 1932-1936

American Youth for Democracy (AYD), 1943-1948

Young Progressives of America (YPA), 1948-1952 (Students for Wallace)

Labor Youth League (LYL), 1948-1957
Progressive Youth Organizing Committee (PYOC), 1960s
W.E.B. DuBois Clubs, 1960s
Young Workers Liberation League, 1971-

c) *Antiwar and pacifist groups*

Fellowship of Youth for Peace, 1920s
Youth Committee Against War (YCAW), 1935-1941
Student Peace Union (SPU), 1959-1964
Student Committee for a SANE Nuclear Policy, 1958-1961
United Student Peace Committee, 1930s

d) *Civil rights groups*

Student Nonviolent Coordinating Committee (SNCC), 1960-1970
Southern Student Organizing Committee (SSOC), 1960s
Northern Student Movement (NSM), 1960s
Black Student Unions, 1960s

Liberal

Intercollegiate Civic League, 1905-1917?
Young Intellectuals, 1908-1915?
National Student Forum (Stemmed from the Intercollegiate Liberal League and the National Student Conference), 1921-1929
National Student Federation of America (NSFA), 1925-1946
United States National Student Association (USNSA), 1947-
U.S. Student Assembly, 1943-1947
Students for Democratic Action (SDA), 1948-1959
Student World Federalists, 1946-1951

Conservative

Intercollegiate Society of Individualists (ISI), 1958-
Young Americans for Freedom (YAF), 1960-
Students for America (SFA), 1952-1955?

"Establishment"

Campus Young Democrats

Campus Young Republicans

Religious

YM-YWCA, 1877

Intercollegiate Christian Volunteer Movement (ICVM)

Protestant denominational student affiliates (largely from 1920 to the present), including Methodist Student Movement, Liberal Religious Youth, and others

National Student Christian Federation (NSCF), 1950s and 1960s— University Christian Movement (UCM), 1969-1971

Young Christian Students (YCS—Roman Catholic Radicals), 1960s

Index

Academic freedom, 33, 58, 79
    91, 93, 125, 126, 135, 149,
    155
Academic Freedom Newsletter,
    179
Addams, Jane, 14, 29, 66
American Association of Univer-
    sity Professors, 179
American Association of Univer-
    sity Students for Academic
    Freedom, 179
American Civil Liberties Union,
    180
American Federation of Teachers,
    58
American Friends Service Com-
    mittee, 70, 115, 173, 181-
    183, 186-188
American Labor Party, 145
American Liberty League, 97
American Student Union, 7, 9,
    61, 66, 68, 70-78, 81,

American Student Union:
    83-86, 88-95, 98, 107*n*,
    110-112, 145, 153, 217
American Veterans Committee,
    122
American Youth Act, 75, 85
American Youth Congress, 67,
    75, 76, 78, 83, 84, 85, 89,
    95-96, 98, 100, 107*n*
American Youth for Democracy,
    111, 145-146
American Youth for Socialism,
    162
Americans for Democratic Action,
    132-135, 136, 137
Antimilitarism, 25, 26, 44, 46,
    47-49, 51, 91, 172
Anti-Semitism, 97
Antiwar activism, 46, 52-53,
    62-64, 65-72, 85, 90, 92,
    110, 148, 161, 177, 205,
    218

Apathy, 20, 31, 174
Aptheker, Bettina, 150
Associated Student Governments, 127

"Beat generation," 112, 115, 204, 207n, 210, 216
Black Panther Party, 200
Black Power, 195, 199, 200, 221, 224
Blanchard, Paul, 43, 51
Bourne, Randolph, 31
Buckley, Jr., William F., 202

California, University of, at Berkeley, 26, 30, 40, 61, 68, 93, 97, 117, 118, 119, 141, 150, 159, 161, 179, 180, 190, 197, 212, 213, 216
    Berkeley Student Revolt, 1964, 201, 206n, 225, 226
    Daily Californian, 179
    Free Student Union, 226
Cambodian invasion, 4, 213
Carmichael, Stokely, 200
Censorship, administrative, 33-34
    of organizations, 60, 134-135
    of student press, 41, 61, 79, 93
Center for Educational Reform, 129
Central Intelligence Agency, 119, 120, 123-124, 128-131, 139n

Chicago, University of, 35, 45, 68, 117, 119, 135, 141, 148, 154, 159, 161, 167, 168, 181, 187, 190, 193, 197, 225
Christian Youth Council of North America, 100
Civil liberties, 9, 64, 92, 126, 135, 144, 146, 152, 155, 157, 161, 172, 177, 182, 205
Civil rights, 7, 9, 11, 64, 83, 84, 91, 92, 110, 125, 135, 177, 191, 192, 194-202, 205, 206n, 210, 221, 228
Civilian Public Service camps, 111
Cold War, 112, 129, 131, 134, 142, 143, 146, 147, 148, 152, 164, 178, 184, 187
Collective security, 91, 92
College Peace Union, 186
Collegiate Anti-Militarist League, 46
Collegiate Council for the United Nations, 122, 138
Columbia University, 63, 68, 93, 135, 141, 145, 146, 190, 225
    Spectator, 59, 61
Committee for Non-Violent Action, 183
Committees to Abolish the House Committee on Un-American Activities, 181
Communist:
    devotion to Soviet Union, 66
    leadership, 9
    literature, 63

Communist:
    manipulation, 71, 76
    party, 7, 11, 32, 42, 43-44,
        63, 88, 142, 147, 227
    -s, 44, 112, 113, 133, 135, 148
    student activity, 45, 76, 110,
        111, 117, 125, 142, 144-
        151, 159, 180, 182, 183-
        184
    support, 185
    youth movement, 45, 52, 68,
        72, 74, 76-84, 86-87, 89,
        91-92, 94-102
Communist International, 42
Congress of Industrial Organiza-
    tions, (CIO), 57, 75, 87
Congress of Racial Equality
    (CORE), 10, 110, 135, 194,
    196, 197, 198, 200
Conscientious objectors, 63, 71,
    110, 111
Conservative:
    activism, 96-102, 231
    organizations, 19
    sentiment, 112, 113, 116, 118,
        164-168, 202-203, 205
Cosmopolitan Club, 9, 28, 46, 55*n*
Cosmopolitan Student, 28
"Counter culture," 32, 115, 210,
    219, 229, 233*n*
Cuba:
    revolution, 190
    missile crisis, 192

Debs, Eugene, 22, 26
Debsian Socialist movement, 162
Dellinger, David, 190

Democratic Convention, 1968, 4
Democratic Party, 136
Depression, 58, 59, 65, 87
Desegregation, 116, 120, 195, 196
Dialectical materialism, 64
Discrimination, 125, 126, 135,
    136, 148, 149, 155, 170
Dow protests, 1968, 10, 225
Draper, Hal, 159

Easter peace marches, 191
Eisenhower, Dwight, 136, 178
Evans, M. Stanton, 166
Expulsion:
    due to administration
        criticism, 79
    in black colleges, 51
    due to demonstrations, 48, 60,
        93

Fabianism, 23, 25
Faculty, 114
    dismissals, 61, 79, 93, 118,
        179, 180-181
    evaluation, 211
    petitions, 62
    salaries, 113
    sentiment, 58, 207*n*
Farmer, James, 110, 155, 196
Federal Bureau of Investigation
    (FBI), 77
Federalist movement, 120
Fellowship of Reconciliation, 47,
    66, 70-71, 99, 110, 182-
    183, 186, 196
Fellowship, 70

Fellowship of Youth for Peace,
    46, 47
Feminist movement, 29
Field Foundation, 127
Ford Foundation, 129
Fraternities and sororities,
    38, 41, 47, 97, 113, 118,
    135, 197
Freedom of expression, 9, 27, 34,
    64, 205
    movements, 30, 61
Freedom rides, 10, 152
Freedom Summer, 201
Friedenberg, Edgar Z., 129

Gandhian tactics, 196
Garvey, Marcus, 51
Goldwater, Barry, 168, 203
Goodman, Paul, 219

Harding, Warren, 47
Harvard University, 14, 27, 31,
    35, 61, 73, 93, 117, 141,
    146, 167, 168, 190
    Gadfly, 33
    Harvard-Radcliffe Committee
        to Study Disarmament,
        168
    Tocsin, 186, 191
    tutorial system, 33
Hayden, Tom, 201
High school organization, 80, 81,
    92-93
Hoover, Herbert, 59
House Un-American Activities
    Committee, 119, 145, 146,

House Un-American Activities
    Committee: 179, 181, 202
Hungarian Revolution, 149, 178,
    183

Illich, Ivan, 129
Independent Socialist League,
    158, 160, 161, 175-176n
    Labor Action, 160
Industrial Workers of the World
    (IWW), 29
In loco parentis, 13, 211, 230
Intercollegiate Civic League (ICL),
    28
Intercollegiate Disarmament
    Council, 63
Intercollegiate Liberal League
    (ILL), 34
Intercollegiate Peace Association,
    46
Intercollegiate Socialist, 25, 26,
    27
Intercollegiate Socialist Society,
    11, 19, 22-28, 29, 42, 46,
    52, 54n, 72, 144
    motto, 27
    (*See also* Student League for
        Industrial Democracy)
Intercollegiate Society of
    Individualists, 167
    Human Events, 167
    New Individualist Review, 167
    Insight and Outlook, 167
International Confederation of
    Students (CIE), 41
International Relations Clubs,
    Association of, 122, 138,

International Relations Clubs, Association of: 164
International Student Conference, 130
International Student Service, 86, 89, 111
International Union of Students, 124, 130, 140*n*, 149
Interseminary Movement, 69, 70, 98, 171
Isolationism, 62, 66

Johnson, Lyndon, 210, 224

Kempton, Murray, 81-82
Keniston, Kenneth, 115-116
Kent State University, 4, 6, 213
Kerr, Clark, 113
Khruschev, Nikita, 149
King, Jr., Martin Luther, 183, 195, 199, 205
Kinsey, Alfred, 18
Korean conflict, 116, 144, 164, 183, 219
Ku Klux Klan, 97

Labor Youth League, 114, 143, 144, 147-151
   New Foundations, 147, 148
   Challenge, 148
Ladd, Jr., E. C., 217
Laidler, Harry, 23-26
Lash, Joseph, 91, 92, 95
League Against War and Fascism, 92

League for Industrial Democracy, 11, 19, 21, 27, 34, 35, 42, 72, 73, 78, 100, 153-154, 155, 156
League of Nations, 20, 41, 51, 65
League of Nations Associations, 89
Leviathan, 231
Liberal Religious Youth, 173
"Liberal Summer School," 35
Lipset, S. M., 217
Literary Digest, 62
London, Jack, 23-24
Loyalty oaths, 61, 118, 178, 179, 180, 206*n*
Lucy, Autherine, 196

MacArthur, Douglas, 166
Mao Tse-tung, 219
Marcuse, Herbert, 219, 232
Marxism, 19, 22, 45, 74, 148, 153, 219, 221
Mass media:
   views on students, 62, 86, 90, 115, 117, 212, 213, 229, 232
   reactions, 68
May Second Movement, 227
McCarthy, Eugene, 128, 228
McCarthyism, 116, 119, 126, 135, 143-144, 145, 157, 164, 165, 168, 169, 178, 185, 204
McGovern, George, 128, 210, 213
McReynolds, David, 190, 191
Methodist Student Movement, 170, 171

Michigan, University of, 62, 93,
    146, 159, 180, 197, 213,
    216
    Intercollegiate Socialist Society
        movement, 25
    Michigan Daily, 34
    Tempest, 33
Middle class, 17, 19, 28, 31, 45,
    46, 48, 57, 63, 64, 65-66,
    87, 215
Mills, C. Wright, 232
Montgomery Bus Boycott, 195
Morrill Act, 80
Movement for a Democratic
    Society, 11
"Multiversity," 113
Muste, A. J., 14, 25, 29, 44, 47,
    190

National Assembly of Student
    Christian Association, 100
National Association for the
    Advancement of Colored
    People, 194, 195, 197, 207n
National Civic Federation, 36
National Collegiate MacArthur
    Clubs, 166
National Committee for a Sane
    Nuclear Policy, 119, 162,
    184-185, 190, 206n
    Sanity, 186
National Committee for the
    Limitation of Armaments,
    46
National Conference on Students
    in Politics, 89

National Council of Methodist
    Youth, 170-171
National Federation of Catholic
    College Students, 172-173
National Federation of Methodist
    Youth, 98
National Negro Congress, 93
National Newman Club Federa-
    tion, 173
National Student Christian
    Federation, 171
National Student Committee, 75
National Student Conference of
    the Student Christian
    Movement, 49
National Student Conference
    for the Limitation of
    Armaments, 34
National Student Council, 169
National Student Federation of
    America, 9, 19, 39-42, 43,
    46, 47, 67, 84-86, 89, 90,
    95, 96, 101
    conferences, 35
    National Student Mirror, 33, 85
    NFSA Reporter, 88
National Student Forum, 34-36,
    37, 39, 46-47, 52
National Student League, 67, 73,
    74, 76, 78-81, 89, 90,
    97-98, 153
    Student Review, 79, 92
National Youth Act, 83, 96
National Youth Administration,
    91
National Youth Committee to
    Defeat the Mundt-Nixon
    Bill, 180

New Deal, 74, 87, 94
New Left, 3-4, 6, 11, 12, 15*n*,
    112, 116, 144, 150, 175*n*,
    182, 189, 191, 193, 194,
    203, 205, 219-220, 231,
    232, 233*n*, 234*n*
New Student, 10, 21, 32, 33,
    34, 35, 36-39, 41, 42, 46,
    55*n*
Newton, Huey, 200
New University Conference, 10
New University Thought, 193,
    231
New York Student League, 78
Northern Student Movement,
    198-199, 207*n*
Nuclear testing, 9, 144, 191-192
    issue, 184
    treaty, 184, 185, 192

Ohio State University, 62, 90, 93
"Operation Brotherhood," 137
"Operation Free Thought," 136
Oxford Pledge, 66-68, 75, 91, 92,
    94, 218

Pacifism:
    activity, 69-71, 182
    issue, 16, 17, 18, 19, 66, 188,
        206*n*
    organizations, 99
Panty raids, 118
Participatory democracy, 222
Paul Revere Society, 97
Peacemakers, 183

Peace strikes:
    1935, 67
    1935, 67-68
    1936, 68
"People's Peace Treaty," 129
Picketing:
    missile bases, 191
    Woolworth's, 198
Political repression, 77, 97, 112,
    113, 117, 148
Polls and surveys:
    on capitalism, 104
    on pacifism, 62-63
    on political attitudes, 49, 59-
        60, 82, 97, 116, 117,
        119, 228, 233*n*
    in *New Student*, 37, 46
Popular Front, 147, 150
Port Huron Statement, 221, 224,
    234*n*
Princeton, 39, 68, 167
Progressive Labor Party, 225,
    227
Progressive Party, 22
Progressive Youth Organizing
    Committee, 250
    New Horizons for Youth, 150
Prohibition, 41, 58
    and drugs, 18
"Proletarian culture," 63

Radical America, 231
*Radicals in the Profession News-
    letter*, 11
Rand School of Social Science,
    44
Reich, Wilhelm, 219

Religious group publications:
  Campus Resource, 169, 171
  Inter-collegian, 169, 171
  Motive, 169, 171
  The Source, 169, 171
  Wind and Chaff, 169, 171
Religious groups:
  activism, 9-10, 96-101, 168-
    174, 180, 215, 216, 231
  Baptists, 51
  Disciples, 49
  Jews, 49, 64, 98, 122, 168,
    173
  Methodists, 49, 51, 67, 70,
    75, 98, 99, 168, 170
  Protestant, 98, 122
  Quakers, 99, 115, 168
  Roman Catholics, 49, 51, 98,
    122, 125, 172
  Unitarians, 49, 99, 168
Republican sentiment, 20, 38,
  168
Revolt, 73
  (*See also Student Outlook*)
Riesman, David, 116
Robin Hood Clubs, 180
Robinson, Frederick, 60
Roosevelt, Eleanor, 89, 96
Root and Branch, 231
R.O.T.C., 3, 26, 37, 38, 41, 42,
  46, 47, 48, 61-62, 73, 80,
  84, 91, 92, 94, 121, 161,
  170, 191
Russian Revolution, 18, 26-27,
  42
Rustin, Bayard, 190, 191, 196,
  198

Savio, Mario, 201
Schachtman, Max, 159
School segregation, 199, 200
Scottsboro Boys, 81
Seale, Bobby, 200
Selective Service System, 71, 136,
  159
Senate Internal Security Subcommittee, 185
Settlement house movement, 14,
  19, 21, 50
Sinclair, Upton, 22, 23-24, 27,
  37, 87
Sit-ins, 196, 198, 200-201
Smith Act, 148
Social Problems Clubs, 74, 80
Socialism, 17, 189
  anti-Stalinist socialism, 76
Socialist:
  groups, 29
  leadership, 9
  party, 11, 22, 26, 42, 43-44,
    73, 75, 76-78, 160-161,
    162
  -s, 44
  student activity, 45, 151-163,
    174, 183
  support, 186
  viewpoint, 64, 73, 99
  youth movement, 52, 66, 68,
    72-77, 86-87, 89, 91-92,
    94, 121, 136, 142-143
Socialist Review, 25, 26-27, 33
Socialist Workers Party, 143, 162,
  163, 226
Socialist Youth League, 152, 156-
  160

Socialist Youth League:
  Anvil and Student Partisan,
    158
Southern Christian Leadership
    Conference, 110, 115, 195,
    200
Soviet Union, 77-78, 80, 83, 88,
    95, 110, 112, 120, 142,
    150, 152, 153, 157, 193
Spanish Civil War, 65, 85, 93
Sparticists, 163
Stalin-Hitler pact, 83, 86, 95
Stevenson, Adlai, 135
Stockholm Peace Petition, 183
Strikes:
  antiwar, 80, 93
  coal miners', 78
  peace, 67-68
  San Francisco waterfront, 97
  University of California at Los
    Angeles, 60
  workers', 93
Student activism:
  American, 15n, 16n, 20, 42,
    205, 209-233
    black, 51
    effectiveness, 87, 194, 210
    ineffectiveness, 4-11, 71,
      75, 103
    influence on student com-
      munity, 229
    pro-war, 101
    radical, 72
  in foreign countries, 4, 6, 15n,
    210-211, 212, 233
Student Advocate, 91, 92, 97
Student Bill of Rights, 125

Student Christian Volunteer
    Movement, 14, 30, 36,
    43, 47, 48, 50-51, 69, 70,
    99, 170, 171, 218
Student Civil Liberties Union, 180
Student Congress Against War, 66
Student Defenders of Democracy,
    101
Student Federalist, 120-121
Students for America, 166
Students for Democratic Action,
    125, 132-138, 140n, 147,
    152, 160, 179
Students for a Democratic Society
    (SDS):
  activities, 10, 221-226, 231
  alumni activities, 11
  civil rights involvement, 194,
    205
  early leaders' activities, 132,
    184
  history, 21, 43, 153, 155-156
  ideology, 217, 219
  internal functioning, 234n
  size, 24, 217
Student League of America, 101
Student League for Industrial
    Democracy (SLID), 21, 42,
    67, 72-75, 77, 79, 89, 90,
    152, 153-156
  alumni, 73
  SLID Voice, 155
  Student Outlook, 92
  (*See also* League for Industrial
    Democracy)
Student League for Progressive
    Action, 101

Student Merger Committee, 101
Student Mirror, 41
Student Nonviolent Coordinating
    Committee, 110, 115, 144,
    194, 195, 198, 199-200,
    204
Student Outlook, 73
Student Peace Union, 115, 119,
    144, 147, 152, 157, 162,
    185-194, 200, 204, 206*n,*
    223
    Bulletin, 186
    Discussion Bulletin, 188
    "Students Speak for Peace,"
        191
Student Review, 79
Student Workers' Federation, 62
Students for Wallace (Henry), 146-
    147
Studies on the Left, 231
Supreme Court desegregation
    decisions, 144, 148, 177,
    194, 205

"Third Camp" Socialists, 156-
    158, 159, 161, 175*n,* 187,
    188, 189, 193
Thomas, Norman, 14, 29, 44, 59,
    71, 76, 155, 190, 191
Trotskyists, 75, 83, 142, 156,
    157, 162, 163, 189, 193

Union Theological Seminary, 183
United Auto Workers Union, 137,
    154

United front:
    of American Student Union,
        74, 77, 84, 85, 86-96
    demise of, 88
United Nations, 9, 112, 120, 122,
    136
United States National Student
    Association, 39, 40, 41, 102,
    111, 114-115, 119-120,
    122-132, 135, 137, 139*n,*
    145, 149, 152, 164, 166,
    179-180, 200, 203
    Student Government Bulletin,
        126
United States Student Assembly,
    111, 121, 124, 133
United Student Christian Council,
    171
United Student Peace Committee,
    68, 69, 85
United World Federalists, 120, 121
University Christian Movement,
    171, 231

Veterans of Future Wars, 68
Vietnam war, 3-4, 65, 128, 192,
    213, 218-219, 221, 224

Wallace, Henry, 122, 144, 146-
    147
War Resisters' League, 111, 188,
    193
Washington Action Project, 192
Washington Disarmament Con-
    ference, 47

Weathermen, 220, 225, 234n
W.E.B. DuBois Clubs, 150, 227
Wechsler, James, 66, 73
"Witch hunting," 137, 148
Wisconsin, University of, 28, 45,
    73, 84, 93, 95, 97, 117,
    119, 124, 141, 148, 154,
    159, 161, 167, 180, 197,
    213, 216, 225,
    Daily Cardinal, 117
    Proletarian, 33
Women's liberation movement,
    220, 234n
Women's suffrage, 27
Worker Student Alliance, 225
Workers Party, 45
Working class, 50
    collaboration with students,
        49, 80-81, 91
World Court, 20, 39, 50, 51
World Order Realized under Law
    and Democracy, 121
World Student Christian Federa-
    tion, 50, 170, 193
World Student Relief, 50
World Tomorrow, 47, 70
World War I, 17, 19, 26, 30, 42,
    44, 51, 52-53, 67, 87
World War II, 9, 11, 62, 65, 69
    71, 100-101, 109-112

Yale, 14, 35, 61, 80, 118
    Saturday Evening Pest, 33
YM-YWCA, 14, 16n, 19, 21-22,
    29-30, 35, 36, 39, 43, 46,
    47, 48-52, 61, 62, 66, 70,

YM-YWCA:
    89, 90, 98-99, 115, 168,
    169-171, 201, 205, 218
Young Americans for Freedom,
    167, 202-203
    Young Guard, 202
Young Christian Students, 172-
    173
Young Communist League, 19,
    45, 61, 63, 76, 77, 81-84,
    96, 216
    (*See also* Communist)
Young Democrats, 138
Young Intellectuals, 28, 29
Young Peoples Socialist Leagues,
    19, 44-45, 71, 74-75, 83,
    98, 110, 143, 152, 156-158,
    160-162, 188, 198, 200,
    216, 227
    Anvil, 161
    Free Youth, 45
    Young Socialist Review, 74-76
Young Progressives of America,
    146-147, 151
Young Republicans, 203
Young Socialist Alliance, 152, 157,
    160, 162, 163, 189, 207n,
    226-227
Young Socialist League, 134, 143,
    152
Young Workers League, 45
Young Workers Liberation
    League, 151
Youth Committee Against War,
    69, 70, 72, 76, 98, 110
Youth March for Integrated
    Schools, 152, 162, 197-198